Secondary Data Analysis

POCKET GUIDES TO
SOCIAL WORK RESEARCH METHODS

Series Editor
Tony Tripodi, DSW
Professor Emeritus, Ohio State University

THOMAS P. VARTANIAN

Secondary Data Analysis

OXFORD
UNIVERSITY PRESS
2011

12 - 8 - 11

OXFORD
UNIVERSITY PRESS

Oxford University Press, Inc., publishes works that further
Oxford University's objective of excellence
in research, scholarship, and education.

Oxford   New York
Auckland   Cape Town   Dar es Salaam   Hong Kong   Karachi
Kuala Lumpur   Madrid   Melbourne   Mexico City   Nairobi
New Delhi   Shanghai   Taipei   Toronto

With offices in
Argentina   Austria   Brazil   Chile   Czech Republic   France   Greece
Guatemala   Hungary   Italy   Japan   Poland   Portugal   Singapore
South Korea   Switzerland   Thailand   Turkey   Ukraine   Vietnam

Copyright © 2011 by Oxford University Press, Inc.

Published by Oxford University Press, Inc.
198 Madison Avenue, New York, New York 10016
www.oup.com

Oxford is a registered trademark of Oxford University Press

Library of Congress Cataloging-in-Publication Data

Vartanian, Thomas P.
Secondary data analysis / Thomas P. Vartanian.
p. cm. — (Pocket guides to social work research methods)
Includes bibliographical references and index.
ISBN 978-0-19-538881-7
1. Social service—Research. I. Title.
HV11.V347 2011
361.0072'3—dc22   2010016027

1 3 5 7 9 8 6 4 2

Printed in the United States of America
on acid-free paper

Acknowledgments

I would like to thank Barb Toews, Marie Guldin, and Molly Graepel for their research assistance on this book, and Philip Gleason and Linda Houser for their helpful comments during the writing of this book. Funding for this research was provided by Bryn Mawr College.

Contents

Secondary Data Analysis

1

Introduction

Social work research has become increasingly reliant on large secondary data sets. These data sets, generally collected by governments, research institutions, and, in some cases, agencies, provide researchers with readily available resources to examine characteristics of populations or particular hypotheses. These data differ from primary data in that primary data sets are collected by the researcher who will also examine that data. Researchers collect primary data directly through interviews, questionnaires, focus groups, observation, the examination of primary sources such as writings or speeches, or a variety of other such collection methods. While collecting data is often the best way to obtain the information necessary to analyze particular hypotheses, it is not always economically or practically feasible. Using large secondary data sets provides an alternative to the collection of primary data, often giving the researcher access to more information than would be available in primary data sets. Secondary data can include any data that are examined to answer a research question other than the question(s) for which the data were initially collected. Large institutions are able to obtain far larger samples and often are able to ask more questions than researchers who are in smaller settings (such as individual or small-group researchers). Over time, data sets have become richer, as researchers refine the types of questions asked in surveys. That being said, many secondary data sets available were primary data sets when they first started, and they grew to become the larger data sets that they now are. Also, many of the secondary data sets available today look to primary researchers, often qualitative researchers, for the questions that they ask their sample members. Without such fieldwork by primary researchers, larger secondary data sets would not be as rich as they are.

To give an example of how research has changed over time, I examine *Social Service Review(SSR)* during 1980 and 2007 (I randomly picked these two years) to determine the data sources for articles published in those years. In 1980, approximately 32 articles were published in *SSR* as main articles or notes, and, of these, six used some form of secondary data, either administrative or survey data; nine used primary data sources; and 17 of the articles used no data. Things changed dramatically by 2007, when, of the 22 articles published that year, 18 used some form of large data set, primarily secondary survey data; one used primary data; and three used no data. Although this is only a "snapshot" of a trend based on one elite social work journal, it would appear that the use of secondary data is becoming increasingly important.

In this book, I will briefly discuss what secondary data sets look like, as well as some of the advantages and disadvantages of collecting and using primary, and secondary, data in a research study. I will take you through a series of questions to help you decide which type of data will work best for your research question. I then turn my attention to the central topic of the book, the use of secondary data sets.

This book examines the types of secondary data sets available to researchers and how these have been used in the past and may be used in the future. While thousands of secondary data sets are available from private sources, universities, federal and other government agencies, and other public sources, I focus on data sets that are often used by social work and other social science researchers. Many of these data sets cover a wide variety of topics; others focus on particular topics or populations. Some are longitudinal, while others are cross-sectional, and they can cover either short or long periods of time. Some data sets use monthly information;others use annual or biannual information. Some data sets are nationally representative; others cover only specific populations. I examine the costs and benefits of using these different types of data sets and the reasons for using particular data sets given particular types of research questions or populations. I also describe how to get the data, where to find the codebooks that describe the variables contained in the data, the costs involved in the use of the data, and, in some instances, how to best use the data for analyses. Some of these data are relatively easy to access, generally by downloading them from websites, while others require contracts and cost a good deal of money to obtain.

I describe surveys that cover a wide range of populations and topics. I first do this by going over some of the details, characteristics, populations, and variable types of 29 popular and informative surveys. I also examine which of these data sets are best used for particular types of research questions. For example, if you are interested in the study of the effect of childhood factors on particular adult outcomes, a number of longitudinal data sets span a great number of years and include children who become adults over the years of the survey.

Below, I give an overview of some of the populations and topics I cover in the book. Many of the data sets that I examine contain numerous populations and topic areas, and I include particular data sets in several topic or population areas.

For childhood data sets, I look at several data sets in which children's mental, emotional, and physical health; bonds with parents; and economic well-being are examined. These include:

- The Panel Study of Income Dynamics, Child Development Supplement (CDS),
- The Project on Human Development in Chicago Neighborhoods (PHDCN),
- The National Institute of Child Health and Human Development (NICHD) Study of Early Child Care And Youth Development,
- The Fragile Families and Child Wellbeing Study (FFCWS),
- The National Survey of Child and Adolescent Well-Being,
- The National Survey of American Families (NSAF),
- The National Longitudinal Study of Adolescent Health (Add Health),
- The Early Childhood Longitudinal Survey (ECLS),
- The National Educational Longitudinal Survey (NELS),
- Welfare, Children and Families: A Three-City Study, and
- The Adoption and Foster Care Analysis and Reporting System (AFCARS).

I describe data for child populations that suffer from abuse and neglect, such as:

- The National Child Abuse and Neglect Data System (NCANDS),
- Longitudinal Studies of Child Abuse and Neglect (LONGSCAN),
- Developmental Victimization Survey (DVS),
- Child Neglect: Cross Sector Service Paths and Outcomes (CN), and
- The Project on Human Development in Chicago Neighborhoods (PHDCN).

I also look at a number of surveys related to schooling, which include information relating to grades completed, types of schools attended, grades in particular subject areas, and level of education of populations:

- The National Educational Longitudinal Survey (NELS),
- School Data Direct (SDD),
- Common Core of Data (CCD),
- The Panel Study of Income Dynamics, Child Development Supplement (CDS),
- Fragile Families and Child Wellbeing Study (FFCWS),
- The Project on Human Development in Chicago Neighborhoods (PHDCN),
- The Early Childhood Longitudinal Survey (ECLS),
- The Survey of Income and Program Participation (SIPP),
- The U.S. Census, and
- Welfare, Children, and Families: A Three City Study.

I examine surveys that ask about adult and children's health outcomes, including:

- The Panel Study of Income Dynamics, Child Development Supplement (CDS),
- Fragile Families and Child Wellbeing Study (FFCWS),
- The Health and Retirement Study,
- The Survey of Income and Program Participation (SIPP),
- The National Longitudinal Study of Adolescent Health (Add Health),

- The Early Childhood Longitudinal Survey (ECLS),
- The General Social Survey (GSS),
- The National Longitudinal Survey (NLS),
- The National Survey of American Families (NSAF),
- National Survey of Child and Adolescent Well-Being (NSCAWB),
- The National Institute of Child Health and Human Development (NICHD) Study of Early Child Care and Youth Development, and
- National Medical Expenditure Survey (NMES)/Medical Expenditure Panel Survey (MEPS).

I also examine which data sets are best for use to study those who use government programs, such as Temporary Assistance for Needy Families (TANF, formerly Aid to Families with Dependent Children), Supplemental Nutritional Assistance Program (SNAP, formerly the Food Stamp Program), Supplemental Security Income (SSI), Social Security (SS), Medicaid, Medicare, and other such programs. These data sets include:

- The Panel Study of Income Dynamics (PSID),
- The Child Development Supplement (CDS),
- Fragile Families and Child Wellbeing Study (FFCWS),
- The National Longitudinal Survey (NLS),
- Survey of Program Dynamics (SPD),
- Welfare, Children and Families: A Three-City Study,
- Early Childhood Longitudinal Survey (ECLS),
- Continuing Survey of Food Intake by Individuals (CSFII),
- National Survey of American Families (NSAF), and
- The Survey of Income and Program Participation (SIPP).

I also examine data sets that work best for those who are elderly or going into retirement:

- The Health and Retirement Survey (HRS),
- The National Longitudinal Survey of Older Men (NLS),
- The National Longitudinal Survey of Older Women (NLS),
- The Panel Study of Income Dynamics (PSID), and
- The Current Population Survey (CPS).

Other topic areas that can be examined with these data sets and will be discussed in the book include child care, mental health, neighborhood perceptions and characteristics, food insecurity, housing, income and poverty, birth weight, sexual activity, sexually transmitted diseases, physical activity, prescription and illegal drug use, dating and domestic violence, home environment, and emotional and general well-being.

2

What is a Secondary Data Set?

A large secondary data set typically covers a broad sample of individuals or other entities (e.g., schools, hospitals) and is generally representative of some broader population—if not for the entire U.S. population, then for some subpopulation or region of the country. Most primary data sets are not as comprehensive as many large secondary data sets in representing either the entire population or large segments of the population. Some of the data sets covered in the book are nationally representative of the U.S. population, such as the Panel Study of Income Dynamics (PSID) (for the nonimmigrant U.S. population), the National Longitudinal Study (NLS), and the Survey of Income and Program Participation (SIPP). Other samples are representative only of certain populations; for example, the Project on Human Development in Chicago Neighborhoods (PHDCN) is representative of all individuals in the city of Chicago; the National Child Abuse and Neglect Data System (NCANDS) is representative of those children whose alleged victimization was reported to child and protective services; the National Educational Longitudinal Survey (NELS) is representative of eighth graders in 1988; and the Developmental Victimization Survey (DVS) is representative of children aged 2–17 years old living in the contiguous United States. The data sets for the entire population generally have smaller sample sizes for specific subgroups, posing potential problems for researchers interested in those subgroups. On the other hand, surveys for specific populations may have larger samples than the more general surveys (such as the PSID), but may offer researchers limited opportunities for comparison with other populations.

The data sets being examined in this book generally use sophisticated sampling designs to obtain, at a reasonable cost, a sample that is both fairly large and representative of either the broad population or the specific population of their study. For example, the PSID, which started in 1968, comprises two independent national samples: a cross-sectional sample [called the Survey Research Center (SRC) sample], based on stratified multistage selection of the civilian noninstitutional population of the United States, and a sample of low-income families [called the Survey of Economic Opportunities (SEO) sample]. Both of these are probability samples (samples that use some form of random selection within a known population). Some groups in the PSID, such as African Americans and those living in large, urban areas, were oversampled in order to obtain large sample sizes for these groups. Sampling weights are then used to make the PSID representative of the U.S. population.

Other data sets use similar types of methodology to make them nationally representative, often oversampling particular groups of interest (such as welfare recipients or those who are food insecure), and providing sampling weights so that the data is representative of some population. These types of sampling strategies are possible for data sets such as the PSID because the PSID is funded by a large variety of government agencies, including the Office of Economic Opportunity of the U.S. Department of Commerce, the National Science Foundation, the National Institute on Aging, and the National Institute of Child Health and Human Development. Several private foundations also help support the PSID. The annual cost of running the PSID, including interviewing, is somewhere in the area of $3.24 million (in 2009 dollars) (Duncan, 1999).

Other organizations that collect survey data use similarly complex sampling strategies to obtain representative samples. The Fragile Families and Child Well Being study, for example, is administered through a joint effort by the Center for Research on Child Wellbeing and the Center for Health and Wellbeing at Princeton University, and the Columbia Population Research Center and The National Center for Children and Families at Columbia University. The Fragile Families sample is drawn by randomly sampling births, from within randomly selected hospitals, from large U.S. cities using stratified random selection. Prior to random sampling, large U.S. cities were grouped (i.e., stratified) according to their policy environments and labor market conditions in order to ensure representation from a range of policy environments. The complexity of the sampling strategy demanded equally complex techniques for weighting the data to be representative either of large U.S. cities with populations of 200,000 or more or of the 20 sampled cities. Data were collected by Mathematica Policy Research, a firm specializing in such data collection. The resultant sample is distinguished by its utility for studies of state and city policy environments, its focus on nonmarital households, and its efforts to interview fathers, both at their children's birth and thereafter. The researchers were able to get information from three-quarters of nonmarital fathers, making these data richer and more complete than previous studies of single mothers.

Some large data sets, such as the Survey of Income and Program Participation (SIPP), the U.S. Census, the Public-Use Microdata Samples, the Current Population Survey (CPS), and the National Educational Longitudinal Survey, are conducted by the Federal Government. Each of these data sets has complex survey methods and large sample sizes, and is nationally representative (or a survey of the entire population) for either specific populations (such as eighth graders for the NELS), or for the entire population (such as the SIPP or the CPS).

Most of the data sets that will be examined in this book are not only nationally or locally representative, but also cover a very broad range of topics. For example, the PHDCN currently has three waves of data, and it includes individual and family information, such as basic as well as detailed demographics, family mental health, exposure to violence, parental warmth and involvement, social support, community involvement, neighborhood structure, legal and health history, and family relationships. Because the focus of the study is on the very young, a vast amount of information is available on infants' temperament, physical growth and development, cognition, and maternal pregnancy conditions. Roughly 27 instruments and scales are used in the first wave of data collection study (with as many or more instruments and scales in subsequent waves), including the Kagan Mobile Task/Latency to Grasp, the Infant Behavior Questionnaire, the Infant Behavior Rating, and the Growth Assessment Form. Other instruments in the survey measure emotional and physical home environment and child maltreatment. The PHDCN also includes a community survey; systematic, in-person social observations and videotape of physical, social and economic neighbor-hood characteristics; and neighborhood data from 343 neighborhood clusters (where neighborhoods are determined by ecologically meaning-ful physical areas). Likewise, the SIPP includes a wide array of variables, to examine a wide range of topics. Generally, each variable is collected for each family on a monthly basis over a 2-½ to 4-year period. Special modules are included in the SIPP data, however, so that those with par-ticular types of disabilities can be identified, and wealth and school financing can be examined (to give just a few examples of modules).

While most of the data sets described so far are longitudinal, many data sets are cross-sectional, such as the CPS, administered by the Bureau of the Census for the Bureau of Labor Statistics. In the CPS data, the same questions are asked for each of the different months of the survey, but new samples are drawn for each sampling period (with some overlap of sample members from one month to the next). Other cross-sectional data sets examined in this book include the Public Use Microdata Sample (PUMS), the U.S. Census, and the Continuing Survey of Food Intake by Individuals. Often, the sample sizes for these cross-sectional data sets are larger than for the longitudinal data sets, allowing for greater precision in estimation. It is possible for a cross-sectional data set to be for a single year, or for many years. Generally, when using a single cross-sectional year of data, it is difficult to examine cause-and-effect relationships because the cause must precede the effect (although it is sometimes pos-sible when retrospective questions are asked). When using a data set such as the CPS, which contains many cross-sectional years, we may be able to examine how factors in previous years affect outcomes in subsequent years.

In this book, I refer to data sets as large, in terms of both the number of observations and the number of discrete pieces of information about each observation. Data collection may have occurred over relatively short or long periods of time. They generally contain hundreds or thousands of questions.

3

Advantages, Disadvantages, Feasibility, and Appropriateness of Using Secondary Data

As noted earlier, there are some good reasons for using secondary data, including access to large amounts of information, coverage of a broad range of individuals or other entities (e.g., schools, hospitals), and the facts that secondary data generally are representative of some broader population and cover a broad range of topics. In this chapter, I will briefly examine benefits and costs associated with the use of such and how these compare to the design, collection, organization, and use of primary data. A number of questions will then be posed to help readers determine the feasibility and appropriateness of using either secondary or primary data.

ADVANTAGES OF SECONDARY DATA

As noted earlier, secondary data sets tend to be far less costly and take far less time to organize (in terms of putting the data together in working form for data analysis) relative to primary data sets. It can take a considerable amount of time to design, collect, and then organize the data in a primary data set. Often, secondary data are available for no cost on the Internet or through arrangements with the sponsoring organization or government agency. Whereas 20 or 30 years ago the breadth and quality of these data sets may have been in question, secondary data sets today cover a broad array of topics, and the quality of these data sets, from reputable organizations, is often high. Generally, the sample size and the number of discrete units of data collected for each sample member are much higher than what can be collected in a primary data set. Having several hundred observations with a limited amount of information from each of those observations is more the norm for primary data sets, due to cost considerations. These limitations on primary data sets often make it difficult to apply advanced analysis techniques. With large data sets, researchers often can take advantage of advanced statistical techniques, such as fixed-effect modeling or hierarchical linear modeling.

Using existing data may allow for the prompt examination of current policy issues. Because many existing data sets have been designed to capture policy-relevant outcomes (such as income, food security, or well-being), they have the potential to begin capturing policy effects as soon as policy shifts. For example, welfare policy and food stamp policy were changed in 1996, and a number of data sets (such as the *National Survey of America's Families, Survey of Program Dynamics*, and *Welfare, Children, and Families: A Three-City Study*) were set up specifically to capture immediate policy effects.

Large secondary data sets often span a great length of time, in years or months. Some secondary longitudinal data sets, such as the *Panel Study of Income Dynamics* and the *National Longitudinal Survey*, have been collected for decades. This means that individuals or families can be followed for a very long period. Thus, with this type of data, you are able to capture intergenerational effects, factors that affect long-term mobility, or long-term consequences of particular events.

Secondary data often come prepared for use with software (including SAS, STATA, and SPSS) to assist in data organizing, coding, and analysis. Thus, instead of having to code all of your variables, an often time-consuming process, you can sometimes go straight to your analyses, or do minimal amounts of programming to get to your analyses. For example, when you download data from the PSID web page, the data come in SAS, Stata, Excel, SPSS, Database File (DBS), or a SAS transport file. The PSID also includes data books, for only the variables you have chosen, that can be downloaded in PDF, XML, or HTML formats. The Interuniversity Consortium for Political and Social Research (ICPSR), which contains a very large number of data sets, often provides users with similar types of SAS, SPSS, and Stata files that go along with the data to make for easier use. Some data sets come with programming code that can be used to identify missing values for variables, which again saves time for the end user.

Once users become familiar with one or several of the large data sets, users often find that they can address a great variety of questions using these data sets. Thus, while one may be interested in one set of questions when first using the data, once familiar with the data, other questions come to mind, and these questions can be answered in a fairly straightforward way. For example, in the PHDCN data, you may first be interested in how neighborhoods affect child behavioral outcomes. In working with the data, you may find that other interesting variables are available in the data, such as the potential effects of crime and violence, illegal drug use, and sexual activity. You can then use these new variables as either predictor or outcome variables.

DISADVANTAGES TO SECONDARY DATA

While secondary data present many opportunities for researchers, there are still good reasons for using primary data. One of the problems with using secondary data is lack of control over the framing and wording of survey items. This may mean that questions important to your study are not included in the data. Also, subtleties often matter a great deal in research, and secondary data may get to broader or related questions, but not to the exact question being posed by your research. Thus, you may be looking at particular definitions of concepts such as abuse, depression, or intelligence that may differ greatly from the definitions of such concepts in the survey data. Often, the survey may get to broader conceptualizations, whereas you may be looking for more specific aspects of a concept. For example, race may be limited to a few, mutually exclusive categories, whereas your study focuses on a nuanced understanding of race, including the multiplicity of ways in which individuals understand their own racial identities. It is also possible that the questions you desire may be asked, but of the wrong people. For example, many data sets include information gathered from a single source, often whoever is considered to be the head of household, about the entire household or family. Thus, the questions may ask about how much a grandmother takes care of the children or the amount of play time for children. While the source of the information may have a good idea of these answers, it is always possible that they do not and yet may feel a need to answer the questions that are asked of them.

While sample sizes are usually larger for secondary data sources, this may not always be the case. When researchers are examining specific subpopulations, such as children with autism, single fathers, or cohabitating gay or lesbian families, large data sets, representative of broad or even national populations, may have insufficient sample sizes to conduct valid analyses for these groups. Some data sources may have only recently started looking for or using questions to identify such groups. Thus, it may be difficult to find an existing data source that will allow you to study a topic like the long-term effects of autism.

All large-scale data sets contain identifiers for families and individuals within the families, and they may contain household identifiers as well. This doesn't mean that you will be able to identify the individuals in the data set, for example, to obtain additional information from them from outside of the data (and shouldn't be able to identify such individuals, given standard research participation protections). Thus, it is impossible to get additional or follow-up information from the people who have participated in the survey. In contrast, the opportunity to re-contact participants to request additional interviews or to follow-up with specific questions may (or may not) be built into the collection of primary data. With primary data, there is the possibility of attaining following-up answers to additional questions; this is not the case with secondary data. Of course, secondary longitudinal data may add questions that are of interest to the researcher in the next phase of the survey. Depending on the size of the ongoing data-collection efforts, interested researchers have at times advocated successfully for the inclusion of additional questions in subsequent data collection waves.

Data sets collected in the past cannot answer questions about a just-implemented policy change. For these recent issues, one can wait for questions relating to this topic to appear on an existing data set, or go out and collect the data in a primary research sample.

In many ways, users of secondary data trade control over the conditions and quality of the data collection for accessibility, convenience, and reduced costs in time, money, and inconvenience to participants. This lack of researcher control manifests itself in several ways. For example, you may know the questions comprising the survey, but you probably will not know *how* they were asked. Were there great differences among the interviewers? How many interviewers were there? Did respondents understand the questions? Are there particular questions that may be difficult for respondents to understand and that may have great variability in responses? Is there information about the response rate? If it is low, what does this mean? Who are the sponsors of the data collection and do they have an agenda to find particular outcomes? How has the data been "cleaned" or, in other words, have missing data been imputed in some way? If so, how? Is this a good method for imputation? Some of these same questions could be asked of primary research, but, generally, primary researchers will have more control over these issues relative to those using secondary data.

Many of the secondary data sets discussed in this volume are very large and complex, and they may take researchers a long time to fully understand. This may make starting to work on one of these data sets a bit daunting. Before beginning, it is important to fully research types of available data sets and understand which groups are included in the survey, how the sample was constructed, and what kinds of sampling weights to use if weighting of the data is necessary. Weighting the data in your analyses can be a particularly difficult process. Do you use individual weights, family weights, or household weights, and for what years do you use these weights? If you are examining a longitudinal data set, you may wonder if you use weights from the first year or years or from the last years.

Secondary data may subvert the research process by "driving the question," or only looking at questions that can be answered by the available data. Researchers need to keep in mind that this sort of approach may be appropriate for doing exploratory work and for developing hypotheses, but not for testing hypotheses.

DETERMINING THE FEASIBILITY AND APPROPRIATENESS OF USING SECONDARY DATA

This section will take readers through a list of questions that they should ask themselves before starting a research project to determine whether using primary or secondary data would best serve their research. It gives some guidance as to whether using secondary data is appropriate, and which data set to use if it is. The questions are intended to help readers determine, first, which would be the most appropriate of a variety of available data sets, and, second, whether the data set, once chosen, contains key information.

1. Is the population from which the sample is drawn appropriate for the planned research?
   Researchers need to make sure that they are sampling from the appropriate populations in order to be able to do their research. If they fail to get an appropriate sample, they will not be able to do the research they wish to do. For example, if you wish to examine patients from mental health institutions, and such patients are not included in the sampling frame, the data will not be appropriate for such a study. Even if the sample includes people from mental health hospitals, variables in the data must contain information about whether the respondent was in a mental health hospital. Often, sampling frames (or the population surveyed) do not include those in institutional settings or the military.

2. Is the dependent variable contained in the data?
   This is one of the most important questions to ask. If the answer is "no," the question then becomes: Is there a variable that is conceptually comparable to the variable that you would like to use? If the answer to this is also "no," then you will not use these data. However, if the answer is yes, then you may want to consider these data. You will need to determine how conceptually far away this variable is from the variable you would truly like to use, and the consequences of this. For example, you are using longitudinal data and hypothesize that childhood health affects the type of neighborhood the individual will live in as an adult. The longitudinal data may have information on average income in the adult neighborhood or the respondent's perception of the adult neighborhood (Is it safe? Is it poor? Is it really poor?). Your preferred variable may be the percentage of the population living below the poverty line in the adult neighborhood. Are these measures close enough for you to use these data for your work?

3. Are the necessary independent variables of interest available?
   This is sometimes a trickier question than the dependent variable
   question because there are oftentimes many variables that you
   will need as both primary independent and control variables. You
   first need to develop (either formally or informally) the
   conceptual model at the basis of the issue you are analyzing,
   which should suggest which are the main independent variables
   you hypothesize will influence your dependent variable, as well as
   the other variables that might be related to that dependent
   variable and should be included as control variables. Once you've
   done this, you could then check the literature to see if there are
   alternative hypotheses that suggest additional variables to
   include. Equally important is the specificity of the measurement.
   For example, if you are examining the effects of childhood mental
   health problems as a primary independent variable, you must ask
   yourself whether having this as a yes/no question is sufficient for
   testing your hypothesis. Do you instead need the degree of
   impairment or specific type of mental health problem to better
   examine the effects of mental health on some outcome? Who is
   asked the question? Who has determined that the child has
   such a diagnosis: a physician or specialist, or a parent or other
   caregiver?

   The same kinds of questions can be asked about other control
   variables or variables that examine alternative hypotheses. First,
   are variables available to test alternative hypotheses? Is it truly a
   mental health problem that is affecting the outcome, or is it some
   other variable that others have found to be important and that
   you may need to control? If the data does not include variables
   for these alternative hypotheses, you may get biased results.

4. If replicating a study, how do these data differ from those used
   previously, and will this make a difference in running and
   interpreting analyses?
   It may make little difference that the variables available in your
   data differ somewhat from the variables in the original study,
   if you are concerned not about completely replicating the
   previous work, but only in finding whether results differ when
   variables are specified in a slightly different way. If you are mainly
   concerned with using a different set of data to see if the results

from a previous study hold, however, then finding a data set with the same variables will be important.

5. Does the available data have adequate identifiers for the target groups for analysis (women with Alzheimer's, adolescents with eating disorders, children of gay couples)?
Without such identifiers, it will be impossible to conduct the planned analyses for your study. If these identifiers are available, you must then determine if the sample sizes for sub-groups are large enough to run analyses. It's often difficult to determine what sample size is "big enough." Obviously, having more observations per included variable will help you find relationships when they exist in the population. If you are running nonparametric analyses, this need for larger sample sizes becomes greater in order to adequately test your hypotheses.

6. Is it important to be able to generalize results to the general population (of the United States, for example), to specific populations (such as the elderly), or to a far lower-level population (such as clients of a particular clinic)?
If you need to generalize to a more broadly defined population, then using a secondary data set will likely be the way to go. If you need only to generalize to a lower-level group, then using primary data may be a more feasible and appropriate option. It is possible that data have already been collected from some lower-level group, such as a clinic, but this isn't likely. Even if the data have been collected, it's unlikely that such data will contain the kinds of information that you need, so collecting data will probably be the best way to examine your hypotheses.

7. Does the data set of interest require special authorization to obtain?
Some data sets are available only with special contracts because of the confidential nature of the data and risk that its specificity may compromise individuals' identities. Often, these contracts require the researcher and his or her institution to sign contracts, with fees attached, for use of the data. You will need to determine whether your institution will be willing to incur the risks of your use of such data. Generally, institutions with such data, such as

the federal government and universities, have become more stringent in their requirements for granting data access. Doctoral students often cannot receive such data without having the doctoral chair or some other high-ranking person or fiduciary agent accept the data for the doctoral student. Such data must be kept off-line, and it cannot be kept on networks that back up the data. Passwords for accessing the data and data encryption are often necessary as conditions for receiving the data. Often, contracts for specific periods of time must be signed, and the data must be destroyed after the contract expires. Generally, the data must be used only at the institution, not at home. The use of such data sets sometimes costs money, as well. For example, for using the restricted version of the PSID, $750 must be paid to the Survey Research Center at the University of Michigan for each project that uses the data. Often, these data sets will contain a public-use component that does not include the potentially identifying information, which is available to researchers without special permission.

8. Do you, or someone you can hire, have the programming skills to use the data?
Some data sets are quite complicated and require advanced skills in programming in SAS, Stata, or SPSS. If you lack these skills, you will not be able to use some of the data sets described in this book, or you may need to hire a programmer to work with you. On the other hand, many data sets are far less complicated than they were only several years ago. For example, many data sets available on the web include SAS, Stata, and SPSS programs that allow you to input and format the data without having to write your own code. This doesn't mean that you don't have code to write. Eliminating missing values, combining and constructing variables, and extracting data for particular years or subpopulations will require some degree of programming skill. In my own work, much of my day is spent programming, in SAS or Stata, to get variables in the proper working condition. Once the data have been "cleaned" (i.e., missing values imputed or deleted and variables put in a usable format), the more difficult programming begins. For example, you may want to look at

longitudinal data for children when they are between the ages of 0 to 4, examining their income, child care, health care, or other variables, and different children may be ages 0 to 4 in different waves of the data. To do this, you will need to use data loops and arrays, with which you should be familiar before starting such a project. Obviously, different software programs have different programming languages (SAS, SPSS, Stata), and it will be helpful to know how to program in at least one of the programming languages.

9. How quickly do you need results?
   If you are examining a new policy and need to determine if it is helping or hurting, secondary data, if it's available, may aid in getting quicker results. Of course, the speed with which you can generate an analysis depends on how well put together the secondary data are and on your programming skills, as noted above. The use of secondary data can save time and resources for the researcher. Even more important, however, using existing data bypasses the need to ask for time and a certain degree of trust from new research participants who, by the purview of the social work profession, are often among the most vulnerable. If the data are not available, and quick results are needed, collecting primary data may the best way to examine new policies.

4

Secondary Datasets

In this chapter, I will describe several social work, social science, and related datasets, along with where and how to access them and their key characteristics. Of course, there are thousands of secondary datasets available in myriad places, and I will cover only a portion of the largest and most widely used datasets. I will indicate where to find these data, and, in some cases, the types of analyses that one can undertake using them. I will also indicate whether datasets have public use versions, which generally strip the data of geographic identifiers or other potentially identifying information and which, in addition, have another version that includes these identifiers. The datasets will be described by various features, including:

1. Cross-sectional, longitudinal
2. Years covered
3. Unit of analysis
4. Sample size
5. Population(s) covered and
6. Basic categories of information covered

I also summarize much of this information in Appendix Tables 1 and 2.

One of the best places to find many of the datasets that will be described here is the Inter-University Consortium for Political and Social

Research (ICPSR), the largest archive of social science datasets (http://www.icpsr.umich.edu). There are not only original datasets in this collection, but also datasets that have been assembled by other researchers. For example, I recently needed the Current Population Survey (CPS) from the 1960s to the present. The CPS website (http://www.census.gov/cps/) contains data only from recent years. I went to the ICPSR and found many of the supplements to the CPS (such as the Veterans Supplement, the Food Security Supplement, and the Tobacco Use Supplement), but also found the March, individual-level extracts from 1968 to 1992, which were put together by Robert Moffitt (Study Number 6171, http://www.icpsr.umich.edu/cocoon/ICPSR/STUDY/06171.xml). Thus, instead of having to put together each individual year of the CPS, the ICPSR contained merged data that were ready to use. In looking for the General Social Survey, I was able to find information about the Japanese General Social Survey, the Chinese General Social Survey, and the Polish General Social Survey, among many others. Many of these datasets are ready for downloading, and many have been cleaned (e.g., putting in missing value codes for missing data, assembling data by person, family, or household) by those putting them together.

The Data Ferret from the U.S. Census Bureau, located at http://dataferrett.census.gov/, is another key source for obtaining data. The data included from this website include the American Community Survey; the American Housing Survey; the Consumer Expenditure Survey; County Business Patterns; the Current Population Survey; the Decennial Census of the Population and Housing; Decennial Public Use Microdata Samples; the Mortality Sample; the National Ambulatory Medical Care Survey; the National Health Interview Survey; the National Hospital Ambulatory Medical Care Survey,; the National Survey of Fishing, Hunting, and Wildlife Associated Recreation; the New York City Housing and Vacancy Survey; Small Area Health Insurance Estimates; Small Areas Income and Poverty Estimates; The Social Security Administration Survey of Income and Program Participation; and the Survey of Program Dynamics. To get the Data Ferret program, go to the web page given above, then click on "Launch DataFerrett." You will be asked for your e-mail address, which you will use when you log into the system. Once you are in DataFerret, you can choose any of the above datasets and download the data in a variety of formats, create tables, or create tables for downloading.

One more excellent site that I will often refer to in the book is the Pennsylvania State Simple Online Data Archive for Population Studies (SODA POP). There are hundreds of secondary datasets available at this site (http://sodapop.pop.psu.edu/data-collections), many of them accessible to those outside of the Penn State system (see http://sodapop.pop.psu.edu/help/sodapop-for-users-outside-of-penn-state for gaining access to the datasets on this site). A truly nice aspect of this site is that you can search all of the datasets by keyword (see http://sodapop.pop.psu.edu/explore/codebooks/sodaforms/searchall_form.html). Thus, if you are interested in mental health, you can type this phrase into their search engine and it will show you all the variables and datasets that contain that phrase (variables, labels, or anywhere else in the description of the data/variables).

For educational datasets, an excellent archive is the International Archive of Educational Data (http://www.icpsr.umich.edu/IAED/index.html). Here, you will find datasets and online tools to examine a wide range of educational surveys.

Large secondary datasets not covered in this book are numerous, and I will mention a few here that may be of interest to social work and other social science researchers. One is the Combine study, which examines treatment options for alcoholism; it included 1,383 alcohol-abstinent volunteers and ran from 2001 to 2004 (Anton, 2006). Second, the National Institute of Justice (NIJ) Data Resources Program is a repository of datasets collected through NIJ-funded grants. These datasets are archived in the National Archive of Crime Justice Data within the ICPSR. A few of these datasets include the National Evaluation of the National Institute of Justice Grants to Combat Violent Crimes Against Women on Campus Program, 2000–2002; Arrestee Drug Abuse Monitoring (ADAM) Program in the United States, 2003; The National Crime Victimization Survey, through 2008; and the National Crime Victimization Survey: School Crime Supplement, 2007. Also, see Boslaugh (2007) for more information on health-related datasets.

Most of the rest of this book goes into greater detail about all of the secondary datasets previously mentioned. For some the datasets, I go into where and how to access the data and, for some datasets, I show you screen shots for using the data. I find that the screen shots are often helpful in seeing what the datasets look like to help users access or use the data. Other datasets, in which less information is given on accessing or using the data, are fairly straightforward (download the data and start working), or are so complicated that they would take up too much space to present such information here. When codebooks or descriptions of the data are available online, I indicate where you can find those descriptions or codebooks. I sometimes give brief SAS code for using some of the data as well, to give readers the feel for what to do when accessing and using some of these data. I will often indicate which datasets are best for particular types of research—such as the study of children, health, education, poverty, intergenerational studies, etc.—often by presenting what kinds of studies have come from these datasets. For some datasets, response rates are easily available, and I indicate these response rates when discussing the dataset, while for others, response rates could not be found. I present the datasets in alphabetical order.

ADOPTION AND FOSTER CARE ANALYSIS AND REPORTING SYSTEM (AFCARS)

The Adoption and Foster Care Analysis and Reporting System (AFCARS) collects case-specific data on all finalized adoptions and foster care placements facilitated through state welfare agencies, or private organizations contracted by public welfare agencies, in all 50 states, the District of Columbia, and Puerto Rico. The children in the dataset range in age from under 1 year through 20 years. Data is available from 1995 through 2005. Data collection became more efficient in 1998, meaning better data was collected for more states. States submit data twice over the course of a year that begins on October 1 and ends the following year on September 30. The original purpose of AFCARS was to gather information for state and federal level policy- and program-management uses and to research the nature of adoption and foster care. The information is cross-sectional.

States are federally mandated to provide this data on an annual basis under Title IV-B/E of the Social Security Act (Section 427). The dataset includes all cases of foster care and adoption that occur through public welfare agencies. The dataset represents only those types of arrangements. Agencies securing adoptions outside of state agencies provide information voluntarily, and this information is not included in the publicly available dataset.

The number of states reporting and number of observations vary across years. In 2005, 52 states/districts reported data for both adoptions and foster care, totaling 51,485 and 801,200 observations, respectively. Efforts are made to remove duplicated adoption observations, but beware of such duplication. The foster care data include only one observation per child; for those children with multiple observations, only the most recent is included.

The dataset provides separate information on a variety of variables for children who are adopted and those who are in foster care. The 37 adoption variables include child demographics, the presence of disabilities (e.g., physical, mental retardation, visual/hearing impairment, emotional disturbance), birth parents' dates of birth and dates of termination of rights, date of adoption, adoptive family structure, adoptive parents' demographics and any pre-adoptive relationship to the child, and information about the agency placing the child, as well as whether the adoptive family is receiving Title IV-E support and if so, the amount.

The 66 foster care variables include child demographics, the presence of disabilities, information about previous removals from home and adoptions, manner of removal (e.g., voluntary or court ordered), reason for removal (e.g., abuse/neglect, alcohol/drug abuse by parent or child, child disability or behavior problems, parent death or incarceration, abandonment), placement setting (e.g., pre-adoptive home, relative or nonrelative foster home, group home), case plan goal (e.g., reunification with parent, live with relatives, adoption, long-term foster care, emancipation, guardianship), information about the principal caretaker and foster caretaker as well as the family structure of each, reasons for discharge from foster care (e.g., reunification, living with other relatives, adoption, emancipation), and use of state support. Foster care variables include whether AFDC/TANF, SSI, and SS payments supported relative caretakers.

Researchers using AFCARS data can study case-level data at a state or national level and examine descriptive data about children and their birth, adoptive and foster parents; placement types, lengths and goals; and the amount and impact of social assistance. Researchers also can examine trends and predictors of a variety of foster care and adoption outcomes. The dataset allows for policy analysis, given that one can study and compare data across states. Each annual dataset includes state-specific notes that inform this type of analysis.

Annually, the U.S. Department of Health and Human Services publishes *The AFCARS Report*, outlining descriptive information about children in foster care, waiting for adoption and adopted. This report is available through http://www.acf.hhs.gov/programs/cb, the Children's Bureau web page. Other researchers recently have used AFCARS to study trends in kinship care (Vericker, Macomber & Geen, 2008), the factors that influence foster care discharge rates after termination of parental rights (Smith, 2003), predictors of reunification for foster children with an incarcerated parent (Hayward and DePanfilis, 2007), and the relationship between child developmental and medical conditions on out-of-home placement (Rosenberg & Robinson, 2004). Another researcher used AFCARS to examine the impact of subsidies on adoption (Hansen, 2007).

These data are available from National Data Archive of Child Abuse and Neglect (NDACAN), http://www.ndacan.cornell.edu. The codebook for the 1995 to 1999 versions of the data is available at http://www.ndacan.cornell.edu/NDACAN/Datasets/UserGuidePDFs/AFCARS_Guide_1995-1999.pdf.

CHILD NEGLECT: CROSS SECTOR SERVICE PATH AND OUTCOMES

Child Neglect: Cross Sector Service Path and Outcomes uses administrative and census data to gather longitudinal, child-level information about cross-sector service use and patterns, caregiver characteristics, and later child and adolescent outcomes. The sample comprises those receiving AFDC or TANF, with approximately half the sample including children with reports to child welfare for maltreatment and half without such reports. All children in the sample were born between 1982 and 1994, were under 12 years old when data collection began, and lived with a family that received AFDC. Data collection began in 1993 to 1994 and followed the children through 2001. Samples were drawn and data collected for a Midwestern metropolitan area. It is unclear whether the data are representative of children in this region or of any other groups.

Child Neglect uses a matched, two-group comparison design. The researchers first created a sample of children who had been reported to child welfare services for maltreatment in 1993 or 1994, and then matched these children to AFDC records. These children constituted the maltreatment/AFDC group. Maltreatment categories for this group included neglect, physical abuse, sexual abuse, or mixed types; emotional abuse and other forms of maltreatment were excluded. The comparison group, randomly selected from the remaining children in the AFDC files and matched by birth year and city or county of residence, includes children whose families were not reported to child welfare for maltreatment in 1993 or 1994. Each group contains only one child per family, and the AFDC-only group excludes those children who have a sibling, or who live in a home with other children, with a report of maltreatment. The total sample includes 10,187 children with 5,087 in the maltreatment/AFDC group and 5,100 in the AFDC-only comparison group. Four age cohorts were created in each sample and followed for the eight years of data collection. This accelerated panel design allows for statistical analysis of 19 years' worth of developmental information, not just eight.

Child Neglect collects child-level data through administrative records from education, health, juvenile and adult corrections, and social service organizations. Some adult-level data are available on some variables. Child abuse and neglect information includes age at time of the report, reason for the report, relationship with the perpetrator, substantiation status, type and severity of maltreatment, and occupation of the reporter. Child welfare services data include information about foster care services (e.g., age at entry, reasons for placement and exit, and type, frequency, and length of placements) and in-home services, such as intensive family preservation services and less intensive family services. Income-maintenance variables include information about spells on AFDC or TANF (starting in 1997) and reasons for receipt. Data is gathered on the admission date and offense type for those who spent time in juvenile justice facilities. Adult corrections data provide information about incarceration in state facilities (not local or county jails), including admission year, sentence length and offense (including property and financial crimes or possession/selling of drugs). Medicaid billing information includes data about inpatient, outpatient, and hospital care and problems at birth that may impact development later (collected from both the mother's and the child's records). Educational data include disability type and date of testing. Community-level data include 1990 residential census tract data (e.g., population total, income, race, education, unemployment and mobility) and crime information.

Researchers can use *Child Neglect: Cross Sector Service Path and Outcomes* to examine service utilization among children experiencing abuse and neglect, the association between service utilization and later outcomes, and the relationship between TANF use and child and adolescent outcomes. This information can be compared with those receiving AFDC or TANF but without maltreatment reports. Researchers have explored the relationship between criminal justice system involvement and welfare (Jonson-Reid, 2002) and maltreatment (Bright, Jonson-Reid & Williams, 2008). Research has also examined the association between maltreatment and special education eligibility (Jonson-Reid, Drake, Kim, Porterfield, & Han, 2004) and risk of death (Jonson-Reid, Chance, & Drake, 2007). Researchers also have used the dataset to explore possibilities for improved technology to map referrals and services (Hovmand, Jonson-Reid, & Drake, 2007).

These data are available through National Data Archive of Child Abuse and Neglect, http://www.ndacan.cornell.edu, or see Http://www. ndacan.cornell.edu/NDACAN/Datasets/Abstracts/DatasetAbstract_116. html. The codebook for the data is available at http://www.ndacan. cornell.edu/NDACAN/Datasets/UserGuidePDFs/116user.pdf.

COMMON CORE OF DATA (CCD)

Common Core of Data, a database of public elementary and secondary schools of the U.S. Department of Education's National Center for Education Statistics, annually collects fiscal and nonfiscal data about students, staff, and characteristics of public schools; public school districts; and state education agencies in the United States. The dataset provides an official listing of elementary and secondary schools and school districts nationally and provides basic information and statistics on schools in general. Unlike many datasets, the CCD actually covers an entire national population (that of public elementary and secondary schools/districts) rather than just a sample that is representative of that population. Often, the CCD is used as a sample frame from which random samples of schools or districts are selected as part of the data collection process in other surveys.

The data is collected each year from a population of approximately 97,000 public elementary and secondary schools and approximately

18,000 public school districts. Data come from the 50 states, the District of Columbia, Department of Defense schools, the Bureau of Indian Affairs, and outlying areas, such as Puerto Rico, Guam, American Samoa, and the U.S. Virgin Islands. The data is collected using five surveys sent out to the state education departments and completed by agency officials. Most of the data are acquired through administrative records. The data for schools and districts are meant to be comparable across states.

The CCD comprises five datasets: Public School Universe, Local Education Agency (School District) Universe, state aggregate nonfiscal data, state aggregate fiscal data, and school district fiscal data. The Public School Universe includes information on the location and type of school, enrollment by grade, student characteristics, and number of teachers. The Local Education Agency (School District) Universe has information on the number of current students and the number of high school graduates. The state aggregate nonfiscal dataset has information on students and staff, such as the number of students per grade level and high school graduates and completers. Both the state and school district aggregate fiscal data include revenue and expenditures by function and average daily attendance and enrollment, respectively.

The CCD includes variables pertaining to dropouts; the receipt of diplomas and GEDs; guidance counselors and institutional aides; library and library/media support; Individualized Education Programs for students with disabilities; alternative education schools, charter schools, magnet schools and programs; kindergarten and pre-kindergarten; educational agencies (state, federal and other); migrant students; shared-time schools; supervisory unions; and Title I eligible schools. The CCD also includes information about schools' participation in the Free Lunch Program, Reduced-Price Lunch Program, and Head Start Program, and geographical information, such as community size and whether the school is located in a metropolitan or micropolitan statistical area.

The data are available through the National Center for Education Statistics (http://nces.ed.gov/ccd). Researchers can build tables, search for public schools, and compare the data across states. Data on private schools also can be accessed through the NCES Private School Universe Survey (http://nces.ed.gov/surveys/pss/).

The data can be assembled by state, county, school district, or school—currently for 1987–1988 through 2006–2007—as shown in the following page.

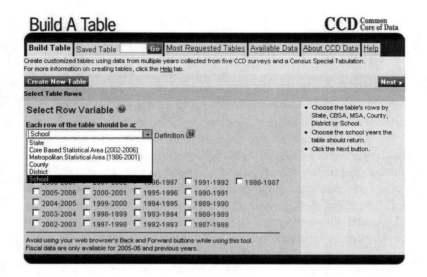

From here, you can examine a limited number of variables by grade level. You also examine the most requested tables, such as grade completers by race and pupil-to-teacher ratios.

A second way to access the data on this site is by downloading entire datasets, with either SAS or SPSS code, or an SAS dataset. Data documentation also is available for download (http://nces.ed.gov/ccd/bat/versions.asp).The download page looks like the figure given in the following page for the local education agency (school district) survey.

From here, click on the 2006–07 SAS zip file, and agree to the terms of use. The file downloads in SAS format (instead of a flat file that would require either SAS or SPSS code to transform the data into SAS or SPSS). From here, the data was put into the c:\SAS directory. Next, go into SAS, and write the code:

```
libname in 'c:\SAS';
data a;set in.ag061c;
proc means n mean std;
run;
```

You then get the result as shown in Table 4.1.

For a second dataset, the State Dropout and Completion Data File: 2005–06, this dataset was again downloaded in SAS format, and the

Local Education Agency (School District) Universe Survey Data

- to provide a complete listing of every education agency in the United States responsible for providing free public elementary/secondary instruction or education support services;
- to provide basic information about all education agencies and the students for whose education the agencies are responsible.

More About - Local Education Agency (School District) Universe Survey Data.

If you have any questions on this data set please contact John Sietsema.

The annual reports using this CCD file's data are the School and Agency Reports.

Year	Data Set	Input Code	Documentation		
			General	*Record Layout*	*Survey Form*
2006–07 (v.1c)**	ZIP (1.8 MB) Flat File (9.3 MB) ZIP (2.1 MB) SAS File (9.9 MB)	SAS Code ZIP (4 KB) SPSS Code ZIP (4 KB)	PDF (470 KB) ZIP (425 KB)[1]	Flat File (21 KB)	N/A
2005–06 (v.1a)	ZIP (1.6 MB) Flat File (9.3 MB) ZIP (1.8 MB) SAS File (10.1 MB)	SAS Code ZIP (4 KB) SPSS Code ZIP (4 KB)	PDF (480 KB) ZIP (215 KB)[1]	Flat File (25 KB)	N/A
2004–05 (v.1c)**	ZIP (1.7 MB) Flat File (9.0 MB) ZIP (1.8 MB) SAS File (9.8 MB)	SAS Code ZIP (4 KB) SPSS Code ZIP (4 KB)	PDF (351 KB) ZIP (229 KB)[1]	Flat File (24 KB)	PDF (267 KB)
2003–04 (v.1b)**	ZIP (1.8 MB) Flat File (12.7 MB) ZIP (2 MB) SAS File (15 MB)	SAS Code ZIP (5 KB) SPSS Code ZIP (5 KB)	PDF (652 KB) ZIP (137 KB)[1]	Flat File (34 KB)	PDF (96 KB)
2002–03# (v.1a)**	ZIP (1.9 MB) Flat File (12.3 MB) ZIP (2 MB) SAS File (6.5 MB)	SAS Code ZIP (5 KB) SPSS Code ZIP (5 KB)	PDF (800 KB) ZIP (121 KB)[1]	Flat File (34 KB)	PDF (24 KB)
2001–02# (v.1a)	ZIP (2 MB) Flat File (13 MB) ZIP (2 MB) SAS File (7 MB)	SAS Code ZIP (4 KB) SPSS Code ZIP (6 KB)	PDF (214 KB) ZIP (84 KB)[1]	Flat File (32 KB)	PDF (8 KB)
2000–01# (v.1a)	ZIP (2 MB) Flat File (12 MB) ZIP (2 MB) SAS File (7 MB)	SAS Code ZIP (4 KB) SPSS Code ZIP (6 KB)	PDF (252 KB) ZIP (110 KB)[1]	Flat File (32 KB)	PDF (9 KB)

sample sizes and mean values as seen in Table 4.2 were obtained for a variety of variables.

Similar downloads are available for Census 2000 School District Demographics, Local Education Agency (school district) Universe Survey Dropout and Completion Data, National Public Education Financial Survey (State Fiscal), Public Elementary/Secondary School Universe Survey, State Nonfiscal Public Elementary/Secondary Education Survey, State-Level Public School Dropout Data, and Survey of Local Government Finances, School Systems. Codebooks for many of these datasets, as well as data downloads, are available from The Pennsylvania State University at http://sodapop.pop.psu.edu/data-collections/ccd/dnd.

Table 4.1   The SAS System The MEANS Procedure

Variable	Label	N	Mean	Std Dev
LATCOD06	Latitude	18208	39.7733226	4.6435224
LONCOD06	Longitude	18208	-91.5740790	14.9207493
SCH06	Aggregate Number of Schools Associated with Agency	18250	5.4871233	18.8966628
TEACH06	Aggregate FTE Classroom Teachers Associated with Agency	18250	106.7183507	423.0605554
UG06	Ungraded Students	18250	14.5500274	234.5235417
PK1206	PK - 12 Students	18250	2713.36	11302.61
MEMBER06	Calculated Total Student Membership of the LEA	18250	2729.48	11365.55
MIGRNT06	Migrant Students Served in a Summer Program	18250	0.3923836	28.2065423
SPECED06	Special Education - Individualized Education Program (IEP) Students	18250	348.0399452	1950.14
ELL06	English Language Learner Students	18250	137.6566575	1210.67
PKTCH06	Teachers - Prekindergarten	18250	2.0001425	16.1675356
KGTCH06	Teachers - Kindergarten	18250	9.3033534	50.7920183
ELMTCH06	Teachers - Elementary v18250	80.7286466	407.9800449	
SECTCH06	Teachers - Secondary	18250	69.1956110	305.0761105
UGTCH06	Teachers - Ungraded	18250	12.5189315	112.6576929
TOTTCH06	Teachers - Total	18250	174.7794521	855.8791411

Table 4.1 The SAS System The MEANS Procedure *(Continued)*

Variable	Label	N	Mean	Std Dev
AIDES06	Instructional Aides / Paraprofessionals	18250	33.1789041	138.3939312
CORSUP06	Instructional Coordinators and	18250	3.3155945	24.7923206
ELMGUI06	Guidance Counselors - Elementary	18250	1.2131836	8.1638505
SECGUI06	Guidance Counselors - Secondary	18250	2.0418630	11.9331475
TOTGUI06	Guidance Counselors - Total	18250	5.5707233	28.7885990
LIBSPE06	Librarians / Media Specialists	18250	2.9306521	14.1227927
LIBSUP06	Librarians / Media Support Staff	18250	1.2083233	7.4469987
LEAADM06	LEA Administrators	18250	3.1864877	15.3907534
LEASUP06	LEA Administrative Support Staff	18250	8.5664274	42.7661939
SCHADM06	School Administrators	18250	8.4452164	41.6789161
SCHSUP06	School Administrative Support Staff	18250	12.1865425	71.1972492
STUSUP06	Student Support Services Staff	18250	13.1183507	65.3746717
OTHSUP06	All Other Support Staff	18250	57.4597151	276.0275388

CONTINUING SURVEY OF FOOD INTAKE BY INDIVIDUALS (CSFII)

The Continuing Survey of Food Intake by Individuals (CSFII), conducted by the U.S. Department of Agriculture, aims to study the food-consumption patterns of the people of the United States, with a particular emphasis on the effects of nutritional policies, exposure

Table 4.2

Variable	Label	N	Mean
RP912	Dropout Rate (Grades 9 through 12)	59	3.3661017
P9	Dropout Rate (Grade 9)	59	2.6237288
DRP10	Dropout Rate (Grade 10)	59	3.1271186
DRP11	Dropout Rate (Grade 11)	59	3.5745763
DRP12	Dropout Rate (Grade 12)	59	4.3711864
DRPAM	Dropout Rate (American Indian / Alaskan Native, Grades 9 through 12)	59	4.7915254
DRPAS	Dropout Rate (Asian / Pacific Islander, Grades 9 through 12)	59	1.9169492
DRPHI	Dropout Rate (Hispanic, Grades 9 through 12)	59	4.7440678
DRPBL	Dropout Rate (Black, non-Hispanic, Grades 9 through 12)	59	4.3474576
DRPWH	Dropout Rate (White, non-Hispanic, Grades 9 through 12)	59	1.9576271
DRPM	Dropout Rate (Male, Grades 9 through 12)	59	2.9661017
DRPF	Dropout Rate (Female, Grades 9 through 12)	59	2.2864407
DRPU	Dropout Rate (Gender Unknown, Grades 9 through 12)	59	1.7457627
EBS912	Dropout Rate Enrollment Base (Grades 9 through 12)	59	239668.68
EBS9	Dropout Rate Enrollment Base (Grade 9)	59	69354.90
EBSAM9M	Dropout Rate Enrollment Base (American Indian / Alaskan Native, Grade 9, Male)	59	377.6949153
EBSAM9F	Dropout Rate Enrollment Base (American Indian / Alaskan Native, Grade 9, Female)	59	365.4745763
EBSAM9U	Dropout Rate Enrollment Base (American Indian / Alaskan Native, Grade 9, Gender Unknown)	59	0.1525424
EBSAS9M	Dropout Rate Enrollment Base (Asian / Pacific Islander, Grade 9, Male)	59	1508.88

to pesticides, and the influence of diet on various health problems. The original study was conducted in 1985 and 1986, with continuations and changes in 1989–1991, 1994–1996, and 1998. The samples are nationally representative.

The 1985 and 1986 data included both an all-income sample and a low-income sample (see http://www.ars.usda.gov/Services/docs.htm?

docid=7889). The all-income sample included 1,500 women aged 19 to 50 and their children, aged 1 to 5 (with around 550 children in each sample year), and a sample of 1,100 men, aged 19 to 50, in the 1985 sample only. The low-income sample had 2,100 and 1,300 women and 1,300 and 800 children in 1985 and 1986, respectively. Food intake was collected for six days, over a one-year period, for each year.

The 1989–1991 study was conducted as three separate one-year surveys with data collected over three consecutive days, with an aim to provide information on the usual intake of foods and nutrients. The first day was an in-home interview in which respondents recalled the food consumed the previous day. The second and third days' data were collected through a self-administered dietary recall. Six weeks after the three-day data collection period, respondents completed the Diet and Health Knowledge Survey. Sample sizes are relatively large, with 15,192 individuals for the one-day dietary intake, and 11,912 for the three-day dietary in-take.

The 1994–1996 continuation, which again aimed to find the "usual intake" of food per individual, collected one-day dietary intake data from 16,103 persons of all ages, 4,253 of whom were children aged 0 to 9 years old. Respondents provided details about their food intake in the past 24 hours, reporting on the specific types of food consumed and the amount of each food consumed. To improve efficiency and minimize error, a computerized coding system (Survey Net) converted food intake into its component foods and nutrients.

The 1998 continuation, called the Supplemental Children's Survey, CSFII 1998, collected data from a larger sample of children (N=5,559) to estimate the exposure to pesticide residues in the diets of children. CSFII 1998 data can be combined with 1994–1996 data. The Department of Agriculture, through the Food Quality Protection Act of 1996, required the collection of this data.

The CSFII contains variables relating to health and diet such as nutrient, vitamin, and supplement intake; dietary fiber; niacin and calcium equivalents; folate content; source frequency of food and beverage intake; household food; identity of the main food preparer; breast-fed children; school and employment of household members over 15 years of age; family income, both absolute and as a percentage of the poverty level; and region and size of the area (metropolitan vs. nonmetropolitan area) of the respondent.

The CSFII data have been used to study many aspects of food intake. Dietary studies involving CSFII data have looked at the relationship between healthy diets and family income (Beydoun, Powell, & Wang, 2009), how demographics affect diet quality (Forshee & Storey, 2006), and the correlation between self-assessed health status and diet intake (Goodwin, Knol, Eddy, & Fitzhugh, 2006). The topic of food intake also has been studied for specific ages, from preschool (Kranz, Hartman, Siega-Riz, & Herring, 2006), to school-aged children (Suitor & Gleason, 2002) to the elderly (Sebastian, Cleveland, Goldman, & Moshfegh, 2007). Other research has studied the relationship between gender and ethnicity and diet (Beydoun & Wang, 2008); the links among nutrition, food security, and obesity (Beebout, 2006); the relationship between school meal participation and nutrient intake (Gleason & Suitor 2003); and calcium requirements (Hunt & Johnson, 2007).

The 1989-1991 CSFII data are available from National Technical Information Service, http://www.ntis.gov. The 1994–1996 and 1998 data and documentation are available at The Pennsylvania State University through Simple Online Data Archive of Population Studies at http://sodapop.pop.psu.edu/data-collections/csfii/dnd, and from the Department of Agriculture (http://www.ars.usda.gov/SP2UserFiles/Place/12355000/pdf/Csfii98.pdf) on CD-ROM.

CURRENT POPULATION SURVEY (CPS)

The Current Population Survey has been conducted as a joint effort between the Bureau of Labor Statistics and the Bureau of Census since the 1940s. The purpose of the CPS is to provide information on characteristics of the labor force in the United States. It is often used to evaluate the number and percentage of unemployed and to measure the potential labor force. It also is used to calculate and analyze wage rates, hours of work, and earning trends for different demographic groups. The study is nationally representative of the civilian noninstitutionalized population. The data can be used to look at the country as a whole and sometimes can be used to examine states or other geographic areas, depending on the sample size of those states.

The CPS collects cross-sectional monthly data from around 50,000 to 100,000 households. Each member of the household aged 16 and above is interviewed. Data is collected by either in-person or telephone interviews. General labor force information is collected each month, and other data on specialized topics are gathered through periodic additional supplements. Each household is a participant in the survey for eight survey periods. When it first enters the survey, it is involved in four consecutive monthly surveys, then it is absent from the next eight, and then it partakes again in another four months.

Outside of employment numbers, the CPS provides data on demographics, displaced workers, computer and internet use, educational attainment, industry, occupation, marital status, minimum wage work, poverty, volunteering, women's employment, and youth employment.

The survey was redesigned in 1994 to take into account changing patterns of life in the United States. The redesign was implemented to collect more monthly data on earnings and hourly wages, child care problems, and problems associated with being laid off.

The March Supplement to the CPS, the Annual Social and Economic Supplement, gives data on income, poverty, and health insurance for the country. Tables for this information are available at the U.S. Census web page, and downloads of these data are available at http://www.bls.census. gov/cps_ftp.html#cpsmarch for 1998 to 2008. Other data in this March Supplement include region, state, principal city, city size, rental subsidies, receipt of food stamps and other government assistance, unearned income, taxes paid, family type, income percentile, disability status and disability income, reasons for missing work, type of worker, involvement in worker training, type of health insurance, health status, and reasons for receiving Social Security income or Supplemental Security Income. All of this information is available at the household, family, and individual levels. Note that the public CPS does not include tax information (and thus no information is given on the earned income tax credit or taxes paid). It also does not include capital gains income. Also note that roughly the top 6 % of income is top coded, meaning that good estimates cannot be made of the top income earners in the country. Internal versions of the CPS that do not contain these top codes are available for researchers willing to work on site (check with the U.S. Census Bureau, Center for Economic Studies for location, at http://www. ces.census.gov).

The CPS data are used by researchers in studies on a variety of subjects. Topics include labor, in which studies have been conducted on union membership and coverage (Hirsch & Macpherson, 2003), job stability (Jaeger & Stevens, 1999), minimum wage (Burkhauser, Couch, & Wittenberg, 2000), and the labor market skills of recent male immigrants (Funkhouser and Trejo, 1995). The CPS also has been used to provide estimates of adult cigarette smoking by state and region (Shopland, Hartman, Gibson, Mueller, Kessler, & Lynn, 1996), income inequality and health status (Burkhauser, Fend, & Larrimore, 2008; Mellor & Milyo, 2002), expectations of work for single mothers (Burkhauser, Daly, Larrimore, & Kwok, 2008), and child support from maritally disrupted men (Cherlin, Griffith, & McCarthy, 1983).

CPS data can be found at the National Bureau of Economic Research (NBER) website http://www.nber.org/data/cps_basic.html and at The Pennsylvania State University Simple Online Data Archive for Population Studies (SODA POP) at http://sodapop.pop.psu.edu/data-collections/cps/dnd, where codebooks for the data also are available. Basic monthly data and supplements are available in SAS, SPSS, and Stata data files. Basic monthly data, however, are available only from 1976 to the present, and supplemental data are available only for 1964 to the present. Data also can be found at the ICPSR, and a number of people have created datasets that include the March Supplement to the CPS from the 1960s to the 1990s. Data Ferret also has all data from the CPS for all months from January 1994 to the present. The variables are well-organized on the Data Ferret web site, so that you can download information on many topical areas, including food security (1995–2007), fertility (1998–2008), Internet (1994–2007) and library use (2002), and work schedules (1997–2004). The Data Ferret screen for the CPS looks like the figure shown in the following page.

From here, you can click on any of the CPS datasets, view the variables for any of the years available, and then choose the variables for downloading by putting them into your data basket. You would then go to Step 2, at the top of the page, and either download them or make a table that can be downloaded. If you are downloading the data (and not the tables), you can do so in all of the popular statistical packages.

DEVELOPMENTAL VICTIMIZATION SURVEY

The Developmental Victimization Survey (DVS) is a longitudinal study that collects data about children's experiences with victimization and

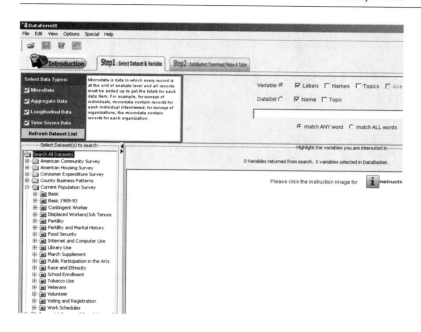

adversity, children's mental health and delinquent behaviors, and child, parent, and household characteristics and demographics. The Crimes Against Children Research Center conducted the research with funding from the U.S. Department of Justice's Office of Juvenile Justice and Delinquency Prevention. The dataset includes information about 2,030 children aged 2 to 17 years, collected in 2002–2003 and again in 2003–2004 (N=1,467). The study uses the Juvenile Victimization Questionnaire to collect victimization information as well as the Trauma Symptom Checklist for Children (TSCC) and Trauma Symptom Checklist for Young Children (TSCYC) for other variables of interest.

The data are nationally representative for children aged 2 to 17 living in the contiguous United States. The data has been weighted to account for the number of eligible children in each household and the undersampling of Black and Hispanic children, and to make the sample equal to the national child population. These weights are based on July 2002 census data.

Researchers collected data during telephone interviews, using list-assisted, random-digit dialing to select participants, with 70% of those eligible agreeing to participate. Caregivers, usually the parents, provided family demographic information. Researchers selected a sample child from all children in the household by selecting the child with the most recent birthday. If that child was under 10 years old, the researchers interviewed the caregiver or parent most familiar with the child's daily routines, using a caregiver version of the survey. If the child was between 10 and 17 years of age, the researcher interviewed the child.

The DVS contains a variety of variables related to child health, victimization, child behavior, and parental, household and neighborhood characteristics. Child health variables include the presence and age of diagnosis for posttraumatic stress disorder (PTSD), anxiety, attention deficit disorder (ADD) or attention deficit hyperactivity disorder (ADHD), oppositional/defiant disorder (ODD) or conduct disorder, autism, developmental delay or retardation, depression, and learning disorders. The survey also provides data on the presence of certain emotions and related behaviors, such as sadness, fear, worry, anger, the feeling that one is hated or disliked, aggressiveness, tantruming, crying, daydreaming, and absentmindedness, in addition to such attitudes or behaviors as calling someone bad, throwing things, wanting to hurt self or wishing for death, and hurting, arguing, or yelling at others. Variables also provide information about participation in counseling or therapy.

DVS collects information about five types of victimization experienced by children using the Juvenile Victimization Questionnaire (JVC). The five categories and the suboffenses include (a) conventional crime (e.g., robbery, personal theft, vandalism and assault); (b) child maltreatment (e.g., physical abuse, psychological/emotional abuse, neglect and custodial interference/family abduction); (c) peer and sibling victimization (e.g., gang or group assault, assault, bullying, and dating violence); (d) sexual victimization (e.g., sexual assault, rape, flashing/sexual exposure, verbal sexual harassment, and statutory rape and sexual misconduct) and (e) witnessing violence and indirect victimization (e.g., witnessing domestic violence, assault, burglary, murder, and shooting). Additional victimization variables include sexual or pornographic photos of child (dropped from the revised JVC), experiences and concern for other adverse life events (e.g., kidnapping, natural disasters, bad accidents, incarcerated parents), and exposure to media violence and subsequent impact (e.g., exposure to the 9/11 attacks and the DC sniper shootings). Behavioral variables include information about delinquency, school, and leisure behaviors. The dataset includes data on 17 delinquency behaviors during the past year, including such variables as breaking things, hitting, stealing, cheating, skipping school, graffiti, loudness, weapon possession, not paying for things, drinking, smoking and using drugs. The DVS also collects information about a child's school attitudes and behaviors, such as whether the child likes school, how often she talks with a parent about school, her grades, special services received at school, involvement in sports or clubs, homework, after-school care, transportation home from school, and where she spends time when in school. If the child attends day care, variables include the type of caregiver and hours spent with someone other than the parent or relative in the home.

Parental variables include status of the parents in the household relative to the child, such as adoptive father, stepfather, biological mother, adoptive mother, stepmother, mother's unmarried partner (not a parent to child), father's unmarried partner (not a parent to child), and the age at which the child stopped living with her biological family (if applicable).

Parental, household and neighborhood characteristics provide information about the environments in which the child resides. Parental characteristics provide data on their warmth, supervision and criticism of their child, communication activities, and knowledge about the child's activities and friends. Household variables include income and public assistance receipt (including TANF, Women Infants and Children [WIC] program, SSI, and SS), exposure to illegal drugs, marital status of parental respondent, household roster, living arrangements of child (e.g., with adoptive or biological family), caregiving information, and experiences with such events as homelessness, removal from the home, and parental incarceration. Neighborhood variables include the degree to which school, neighborhood, and town/city violence is a problem.

The DVS dataset makes it possible to look at both risk factors and outcomes of childhood victimization, adversity, and exposure to violence. Given the array of variables, researchers can control for child, parent, or household characteristics that may contribute to similar health and behavior outcomes to isolate the victimization experience. The data enable the researcher to study specific individual victimizations or multiple victimizations treated separately or together. The Juvenile Victimization Questionnaire was designed to use the same offense categories as the National Crime Victimization survey so that DVS data can be compared with other crime statistics.

Researchers have used the DVS to study polyvictimization (Finkelhor, Ormrod, Turner, & Hamby, 2005) as well as the relationship between victimization and delinquency (Cuevas, Finkelhor, Turner, & Ormrod, 2007), polyvictimization and trauma symptoms (Finkelhor, Ormrod, & Turner, 2007) and family structure and victimization (Turner, Finkelhor, & Ormrod, 2007). Other studies provide information about differences across ages in number and forms of violence (Finkelhor, Ormrod, & Turner, 2008; Finkelhor, Ormrod, Turner, & Hamby, 2005) and in the nature and impact of peer and sibling violence (Finkelhor, Turner, & Ormrod, 2006). Researchers have also studied revictimization risk patterns (Finkelhor, Ormrod, & Turner, 2007), sociodemographic variation in exposure to violence (Turner, Finkelhor, & Ormrod, 2006) and victimization as a predictor of children's mental health (Turner, Finkelhor, & Ormrod, 2006).

Data from the 2002–2003 wave are available through the National Data Archive on Child Abuse and Neglect (http://www.ndacan.cornell.edu/NDACAN/Datasets_List.html). The codebook for the DVS is available at http://www.ndacan.cornell.edu/Ndacan/Datasets/UserGuidePDFs/126user.pdf.

EARLY CHILDHOOD LONGITUDINAL SURVEY

The Early Childhood Longitudinal Survey (ECLS) consists of three longitudinal studies that gather data on children's early life experiences; cognitive, social, emotional, and physical development; home and school environments; school readiness; and pre-school and school experiences. The three studies include one birth and two overlapping school-age cohorts: the birth cohort (ECLS-B), the kindergarten class of 1998–1999 (ECLS-K), and the kindergarten class of 2010–2011 (ECLS-K:2011). Children, parents, child care providers, teachers, and school administrators provide data. Fathers also respond about their relationships with their children. The ECLS allows researchers to study how family, school, community, and individual factors affect school performance and how early childhood experiences affect later developments.

All of the ECLS samples are nationally representative. The birth cohort is representative of children born in 2001, whereas the kindergarten cohorts of 1998–1999 and 2010–2011 are representative of kindergarten children attending public and private, full- and partial-day kindergarten during the respective sampling year. In total, 19,173 children participated in the study, and 1,277 schools were asked to participate. Of these 1,277 schools, 74% agreed to participate. There was a 64% response rate from the children. The study used data from children of varied socioeconomic and racial/ethnic backgrounds and oversampled Asian and Pacific Islander, American Indian, Alaska Native, and Chinese children; twins; and children with low and very low birthweight.

Data is collected in a variety of ways. The information from the ECLS-B and the ECLS-K was obtained through interviews of the sample members' parents and school administrators, teacher questionnaires, and observation of children's participation in one-on-one assessment activities. An English proficiency screener was used for English as a Second Language (ESL) students. The birth cohort also involved a socio-emotional direct assessment, which was carried out by videotaping the child with her parent.

The birth cohort followed children from birth through kindergarten and includes 14,000 children. Data were collected when the children were 9 months old (N=approximately 10,700), 2 years old (2003, N=approximately 9,800), pre-school age (2005, N=approximately 8,900), and age-eligible for kindergarten (2006 and 2007). The birth cohort dataset contains variables relating to the child's health, such as height, weight, and body mass index; general mental ability; fine and gross motor skills; behaviors such as attentiveness and social engagement; attachment to parent; language and literacy development (and related parental behaviors to promote such development); math skills; color knowledge; and education during the years from birth to kindergarten. Community support variables include frequency of visiting with neighbors and receiving community mental help services. Families report receipt of public assistance, such as Food Stamps, WIC, and TANF; they are also asked about periods of food insecurity. A variety of self-reported mental and emotional health questions are asked of parents. Different variables are collected at different ages.

The kindergarten class of 1998–1999 followed children from kindergarten through grade 8. Data collection points included kindergarten (1998-1999) and Grade 1 (1999–2000), and the springs of Grades 3 (2002), 5 (2004) and 8 (2007). This survey collects data on children's cognitive, social, emotional, and physical development, and home environment and school characteristics. Specific questions are asked in the eighth-grade survey about the child's height and weight and the child's feelings about these, amount of exercise, physical education classes taken, availability of certain types of food in school, and the purchasing of food in school, including soda and vegetables. School administrators are asked about characteristics of the school, including percent of students by race; participation in school breakfast and lunch programs; academic options for students; problems with drugs, crime, and racial tensions; and the involvement of parents in academic and nonacademic activities. The kindergarten class of 2010–2011 cohort will follow students from kindergarten through Grade 5.

The two kindergarten cohorts are able to track children from kindergarten during different policy environments, to see how policy changes affect outcomes. Thus, changes in policy, such as the No Child Left Behind Act and expansions in school choice, will allow researchers to see how these policy actions affect child-related outcomes http://nces.ed.gov/ECLS/comparisons2010.asp).

The data from the Early Childhood Longitudinal Survey have been used to study different health factors, such as overweight (Judge & Jahns, 2007), depression and mental health (Huang, Wong, Ronzio, & Yu, 2006), birth complications (Beaver & Wright, 2005), and nutrition (Jacknowitz, Novillo, & Tiehen, 2007). Several research studies have examined the effects of race, such as the effects of racial identification (Brunsma, 2005), segregation, (Reardon, Yun, & Kurlaender, 2006), the effects of racial and ethnic diversity on birthweight (Teitler, Reichman, Nepomnyaschy, & Martinson, 2007), and the impact of computer technology on African American children (Judge, 2005). Other studies have examined kindergarten variables, such as the effects of delayed starts (Datar, 2006), the effects of class size (Milesi & Gamoran, 2006), and effects of full-day versus half-day kindergarten (DeCica, 2007). Also, research has been done using ECLS data pertaining to income, particularly the relationship of material hardship and parenting and child development (Gershoff, Aber, Raver, & Lennon, 2007), food insecurity and hunger and their effect on learning in the classroom (Winicki & Jemison, 2003), religion (Bartkowski, Xu, & Levin, 2007), physical activity (Carlson, Fulton, Lee, Maynard, Brown, Kohl, & Dietz, 2008; Beets & Foley, 2008), inequality in cognitive skills and academic achievement (Downey, von Hippel, & Broh, 2004; Foster & Miller, 2007), and special needs (Park, Hogan, & D'Ottavi, 2005).

Data are available from the National Center for Education Statistics (www.nces.ed.gov). More specifically, the data and codebooks can be found at http://nces.ed.gov/ecls/dataproducts.asp. Some of these data are also available at the International Archive of Education Data (IAED) (http://www.icpsr.umich.edu/IAED/studies.html), including the kindergarten class of 1998–99 and the original kindergarten class in third grade. You can do simple analyses of these data at the IAED site. Some data are available for public use, and other data require a data license. Some data, primarily the birth cohort data, are available through Data Analysis System (DAS) for statistical analysis online.

Below, I use the Survey Document and Analysis system to examine some cross tabulations for the third-grade class, for the variables capturing "litter near the school" and "attentive teachers in school."

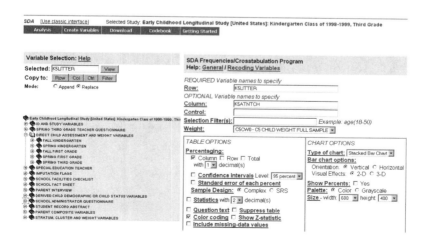

And get the following results.

Variables					
Role	Name	Label	Range	MD	Dat
Row	**K5LITTER**	K5 Q5A LITTER AND TRASH NEAR SCHOOL	1-4	-9--1	
Column	**K5ATNTCH**	K5 Q3B ATTENTIVE TEACHERS IN SCHOOL	1-4	-9--1	
Weight	**C5CW0**	C5 CHILD WEIGHT FULL SAMPLE	.00-3,376.78		

Frequency Distribution						
Cells contain: -Column percent -Weighted N		K5ATNTCH				
		1 STRONGLY AGREE	2 SOMEWHAT AGREE	3 SOMEWHAT DISAGREE	4 STRONGLY DISAGREE	ROW TOTAL
K5LITTER	1: NONE	**77.8** 2,083,606	**62.8** 447,573	**40.0** 19,796	**77.6** 1,271	**74.1** 2,552,247
	2: A LITTLE	**18.5** 494,927	**25.7** 182,947	**34.3** 16,956	**.0** 0	**20.2** 694,831
	3: SOME	**2.7** 73,157	**10.5** 75,199	**17.8** 8,813	**.0** 0	**4.6** 157,168
	4: A LOT	**1.0** 27,840	**1.0** 7,482	**7.8** 3,867	**22.4** 368	**1.1** 39,557
	COL TOTAL	**100.0** 2,679,530	**100.0** 713,201	**100.0** 49,433	**100.0** 1,639	**100.0** 3,443,803

As you can see from the first table, more elaborate statistics can be derived using this system than what are given here, but the scope of these analyses is very limited. By downloading the entire datasets, you can better control the variables and use them for more sophisticated analyses. Below, the data for the kindergarten base and kindergarten-third grade sample were downloaded, and SAS was used to merge the two files together. SAS variable definitions are given when downloading both datasets, but the user must supply the location and filename of the data, which are given below. Both SAS files are very large, and only the top of the data statement for both datasets below are given.

```
data a;
infile 'c\10326250\ICPSR_04075\DS0001\
04075-0001-Data.txt' lrecl=5798 n=2
missover pad;
input
  #1
    @1 CHILDID $8.
    @9 PARENTID $8.
Run;
```

```
data b;
infile 'c:\10326273\ICPSR_03676\DS0001\
03676-0001-Data.txt' lrecl=5250 n=3;
input
  #1
    @1 CHILDID $8.
    @9 PARENTID $8.

Run;

data c;merge a b;by childid;
run;
```

NOTE: There were 15305 observations read from the dataset WORK.A.
NOTE: There were 17212 observations read from the dataset WORK.B.
NOTE: The dataset WORK.C has 17707 observations and 8848 variables.

Data c gives you the merged dataset of the two waves of data.

FRAGILE FAMILIES AND CHILD WELL-BEING STUDY (FFCWS)

The Fragile Families and Child Well-Being Study (FFCWS), a longitudinal study, gathers demographic, relationship, health, well-being, and parental capacity data on non-marital couples, facilitating examination of how these factors, as well as contextual and environmental conditions, affect their children. Particular attention is paid to fathers. To date, the study has followed couples and their children over a nine-year period, with initial interviews occurring between February 1998 and September 2000. The initial interviews involved each parent and were conducted in the hospital within 24 hours of the child's birth. Subsequent interviews occurred when the children were 1, 3, and 5 years old. A nine-year follow-up was conducted between the summer of 2007 and the end of 2009, incorporating the core study, an in-home study, and a teacher study. The survey includes data collected through parental interviews, in-home interviews, and collaborative studies using administrative records, in-depth qualitative interviews, and surveys.

Data were collected from 4,898 families, including 3,712 unmarried couples and 1,186 married couples, from 20 U.S. cities with populations over 200,000. The sample sizes for the follow-up years are: 4,270 mothers of whom 1,029 were married and 3,241 were unmarried at the time of birth (one year); 4,140 mothers of whom 1,012 were married and 3,128 were unmarried (three year); and 4,055 mothers of whom 975 were married and 3,080 were unmarried (five year). Approximately half the sample is non-Hispanic Black and a third is Hispanic. National weights make the data of 16 of the 20 cities representative of nonmarital births in U.S. cities with populations over 200,000. City weights can be applied to make the data representative of the sample cities, an option that may be of particular benefit to those wishing to examine conditions in cities that were strategically sampled so as to maximize variability in economic and policy conditions.

Parental interviews gathered information on attitudes, relationships, parenting behavior, demographic characteristics, mental and physical health, economic and employment status, neighborhood characteristics, and program participation. The mother's questionnaire included far more comprehensive birth father data than are available in most other data sets, which allows for comparisons of fathers' perceptions of their roles and relationships and mothers' perceptions of the same. The in-home interview gathered information on children's cognitive and emotional development, health, and home environment. Studies developed in collaboration with the FFCWS provide additional information on parents' medical, employment, and incarceration histories; religion; child care; and early childhood education.

The mother and father datasets contain 333 and 338 variables, respectively. The FFCWS covers numerous variables including: parental sexual activity; contact with Child Protective Services regarding sexual abuse; incarceration; home environment; neighborhood information; foster care; disability status of parent(s) and/or children; government program participation; and health insurance coverage. The FFCWS also takes into consideration forms of intimate and partner violence, including whether a mother ever reported any abuse; whether either the father or the mother is or has been incarcerated due to domestic violence; whether parents ever witnessed violence, including murder; whether either parent has reported being a victim of violence; and whether violence was cited as a reason for a mother and a father not living together, not being married, or a reason for ending a relationship.

The FFCWS provides extensive information on alcohol and drug abuse, including whether the biological mother drank and/or used drugs during her pregnancy; whether the father was unable to find and maintain a job or friends due to alcohol or drugs; whether help was sought for drug and alcohol problems; the number of alcoholic beverages consumed or drugs used in one month; the problems associated with alcohol or illegal drug use; the presence of emotional and psychological problems due to alcohol or drugs; the dangerous situations that arose because of alcohol and drug abuse; the use of therapy for alcohol or drug problems; the dependence on drugs and alcohol; the relationship problems due to alcohol or drugs; the incarceration of the father; and the father's and/or mother's absence in the child's life because of alcohol or drug issues.

The FFCWS provides information on the presence of mental health issues for the father and mother, regular medications taken, limitations on work, and mental retardation or developmental delay in the child.

The data contain information about foster care, including whether the child spent brief and/or extended separations from the parents with foster parents; whether the mother or father know or are related to the foster parents; or whether the child usually lives with foster parents. There is also information on injuries the child sustained with foster parents.

Princeton University's Bendheim-Thomas Center for Research on Child Wellbeing and Columbia University's Social Indicators Survey Center conducted the FFCWS. Most of the data have been released for public use. To protect respondent identity, however, data with geographic identifiers and medical records are released only through a restricted-use contract. Access to Fragile Families contract data is limited to faculty and research personnel at institutions with an Institutional Review Board/ Human Studies Review Committee, which must be registered with either the U.S. Office for Human Research Protections (OHRP) or the National Institutes of Health (NIH).

Research involving the Fragile Families and Child Well-being Study data covers a variety of topics. These data have been used to examine health topics such as obesity (Whitaker, Phillips, Orzol, & Burdette, 2007), depression (Whitaker, Orzol, & Kahn, 2007; Whitaker, Phillips, & Orzol, 2006; Rees & Sabia, 2007), low birth weight (Reichman, Hamilton, Hummer, & Padilla, 2008; Nepomnyaschy & Reichman, 2007), newborn complications (Smulian, Teitler, Nepomnyaschy, Ananth, & Reichman, 2005), and health insurance and utilization of healthcare (Hamilton, Hummer, You, & Padilla, 2006). Other studies have examined the effects of domestic violence (Burke, Lee, & O'Campo, 2008), acculturation (Kimbro, Lynch, & McLanahan, 2008), religion (Petts, 2007), and household monetary inequality (Kenney, 2006). Numerous studies look at the effects of father involvement (Percheski & Wildeman, 2008; Carlson, McLanahan, & Brooks-Gunn, 2008; Lewis, Garfinkel, & Gao, 2007), as well as a number of outcomes by family structure, especially for those who are unmarried parents (Gibson-Davis, 2008; Gibson-Davis, Edin, & McLanahan, 2005; Heiland, Liu, 2006; Kenney, 2004; Sigle-Rushton & McLanahan, 2002; Edin & Reed, 2005; Curits, 2007), and the effects of neighborhoods (Burdette & Whitaker, 2005; Burdette, Wadden, & Whitaker, 2006; Casciano, 2007; Casciano & Massey, Forthcoming). The effects of government assistance programs — particularly TANF, food stamps, housing subsidies, SSI, and WIC (Teitler, Reichman, & Nepomnyaschy, 2007; Livermore & Powers, 2006) — have also been examined.

Codebooks and data for the FFCW study can be found at the home page for the data at Princeton University, http://www.fragilefamilies. princeton.edu/documentation.asp, or at Pennsylvania State's SODA POP page, http://sodapop.pop.psu.edu/data-collections/ff.

GENERAL SOCIAL SURVEY (GSS)

The General Social Survey is the longest-running project of the National Opinion Research Center (NORC), with 27 rounds of cross-sectional data collection completed since its inception in 1972; it currently runs through 2008. The GSS traces the opinions of Americans and monitors social change and, next to the U.S. Census, is the most examined source of social science information. The survey includes standard, core questions exploring issues such as attitudes to various topics such as race relations, sex relations, civil liberties, and morality, and also includes socioeconomic status and social mobility. The survey also includes topical questions, or modules, of special interest. Since 1982, the General Social Survey has collaborated with the International Social Survey Program (ISSP) to gather crossnational information on the role of the government and social inequality.

Researchers collected data annually starting in 1972, excluding 1979, 1981 and 1992, and biannually since 1994. Annual samples aim to include 1,500 respondents, but they range from 1,372 (1990 round) to 1,613

(1972 round) and, in 1994 with the introduction of a split-sample design of two parallel samples of 1,500 respondents each, from 2,765 (2002 round) to 2,993 (2004 round). A third parallel sample was added in 2006 for a total of 4,150 respondents. Researchers oversampled Black respondents in 1982 (354 respondents) and 1987 (353 respondents).

Researchers originally collected data through 90-minute face-to-face interviews, with the exception of several phone interviews when necessary, and they switched to computer-assisted personal interviewing (CAPI) in 2002.

The GSS dataset contains 5,084 variables with core data topics including age, sex, education, region of residence, and measures of attitudes about issues like gun control or voting attendance. For instance, variables include such information as respondents' astrological signs, trust in public officials and other individuals, whom they voted for in presidential elections, beliefs in abortion or capital punishment, use of contraception (especially teenagers), disabilities, attitudes towards specific countries, and engagement in extramarital sex or adultery. Topical content varies from year to year of data collection, but generally only one or a few topics were covered. For instance, some rounds of data collection include variables for abortion and feminism (1977), role of the military (1982 and 1984), mental health (1992), environmental issues (1993), gender and mental health (1996), and health care, health ethics and religion (1998). With the introduction of the split-sample design in 1994, respondents in each of the subsamples respond to identical core questions and different topical, ISSP modules. In that same year, researchers reduced the number of core questions in order to create mini-modules, which are more flexible to advancements and responsive to new variables of interest. Thus, in 2004, topical modules included work environment, immigration, genes, guns, Catholics, and alcohol; in 2006, topical modules were added for mental health, gun control, and disability.

GSS provides information on neighborhoods, including opinions on segregated neighborhoods, safety, racial makeup, number of gay people, number of cohabiting people, number of regular church attendees, number of conservatives and liberals, number of people in prison, and number of unemployed.

GSS provides information on HIV including HIV testing, the option of suicide if diagnosed with an incurable disease, and opinion if ADHD is a real disease.

GSS includes variables that provide public opinion on topics including homosexual rights, sex education in public schools, sex before marriage, adultery, available information about sex, if homosexuality is inherent or a choice, sex and faith, gender discrimination, prostitution, sexual harassment, number of sexual partners since respondent was 18 years old, age of first homosexual attraction, age first revealed to another that the respondent had sexual relations with someone of the same sex, government programs on safe sex, sex with friends, sex with acquaintances, and frequency of sex in the past year.

Data from the General Social Survey has been used by many researchers in their studies. A popular research topic is relationships, with many different facets studied, such as correlations among social networks, marital status, and well-being (Acock & Hulrbert, 1993); examining the marriage and lifestyle choices of former commune members (Aidala, 1989); and comparing husbands' and wives' family-life satisfaction (Mancini, 1979). Some studies look at ethnicity, including research analyzing whether Black neighborhoods have higher crimes rates (Quillian and Pager, 2001), the involvement of culture to social structure and communities (Jeannotte, 2003), and studying ethnic identity among whites (Alba & Chamlin, 1983). Other studies look at education, such as research that examines shifts in important qualities to children between 1964 and 1984 (Alwin, 1989), teachers' salary satisfaction (Matthews, Weaver, Cisneros, & Franz, 1992), and the correlation between Catholic high schools and academic achievement in rural areas (Sander, 2001). Other areas of study include the public opinion of Roe v. Wade (Adamek, 1994), the perceived strength of religious beliefs (Alston, 1973), the relationship between condom use and HIV risk among adults in the United States (Anderson, 2003), public opinion on economic and political development in China (Andreosso-O'Callaghan, Wang, & Rees, 2004), measuring labor market success (Jencks, Perman, & Rainwater, 1988), the correlation between firearms and suicide (Markush and Bartolucci, 1984), the connection between age and anger (Schieman, 1999), and unethical behavior of political officials (Maule and Goidel, 2003).

The full GSS data can be downloaded online from the ICPSR for those whose institutions are members, or from the Survey Documentation and Analysis website at the University of California, Berkeley http://sda. berkeley.edu/cgi-bin/hsda2?setupfile=harcsda&datasetname=gss08&ui =2&action=subset). All or some of the data (all or some years and all or some variables) can be downloaded in SAS, SPSS, Stata, or several other formats. CD-ROMs can be ordered from Roper Center for Public Opinion Research. The entire datasets, 1972–2008, can also be downloaded at http://www.norc.org/GSS+Website/Download/, in either SAS, SPSS, or Stata formats. The codebook for the 1972–2008 GSS is available at http://publicdata.norc.org:41000/gss/documents//BOOK/Main%20Body.pdf (it is more than 2,000 pages long). GSS data are available six months after the data collection is completed. Proposals from researchers for future GSS rounds are sometimes accepted. They should ideally be sent in two years prior to the GSS round for which they are desired. For more information, see the National Opinion Research Center (http://www.norc.org) or ICPSR (http://www.icpsr.umich.edu).

Also, cross tabulations or frequencies can be calculated online (http://sda.berkeley.edu/cgi-bin/hsda?harcsda+gss08) for many of the variables in the GSS. For example, I examined the level of confidence in financial institutions by political party affiliation. The first table gives the general screen for examining variables in the 1972 to 2008 GSS and the second screen gives the cross tabulations, along with z statistics, for the different groups. These same types of tabulations and multiple regressions can be run at http://www.norc.org/GSS+Website/Data+Analysis/.

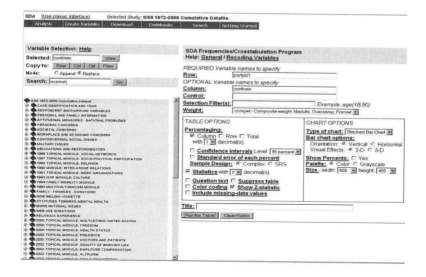

SDA 3.3: Tables

Frequency Distribution					
Cells contain: -Column percent -Z-statistic -Weighted N		CONFINAN			
		1 A GREAT DEAL	2 ONLY SOME	3 HARDLY ANY	ROW TOTAL
PARTYID1	1: DEMOCRAT	**45.0** −.23 175	**46.0** .48 378	**44.1** −.39 83	*45.5* --- *635*
	2: REPUBLICAN	**36.3** 2.46 141	**29.2** −1.99 240	**30.1** −.36 56	*31.3* --- *437*
	3: INDEPENDENT	**16.4** −2.37 64	**22.5** 2.14 185	**20.6** .03 39	*20.5* --- *287*
	4: OTHER	**2.4** −.42 9	**2.3** −1.12 19	**5.1** 2.16 10	*2.7* --- *38*
	COL TOTAL	*100.0* --- *389*	*100.0* --- *821*	*100.0* --- *187*	*100.0* --- *1,397*
Means		1.76	1.81	1.87	1.81
Std Devs		.81	.86	.92	.86
Unweighted N		376	794	186	1,356

HEALTH AND RETIREMENT STUDY (HRS)

The Health and Retirement Study is a national longitudinal study sponsored by the National Institute on Aging and the Social Security Administration with a cooperative agreement with the Survey Research Center at the University of Michigan. The study is a merging of two data sets: HRS and the Study of Asset and Health Dynamics among the Oldest Old (AHEAD). HRS started in 1992 and AHEAD started in 1993; the merging of the datasets occurred in 1998. The ongoing study, which began in 1992, focuses on Americans over the age of 50 and collects information on health, marital, family, and economic status, as well as support systems, both public and private. Data is collected through biennial surveys, using questionnaire interviews, with most questions asked to both people in coupled relationships within the household. Some questions are asked only to a specific respondent, such as the female spouse or the person most responsible for family finances.

New cohorts are added every six years, with the third cohort starting in 2004 (with previous cohorts in 1992 and 1998). African Americans and Latinos were oversampled in order to get good sample sizes for these groups. The original 1992 sample consisted of 8,222 observations. There have been seven waves of data collection: 1992 (N=12,654),

1994 (N=11,597), 1996 (N=11,199), 1998 (N=10,857), 2000 (N=10,377), 2002 (N=10,142), and 2004 (N=9,759 respondents). The next cohort will be added in 2010. The original HRS can be studied back to 1992 and the original AHEAD cohort can be studied back to 1993.

The HRS includes variables pertaining to family structure; employment history; disability status; health and life insurance; finances, including assets, debt, and retirement and pension income; widow and divorce status and their economic impact; Internet use; prescription drug use; and housing, including type and associated costs. HRS includes information on prescription drug use through a two-wave off-year survey, conducted in 2005 and 2007, that tracks changes in prescription drug use after the implementation of Medicare Part D. HRS did a memory study from 2001 to 2005, using in-home assessments to determine the severity of any dementia found. The data also include information on time and money use.

Aspects of widowhood and divorce are examined in detail, including predivorce and death amount of work earnings, work hours, and Social Security benefits; changes to these due to a death or separation; changes in health insurance; receipt of a life insurance settlement or lump-sum pension and amount; expenses associated with spouse's death and illness; assistance from a grandchild; cause of death; state in which death occurred; loss of claim on former/late spouse's pension; and expenses due to legal fees during divorce. Government and private health insurance information is given, including insurance during nursing home stays, military health care plans, loss of eligibility, amount paid through their plan, and length of time on current plan. HRS also provides information on life insurance, such as number of policies, face value of plan, and beneficiaries. Financial information includes assets, debts, capital gains, mortgage crises, retirement plans, and pensions. HRS includes housing variables on type of housing unit; renting versus ownership; ownership of surrounding land; present value; presence of a mortgage, second mortgage, or loan to pay for dwelling; property tax and insurance; and purchase price of the home.

Geographical information is available at the state, county, and census-tract levels. Special signed contracts and IRB approval are necessary for using these geographical identifiers.

Growing Older in America: The Health and Retirement Study outlines research findings using HRS data, describes HRS development, and includes figures and tables (see http://www.nia.nih.gov/NR/rdonlyres/ D164FE6C-C6E0-4E78-B27F-7E8D8C0FFEE5/0/HRS_Text_WEB.pdf).

The HRS data have been used to examine many different areas of study concerning the U.S. population that is over 50 years of age. Researchers have studied health concerns such as the health care costs of moderate and severe obesity (Andreyeva, Sturm, & Ringel, 2004), age differences and depression due to functional impairment (Choi & Kim, 2007), effects of pollution on health conditions and mortality (Evans & Smith, 2005), smoking cessation in middle-aged Americans (Falba, 2005), and the effects of physical activity on older adults with arthritis. Other researchers have studied insurance and benefits, such as the effect of part-time work on wages, looking at Social Security (Aaronson & French, 2004), the correlation between loss of health insurance and a decline in self-reported health issues (Baker, Sudano, Albert, Borawski, & Dor, 2002), and delays in claiming Social Security benefits (Coile, Diamond, Gruber, & Jousten, 2002). Other research focuses have been nursing home use and racial differences (Akamigbo & Wolinsky, 2007) and the effects of personal care and assistive devices on the measurement of disability (Agree, 1999). Others have studied widowhood in older minority women (Angel, Jimenez, & Angel, 2007), the influence of religion on patient satisfaction (Benjamins, 2006), labor dynamics and older couples (Blau, 1998), the importance of cohabitation with regards to marital status and mental health benefits (Brown, Bulanda, & Lee, 2005), and the connection between military service and wealth accumulation (Fitzgerald, 2006).

All nonrestricted data files are available at https://ssl.isr.umich.edu/ hrs/files.php, including the 1992 HRS, 1993 AHEAD, and all other files through 2007. HRS files can be merged together by the use of the household ID (HHID) and the person number within the household (PN). All data must be sorted by these variables before merging. To learn more about merging HRS files, see https://ssl.isr.umich.edu/hrs/ filedownload.php?d=525. To get the codebooks for the HRS files, go to http://hrsonline.isr.umich.edu/index.php?p=showcbk.

In order to access HRS data, researchers register at http://hrsonline. isr.umich.edu. Some of the data are restricted, requiring approval from HRS for use. The Medicare claims and summary data require HRS approval and a data use agreement from the Centers for Medicare and Medicaid Services (CMS) through the Research Data Assistance Center.

Data are in ASCII format, which can easily be transferred into SAS, SPSS, or Stata format.

It is possible to link some of these data with Social Security and Medicare administrative records. It is also possible to link these data with employer surveys, such as pension plans. Contracts and IRB approval are required to obtain such data.

LONGITUDINAL STUDIES OF CHILD ABUSE AND NEGLECT (LONGSCAN)

Longitudinal Studies of Child Abuse and Neglect (LONGSCAN) is based on an ecological-development model. LONGSCAN is a consortium of five longitudinal research studies about child abuse and neglect. The pooled studies follow children and their caregivers from when the child is aged 4 or less until he is 18 years old. Given variation across the five sites, the children enrolled in the study have experienced different degrees of maltreatment and represent different levels and types of risk. The study conducted or will conduct comprehensive interviews with the children and their caregivers when the child is aged 4, 6, 8, 12, 14, 16 and 18. Currently, parent, teacher, and child assessments have been completed for children up to age 12. Researchers facilitated annual phone interviews with the caregivers in the off year and, every two years, reviewed child protective services case files. Child self-reporting begins at age 12. Each of the five study sites used the same measures. Interviewer-based information also is collected.

Researchers determine what data to collect at what age, based on the child's social ecology at that age. The study collects information on the child, the caregiver, the family unit, and the larger social system. The study includes variables related to physical, mental, and emotional health; cognitive functioning; behavior; relationships; substance use; violence; school performance; and service utilization.

LONGSCAN began in 1991 with funding from the National Center for Child Abuse and Neglect. The University of North Carolina at Chapel Hill coordinates the consortium. The creators originally designed the study to gather child abuse and neglect information pertaining to child, family, and community risk factors for abuse as well as similar such factors that impact the degree of harm caused by the abuse and factors that contribute to both negative and positive child outcomes.

The dataset includes 1,354 observations. Of these children, 282 are from the Eastern study, 245 from the Midwest study, 254 from the Northwest study, 243 from the Southern study and 330 from the Southwest study. From baseline to age 8, there was an attrition rate of approximately 16% for the pooled study. Attrition rates vary by each study site.

The five studies vary by region, community type, recruitment site, and selection criteria. The following tables outlines these differences:

Table 4.3

Study	Community Type	Recruitment site	Selection Criteria
Eastern	Urban	Inner-city pediatric clinic	Clinic criteria for risk in first year based on both child and parent risk factors
Midwest	Urban	Child protective services	Those reported to CPS and receiving comprehensive services or only intervention
Northwest	Urban	Child protective services	0-4 years old considered moderate risk after report to CPS
Southern	Suburban	State pubic health tracking system	4-5 years old considered high risk at birth
Southwest	Urban, suburban and rural	County dependency system	Approximately 4 years old with confirmed maltreatment and out-of-home placement with relative or foster family

The survey is not nationally representative. As a consortium of studies, it is only representative of those individuals included in the study. Regionally, the data are representative only of those included in that region.

Information on child characteristics was collected by interviewing caregivers, the child, or both. The dataset includes information pertaining to children's birth and their first year of life, and day care utilization during this time. Information was collected on child health and injuries, pubertal development, employment, resiliency and future orientation, school orientation and problems, life events, abuse (physical, psychological, and sexual), delinquent and violent behavior, sexual experiences and risk behaviors, and sibling/peer/dating/community violence. The dataset also includes instruments on social competence; temperament; developmental status and adaptive behavior; cognitive functioning; behavior problems; tobacco, drugs and alcohol use; suicidality; health risk; affective symptoms; psychopathology; parental relationships and expectations; peer relationships; social problem solving; perceived competence; exposure to alcohol and drugs; risk behaviors of family and friends; academic achievement; delinquency and criminal/judicial involvement; exposure or witness to violence at home or in the community; neglect; victimization; parenthood; attitudes towards parenting; coping style/ strategies; self-esteem; and social desirability. Information is also included on the child's history with child protective services that is gathered through a review of CPS case files and the state's central registry.

Caregiver characteristics collected include physical health, history of loss and victimization, religious and organizational affiliation and involvement and expectations of the child. Other caregiver information includes attitudes towards parenting and deviance; tobacco, alcohol and drug use; mental health; and social desirability.

The data includes information about the family unit such as family supports, health and welfare services used by the family, parental involvement in the child's school, and the accessibility of guns in home. Additional variables include family satisfaction and functioning, daily stressors, household rules and routines, quality of the spouse/partner relationship and the parent/child relationship, domestic/interpersonal violence and the use of physical discipline, father's involvement in parenting, parental monitoring of the child, family use of drugs and alcohol, and information about hunger and poverty. Interviewer-rated information includes home environment characteristics.

Information was collected on caregiver-provided macrosystems in which the child and family live. The group of variables included information about unemployment, income and welfare, neighborhood characteristics, school safety, social support for both the caregiver and the child, risk behaviors of family and friends, and ethnic minority status.

The breadth of LONGSCAN variables makes it possible to examine both risk and protective factors and consequences of maltreatment at a variety of levels—individual child and parent, familial, and community.

Researchers also can study the impact of interventions at the same levels and conduct subgroup analysis or comparisons across different demographics. Given that data is collected in specific regions, researchers can also study the impact of policies and legislation on outcomes.

Researchers have used LONGSCAN to study the relationship between child maltreatment and health (Flaherty, Thompson, Litrownik, Theodore, English, Black, Wike, Whimper, Runyan, & Dubowitz, 2006), depression and suicidality (Litrownik, Newton, & Landsverk, 2005; Thompson, Briggs, English, Dubowitz, Lee, Brody, Everson & Hunter, 2005), childhood aggression (Kotch, Lewis, Hussey, English, Thompson, Litrownik, Runyan, Bangdiwala, Margolis, & Dubowitz, 2008), sexualized behaviors (Merrick, Litrownik, Everson, & Cox, 2008) and weapon possession (Lewis et al., 2007). Studies also examine the relationship among caregiver, familial, and neighborhood factors on children's behavior, health, and service use (Lindsey et al., 2008), discipline and child behaviors (Lau, Litrownik, Newton, Black, & Everson, 2006; De Robertis & Litrownik, 2004). Related studies explore the associations among caregiver, family, and other social characteristics on children's health and service use (Thompson et al., 2007; Thompson & May, 2006; Thompson, 2005). One study examines the impact of services on children's behaviors (Thompson, in press).

Studies examine predictors of re-referrals to child protective services (Thompson & Wiley, in press) as well as the relationship between domestic violence and child maltreatment (Lee, Kotch, & Cox, 2004), mothers' experience with violence and maltreatment (Weisbart et al., 2008; Thompson, 2006), mothers' experience with violence and childrens' behaviors (Thompson, 2007), and the relationship between child characteristics and living arrangements (Romney, Litrownik, Newton, & Lau, 2006).

Researchers have also used the data to compare child, adult and/or child protection services reports on the same variable (Everson et al., 2008; Thompson et al., 2006), test measure validity (Thompson et al., 2007) and explore definitions of maltreatment (Dubowitz et al., 2005).

The data are not publicly available and are only available to faculty and nonstudent researchers at institutions with institutional review boards. The codebook for LONGSCAN can be found at http://www.ndacan.cornell.edu/Ndacan/Datasets/UserGuidePDFs/144.pdf.

NATIONAL CHILD ABUSE AND NEGLECT DATA SYSTEM (NCANDS)

The National Child Abuse and Neglect Data System (NCANDS) is a national data collection process that gathers data from child and protective services in all 50 states, the District of Columbia, and Puerto Rico. States voluntarily submit both child-level and state-level information pertaining to the report, investigation, and disposition of alleged child maltreatment; child-victim characteristics and risk factors; caregiver risks factors; child and family service provision; perpetrator characteristics; fatalities due to maltreatment; and caseworker and agency information. The NCANDS considers a child to be someone under 18 years old. States began submitting state-level data in 1990, with case-level data beginning in 1995. Puerto Rico began submitting data in 2005.

The National Child Abuse and Neglect Data System emerged as a result of the Child Abuse Prevention, Adoption and Family Services Act of 1998 and the Child Abuse Prevention and Treatment Act, which required the National Center on Child Abuse and Neglect (NCCAN) to collect and analyze national child maltreatment data. The NCANDS' principal investigator and funding agency is Children's Bureau, Administration on Children, Youth and Families of the U.S Department of Health and Human Services.

The NCANDS has been collecting both case-level and aggregate state-level data since 1990. States submit case-level data using the Child File or its predecessor, the Detailed Case Data Component (DCDC). The Child file contains information for each child identified on each report made to child and protective services. Researchers have gathered information specific to that child, with up to four allegations of maltreatment. The NCANDS Child File dataset contains seven categories of variables: report data, child data, child maltreatment data, child risk factors, caretaker risk factors, services provided, and perpetrator data. The Combined Aggregate File (CAF) provides aggregate state-level data and includes data about preventative services and their funding, number of referrals and the children that are screened out, response time and number of staff responsible for certain functions, use of preservation services and number of children reunified with their families, contacts with court representatives, and child fatalities among families using preservation services who have been reunified, or among children in foster care, including those not reported in the Child File. The CAF also includes aggregate case-specific information such as the report source; disposition outcomes; type of maltreatment; victim sex, age and race; fatality information; and service provision.

While the NCANDS data is census in nature, it is representative only of those children whose alleged victimization was reported to child and protective services. It is not generalizable to all children experiencing maltreatment, given that not all abuse and neglect is reported.

The number of observations varies from year to year as more states provide detailed case information. For example, in 2000, the dataset included 1,032,362 observations, a number that increased to 3,477,988 in 2006. Currently, all states, the District of Columbia, and Puerto Rico provide case-level data. While the dataset is census data, years 2004 through 2006 include a sample dataset, selected through systematic sampling, in addition to the complete dataset. The reason for providing these samples is because the full sample datasets have grown to be large. These smaller datasets can be more easily run with a similar level of confidence as the larger-population datasets. According to NCANDS, the 2004 and 2005 sample data should be generalizable to the full dataset, though they caution against presenting results from the sample data.

The NCANDS provides data on child abuse and neglect, child and caregiver risk factors, perpetrators, service utilization, foster care and adoption, and use of public assistance. The NCANDS identifies eight types of maltreatment (including physical, sexual, psychological abuse, deprivation of necessities and medical neglect), nine types of dispositions, living arrangements at the time of abuse, and whether death or injuries resulted from abuse. Child and caregivers risk factors include the presence of alcohol and drug abuse or domestic violence in the home, diagnoses of disabilities, behavioral problems or medical conditions, inadequate housing, financial problems, and the use of public assistance. Services utilization variables include post investigation services such as family support and family preservation services, foster care, a juvenile court petition, adoption assistance or education, employment, housing, legal, or health assistance. Perpetrators data includes such variables as demographics, relationship to the child, military status, and history with perpetration. Child data includes child's age at report, sex, race, ethnicity, living arrangements, and whether the child has been a victim of previously substantiated or indicated maltreatment.

Aggregated state level data provide information on a variety of topics required by the CAPTA legislation. These include summary information about investigations and outcomes, preventative services and referrals, staffing and response time, preservation services, and child fatalities among families using preservation services, reunification, foster care, and contacts with court representatives.

Given that NCANDS provides both case-level and aggregate state-level data, researchers can gain information about statewide or nationwide trends, as well as information specific to cases using a variety of multivariate statistical analyses. The data make it possible to gather information not only about descriptive statistics, but also about risk factors for maltreatment and fatality from maltreatment, likelihood of occurrence, and differences in maltreatment across a variety of child and family factors. Several researchers have created longitudinal datasets using data over several reporting years and conducted hazard analyses. NCANDS is just one of several datasets collecting information about child maltreatment and, as such, researchers can compare their analyses with those of other datasets to explore differences across measures. Additionally, both case- and state-level data can be analyzed alongside state laws, and state definitions of abuse, to study the relationship between laws and maltreatment.

Since 1995, the Department of Health and Human Services' Administration for Children, Youth and Families has published annual bulletins detailing its analysis of that year's data. These publications report on outcomes relating to referrals, reports, investigations, and outcomes of maltreatment allegations, characteristics of the children involved in those reports, maltreatment related fatalities, service provision, and perpetrator characteristics. These reports are available on the DHHS website, http://www.acf.hhs.gov.

Researchers have used NCANDS data to study a variety of child abuse and neglect questions, including the risk of nonfatal infant maltreatment (Brodowski et al., 2008), factors that correlate or predict maltreatment (Chance & Scannapieco, 2002), and repeated abuse and re-referrals to child protective services (Connell, Bergeron, Katz, Saunders, & Tebes, 2007; Fluke, Shusterman, Hollinshead, & Yuan, 2008; Palusci, Smith, & Paneth, 2005). Researchers also have compared maltreatment rates and types between military and nonmilitary families (McCarroll, Ursano,

Fan, & Newby, 2004), and across race and ethnicity (Earle & Cross, 2001; Fluke, Yuan, Hedderson, & Curtis, 2003). Others have studied perpetrator characteristics (Shusterman, Fluke, & Yuan, 2005), worker perceptions of neglect (Fox, 2004) and frequency trends across states (Wertheimer & Atienza, 2006).

The multiyear codebook for the NCANDS can be found at http://www.ndacan.cornell.edu/NDACAN/Datasets/UserGuidePDFs/NCANDS_MultiYear_Guide.pdf. All datasets, except the Agency File, are available through the National Data Archive on Child Abuse and Neglect for the years in which they were or are in use (http://www.ndacan.cornell.edu). The data are restricted and the necessary procedures and documentation must be given in order to obtain the data.

NATIONAL EDUCATIONAL LONGITUDINAL SURVEY (NELS)

The National Educational Longitudinal Survey (NELS) is a longitudinal study that follows eighth-grade students as they transition into and out of high school. The study aims to observe changes in children's lives during adolescence and the role of school in promoting growth and positive life choices. NELS observes students' academic growth, features of effective schools, schools' ability to help disadvantaged students, academic performance and school experiences of minority students, and transitions into the working world and/or higher education. The study began in 1988, when the students were in Grade 8, and included four follow-up periods of data collection in 1990 and 1992, when students were generally in Grades 10 and 12, respectively (and also followed those who dropped out of high school as well), and 1994 and 2000, post-high school. Data was collected through questionnaires and, in the first three waves, through achievement tests in mathematics, reading, social studies, and science. NELS makes it possible to link student, dropout, parent, teacher, and school data as well as conduct analysis on subgroups, such as by region, race/ethnicity or private schools.

The nationally representative sample contains 1,000 schools and 24,599 students. The schools are representative of the approximately 40,000 public and private schools in the United States with enrolled eighth graders in 1988. The students represent the 3 million eighth graders attending schools in 1988. It is not, however, representative of students from Bureau of Indian Affairs (BIA) schools, schools for students with disabilities, area vocational schools that do not enroll students directly, and overseas schools for the children of U.S. personnel. The study oversampled, and provides sampling weights, for a variety of subgroups such as Hispanics, Asians, and private-school students. Dropouts remained in the study.

The baseline, 1988, sample includes 24,599 students. Data were collected from students, one parent of each student respondent, school principals (N=1,032) and teachers (N=approximately 5,000). The first follow-up (1990) included approximately 25,000 respondents and a response rate of 99% and 98% for the school districts and schools, respectively. Parents did not participate in the second wave, which gathered information about the transition into high school and from students who dropped out before 10th grade. The second follow-up (1992) wave contained a subsample of the original sample (N=14,000) has approximately 25,000 students, refreshed to create a representative sample of the 12th-grade cohort. This follow-up was designed to provide information about curriculum, student performance, and course-taking opportunities. Baseline through the second follow-up (1992) are available as one dataset and include 27,394 observations. The third follow-up (1994) contains 14,915 observations and looks at employment, access to post-secondary institutions, and family formation. The fourth follow-up (2000) had a sample of 12,144 students.

The student questionnaire inquires about school, work, home, their neighborhoods, academic achievements and aspirations, career goals, educational support and resources, and the role of education in their home and with their peers. Education variables include grades; subjects taken; extracurricular activities; general feelings regarding school and the teachers; boredom in school; school interactions with theft, drugs, and fights; future expectations; amount of time spent on homework; and participation in science experiments. Other education, deviant behavior, and self-assessment variables include smoking and drug (e.g., cocaine) and alcohol use; extracurricular activities; whether ever incarcerated; attitudes toward weapons; the presence of fights, cheating, and stealing at school; feelings about self and other; future aspirations; and beliefs on various issues, such as sex before marriage.

The base-year survey has many questions on languages spoken by the respondents, English proficiency, and participation in language-assistance programs. Respondents are asked whether they have children while in high school (or when they are high school age but are no longer in high school).

The dropout questionnaire includes reason for dropping out, reasons for pre-dropout, long absences from school, encouragement from school to not drop out or offering of alternatives, parental punishment upon leaving school or encouragement to return, participation in alternatives, participation in gangs, receipt of GED, future plans, and parental and personal expectations.

The school administrator questionnaire provides information on average daily attendance, percentage of eighth-grade students who live in a single-parent family, number of students who receive special services, base salary for teachers, admissions process for the school, financial aid, standardized tests, gifted and talented program, school climate, team teaching, college representatives, and outstanding teacher awards.

The parent questionnaire provides information on finance and educational expenses as well as the sexual orientation of the parent and his or her partner. The teacher questionnaire provides in-depth information on teachers' class schedules, materials used for classes, and preparedness.

The fourth follow-up, when students are approximately eight years post-high school, collected data pertaining to work information, degrees attained, activities outside of work, marital status, alcohol use, and income.

The specific data collected each year vary from round to round. Teachers, parents, and school administrators also were surveyed, and the students' coursework and grades were acquired through high school and postsecondary transcripts.

After you have received the NELS CD, you will set up the program and go into the codebook. In the codebook, variable names are based, in part, on when and from whom the information was collected. For example, variables beginning with BY indicate that these were collected in the base year, or 1988. F1 variable were collected in 1990 (Year 1 follow up), F2 is the second follow up, and so on. The following comes from the Quick Guide to Using the NELS: 88/2000 data (http://nces.ed.gov/surveys/NELS88/pdf/QuickGuide.PDF).

1988→	1990→	1992→	1994→	2000
Base Year (BY)	1st Follow-up (F1)	2nd Follow-up (F2)	3rd Follow-up (F3)	4th Follow-up (F4)

The first three to four characters of each variable name identify the section that the variable belongs (e.g., BYS = Base-year Student; F2P = Second Follow-up Parent). At the end of the first and second follow-up student sections, the composite variables (and weights) are followed by responses for freshened students. At the end of the second follow-up freshened student variables, the record contains composite (summary) high school transcript variables.

Quick Guide to Using the NELS:88/2000 Data

Table A-1.—NELS:88 student-level datafile content, by survey and ECB: 1988-2000

List order*	Base year (1988)	1st Follow-up (1990)	2nd Follow-up (1992)	3rd Follow-up (1994)	4th Follow-up (2000)
1.	By student data				
2.		F1 student data			
3.			F2 student data		
4.		F1 dropout data			
5.			F2 dropout data		
6.	BY school administrator data				
7.		F1 school administrator data			
8.			F2 school administrator data		
9.	BY parent data				
10.			F2 parent data		
11.	BY teacher data				
12.		F1 teacher data			
13.			F2 teacher data		
14.				F3 student data	
15.					F4 student data

N2P ECB (27,394 students) Datafile-stmeg.pub

N4P ECB (14,915 students) Datafile-stmeg3.pub

N0P ECB (12,144 students) Datafile-BYF4stu.dat

*List order refers to the order the variables appear on the data file and ECB.

B

These tables describe how the data were collected, and from whom.

Once in the electronic codebook, you can click on particular variables, then click on "View" at the top of the page to see both descriptions of the variable and the frequency for the variable. You'll notice that all variables have missing data codes. You'll need to take this missing data information into account when making up variables. The electronic code

Table A-1.—NELS:88 student-level datafile content, by survey and ECB: 1988–2000—continued

List	Base year	1st Follow-up	2nd Follow-up	3rd Follow-up	4th Follow-up
16.				F3 attendance	F4 attendance
				◄—— NOP (16,459 institutions X students) Datafile-pseF3F4.dat ——►	
17.				F3 institution	F4
				◄—— NOP (3,217 institutions) Datafile-instF3F4.dat ——►	
18.				F3 enrollment	
				◄———► NOP (11,560 students X institutions X number) Datafile-pse1994.dat	

*List order refers to the order the variables appear on the data file.

9

book that you load from the CD received from the National Center for Education Statistics looks like the figure given in page 71.

From this screen, you can either choose variables by clicking on the box next to the variable, or view descriptions of the variables by clicking on view at the top of the page when the variable is highlighted. There are a lot of variables in this list (all variables in the public use data set from all waves of the data) so you may choose to tag some of the variables now, and come back and tag more later. To do this, click on output, then tag file. Please see the the figure depicting this in page 72.

You will then give the tag file a name, and you can come back to it later by clicking on "Import tag files." Once you have finished tagging all of your variables, click on "File, Output," and then choose either SAS or SPSS to output the file. I have output a file to SAS with a few variables. You will next have to go into SAS (or SPSS, if you're using that program), and run the file to get a SAS output file. The code will include format codes, which you can choose to include or not, but it does not include

▓ **ECBW** - **[National Education Longitudinal Study: 1988/2000 --Public]**

File   Move   Tag   View   Search

|◀◀| |◀| |◀| |▶| |▶|| |▶▶|| ↶ ↷   ⊟ 🔍   **BYF4STU: Universe status**

✓	Variable	Label
☐	F4UNIV1	Sample member status in all five waves
☐	F4UNI2A	How sample member entered study
☐	F4UNI2B	Base year status of sample member
☐	F4UNI2C	First follow-up status of sample member
☐	F4UNI2D	Second follow-up status of sample member
☐	F4UNI2E	Third follow-up status of sample member
☐	BYS2A	IS MOTHER/FEMALE GUARDIAN LIVING
☐	BYS4A	MOTHER/FEMALE GUARDIAN EMPLOYMENT STATUS
☐	BYS4OCC	MOTHER/FEMALE GUARDIAN^S OCCUPATION
☐	BYS5A	IS FATHER/MALE GUARDIAN LIVING
☐	BYS7A	FATHER/MALE GUARDIAN EMPLOYMENT STATUS
☐	BYS7OCC	FATHER/MALE GUARDIAN^S OCCUPATION
☐	BYS8A	R LIVES IN HOUSEHOLD WITH FATHER
☐	BYS8B	R LIVES IN HH WITH OTHER MALE GUARDIAN
☐	BYS8C	R LIVES IN HOUSEHOLD WITH MOTHER
☐	BYS8D	R LIVES IN HH WITH OTHER FEMALE GUARDIAN
☐	BYS8E	R LIVES IN HOUSEHOLD WITH BROTHER(S)
☐	BYS8F	R LIVES IN HOUSEHOLD WITH SISTER(S)
☐	BYS8G	R LIVES IN HOUSEHOLD WITH GRANDPARENT(S)
☐	BYS8H	R LIVES IN HOUSEHOLD W/OTHER RELATIVE(S)
☐	BYS8I	R LIVES IN HOUSEHOLD W/ NON-RELATIVE(S)
☐	BYS12	SEX OF RESPONDENT
☐	BYS14	SECTOR OF HIGH SCHOOL R PLANS TO ATTEND
☐	BYS15	IS THERE ANOTHER H.S. R MAY ATTEND INSTD
☐	BYS16	SECTOR OF 2ND CHOICE HIGH SCHOOL
☐	BYS17	R SPEAK ANY LANG OTH THN ENGLISH BFR SCH
☐	BYS18	1ST LANG R LEARNED TO SPEAK AS A CHILD
☐	BYS19	OTHER LANG R SPOKE BEFORE STARTING SCHL
☐	BYS20	LANGUAGE R USUALLY SPEAKS NOW
☐	BYS21	ANY OTHER LANGUAGE SPOKEN IN R^S HOME
☐	BYS22	LANG USUALLY SPOKN BY PEOPLE IN R^S HOME
☐	BYS23	OTHER LANGUAGE SPOKEN IN R^S HOME
☐	BYS24	LANG OTHER THN ENGLISH R USES MOST OFTEN
☐	BYS25A	HOW WELL R UNDERSTANDS THAT LANGUAGE
☐	BYS25B	HOW WELL R SPEAKS THAT LANGUAGE
☐	BYS25C	HOW WELL R READS THAT LANGUAGE
☐	BYS25D	HOW WELL R WRITES THAT LANGUAGE
☐	BYS26A	HOW OFTEN R SPEAKS LANGUAGE TO MOTHER
☐	BYS26B	HOW OFTEN R^S MOTHER SPEAKS LANG TO R

Ready

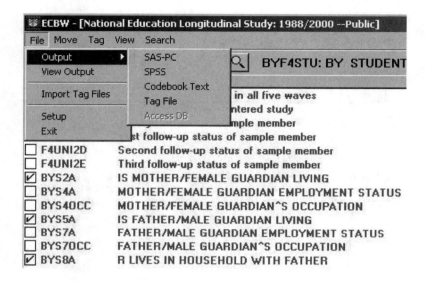

missing value codes, and you will need to take care of missing values. The code looks like the following.

```
LIBNAME NOP 'C:\ECBW\NOP';

DATA X1;INFILE 'D:\ECBW\NOP\DATA\BYF4STU.DAT'
LRECL=1024 PAD;INPUT ID 1-7
 BYS2A 26-26 BYS5A 30-30 BYS8A 34-34 BYS8D 37-37
 BYS8I 42-42 BYS21 54-54 BYS23 57-58 ////////////////;

LABEL
 BYS2A='IS MOTHER/FEMALE GUARDIAN LIVING'
 BYS5A='IS FATHER/MALE GUARDIAN LIVING'
 BYS8A='R LIVES IN HOUSEHOLD WITH FATHER'
 BYS8D='R LIVES IN HH WITH OTHER FEMALE GUARDIAN'
 BYS8I='R LIVES IN HOUSEHOLD W/ NON-RELATIVE(S)'
 BYS21='ANY OTHER LANGUAGE SPOKEN IN R^S HOME'
 BYS23='OTHER LANGUAGE SPOKEN IN R^S HOME';
run;
```

After you run this, you will have your variables in SAS format.

The codebook for the NELS can be found on the CD for the data, which can be obtained from the NCES.

NELS data have been used to study some of the causes of teen abuse of alcohol and smoking and teen delinquency, which include parent's divorce (Jeynes, 2001) and parent/youth conflict (Liu, 2004). The data also have been used to examine the effects of neighborhoods (Ainsworth, 2002), participation in extracurricular activities (Zaff, Moore, Papillo, & Williams, 2003), and entrepreneurial parents (Davila & Mora, 2004) on scholastic achievement and positive life outcomes. Private schools also have been studied, particularly the effects of school uniforms (Bodine, 2003) and Catholic schools, including a study of single-sex versus coeducational Catholic schools (LePore & Warren, 1997) and the effects of religious commitments (Jeynes, 2003). Researchers have used NELS data to observe the causes of school violence (Honora & Rolle, 2002) and victimization (Anderman & Kimweli, 1997), as well as the effects of student mobility on dropping out (Rumberger & Larson, 1998), of growing up mutlilingual (Yeung, Marsh, & Suliman, 2000), of participation in voluntary associations on their voting behavior (Frisco, Muller, & Dodson, 2004), and of substance use by students with disabilities on academic, employment, and social achievements (Hollar & Moore, 2004). Other studies include the consequences of employment during high school (Warren, LePore, & Mare, 2000); the relationship between poverty and teen pregnancy (Young, Martin, Young, & Ting, 2001); the results of at-home computer use (Du & Huang, 2002), single parents (Battle, 2002; Deleire & Kalil, 2003), and gender on mathematics achievement (Bielinski & Davidson, 2001); the effects of inquiry-based teacher practices on excellence in science (Von Secker, 2002); differences in educational attainment among Asian-American and other ethnic groups (Vartanian, Karen, Buck, & Cadge, 2007) and studies into the past looking at racially segregated colleges (Bennett & Xie, 2003).

Data are available through the National Center for Education Statistics (http://www.nces.ed.gov). All years of the data (including all follow-ups to the base year) are available online at the International Archive of Educational Data (http://search.icpsr.umich.edu/IAED/ query.html?col=abstract&op0=%2B&tx0=national+education+longitu dinal+study+of+1988+(nels)+series&ty0=p&fl0=series%3A&op1=- &tx1=restricted&ty1=w&fl1=availability%3A&op2=%2B&tx2=IAED& ty2=w&fl2=archive%3A&nh=50&rf=3). Some data, such as students' transcripts, neighborhood characteristics, and college choice, can be accessed only with an NCES data license. Information on obtaining such licenses can be found at http://www.nces.ed.gov/pubsearch/licenses.asp. Additional information, including a Quick Guide, is available on the NCES website. The codebooks and data are available on a CD-Rom from the NCES.

NATIONAL HEALTH AND NUTRITION EXAMINATION SURVEY (NHANES)

The National Health and Nutrition Examination Survey (NHANES) is a set of cross-sectional studies designed to obtain information on the health and nutritional status of the U.S. population. Sample members are both interviewed and medically examined. NHANES also includes the Epidemiologic Follow-up Study (NHEFS), a national longitudinal study that explores the clinical, nutritional, and behavioral factors assessed in NHANES I (with data originally collected from 1971 to 1975) and studies their relationship to subsequent morbidity, mortality, and hospital utilization. NHEFS also gives information on changes in risk factors, functional limitation, and institutionalization. The NHANES generally collects data on individuals aged 2 months to 74 years old. Researchers collected data through personal and computer-assisted interviews and physical examinations, completed both in home and in research facilities.

The NHANES consists of nine cross-sectional datasets: NHANES I, NHANES II, NHANES III, Hispanic HANES, and NHANES 1999–2000, 2001–2002, 2003–2004, 2005–2006, and 2007–2008. NHANES I, collected from 1971 to 1975, consists of 31,973 individuals. A subsample of participations (N=23,808) also participated in a medical examination at the end of the survey, with those aged 25 to 74 years included in the dataset. The medical examination tested for numerous medical conditions for respondents that are explained below. This study oversampled low-income individuals, preschool children, women of childbearing age, and the elderly, all of whom are more at risk for malnutrition, to help determine the extent of malnutrition in the country. NHANES II, collected from 1976 to 1980, consists of 27,801 individuals with 25,286 interviewed, and 20,322 interviewed and examined. This study oversampled for individuals and children at or below the poverty line. NHANES III, collected from 1988 to 1994, consists of 33,994 individuals, aged 2 months and older. This study included an emphasis on environmental effects on health and nutrition. Hispanic HANES (HHANES), focused on the health and nutritional status of Hispanics, consists of 16,000 individuals with data collected from 1982 to 1984. The sample includes 7,462 Mexican Americans, 1,357 Cuban Americans, and 2,834 Puerto Ricans. NHANES also includes datasets for 2000 (N=9,965), NHANES 2001–2002 (N=9,965), NHANES 2003–2004 (N=10,122), NHANES 2005–2006 (N=12,162), and the soon-to-be released NHANES 2007–2008.

The NHANES Epidemiologic Follow-up Study (NHEFS) is a series of follow-up studies of NHANES I respondents. The sample includes 14,407 individuals, aged 24 to 74 years, who completed the medical examination. Four follow-up studies have been completed, in 1982–1984, 1986, 1987, and 1992. The 1986 NHEFS includes original cohort members aged 55 to 74 years (N=3,980). The 1987 and 1992 NHEFS include the nondeceased members of the original sample, with samples of 11,750 and 11,195, respectively. In the initial study, researchers collected data by tracing the cohort; conducting personal interviews; measuring weight, pulse rate, and blood pressure; collecting hospital records of home and overnight stays; and collecting death certificates.

All the NHANES panels include physical measurements and results of physical examinations (e.g., they drew blood and measured blood content). It is the only national study that includes a wide range of survey-based variables but also many biological measures that can be used as objective indicators of health and nutritional status. Starting in 2002, the NHANES also includes a 24-hour dietary recall, which also includes the amount of plain water consumed over the previous 24 hours and the frequency of consumption of fish and shellfish over the last 30 days.

Researchers collected data on individual and family variables. NHANES includes variables relating to sexual activity and sexually transmitted diseases of those aged 14 to 59 years, including frequency of activity, number of partners, condom use, and sexually transmitted diseases. A mental health questionnaire, for respondents aged 12 to 59 years, includes variables relating to use of illegal drugs, such as marijuana, cocaine, and street drugs. NHANES also includes data on immunizations, reproductive health, obesity, sleep disorders, vision problems, allergies, balance problems, and diseases and chronic illnesses, such as arthritis, diabetes, osteoporosis, cancer, and cardiovascular and respiratory diseases. The dataset also includes variables about food security, smoking and tobacco use, physical activity, TV viewing, and computer use. There is extensive information available about body mass index, including self-reported height and current weight as well as weight one year ago, intentional versus unintentional change over year, loss or gain of weight in the past year, how did the respondent lose weight over the past year or not gain weight, self-reported weight 10 years ago, self-reported heaviest weight and age at this time, and self-reported lowest weight since 18 years of age and the age at this point. Also available is early childhood information, including maternal characteristics such as smoking, birth weight, and participation in Head Start/Early Head Start.

Researchers have used NHANES to conduct research in many areas relating to health and nutrition. For instance, researchers have looked at nutrition and diabetes (Heikes, Eddy, Arondekar, & Schlessinger, 2008) and popcorn consumption (Grandjean, Fulgoni, Reimers, & Agarwal, 2008). Other studies look at obesity (Ogden, Carroll, & Flegal, 2008), and its relationship with functional disability and elderly Americans (Chen & Guo, 2008), the effects of changes in obesity prevalence and smoking prevalence (Flegal, 2007), and cause-specific deaths associated with overweight and obesity (Flegal, Graubard, & Williamson, 2007). Other research explores the association between blood lead levels and osteoporosis (Campbell & Auinger, 2007). Research relating to sexually transmitted diseases explores syphilis (Gottlieb et al., 2008) and gonorrhea and Chlamydia (Datta et al., 2007). Other research topics relate to environmental issues and health, such as the effects of triclosan in urine (Calafat, Ye, Wong, Reidy, & Needham, 2008) and different environmental chemicals that enter the human body (LaKind, Barraj, Tran, & Aylward, 2008), folic acid consumption patterns (Quinlivan & Gregory, 2007), biological risk profiles with education, income, and ethnic differences (Seeman et al., 2008), and the association between calcium and body mass index and body fat in American Indians (Eilat-Adar et al., 2007).

The NHANES data are available through the Centers for Disease Control and Prevention. Publicly released data includes NHANES I, NHANES II, NHANES III, HHANES and NHANES 1999–2000, 2001–2002, 2003–2004, and 2005–2006. NHANES 2007–2008 is in the process of being released. In order to access not-yet-public data, researchers complete a data agreement to garner approval. Most data is available in SAS code or an SAS transport format for use with other statistical software programs, such as SPSS and SUDAAN.

Documentation for the NHANES studies can be found in numerous places, including http://www.cdc.gov/nchs/nhanes/nhanesi. htm, http://www.cdc.gov/nchs/nhanes/nhanesii.htm, and http://www. cdc.gov/nchs/data/nhanes/nhanes3/snh3hrm.pdf for the NHANESI to the NHANESIII datasets, and more generally at http://www.cdc.gov/ nchs/nhanes.htm.

THE NATIONAL LONGITUDINAL STUDY OF ADOLESCENT HEALTH (ADD HEALTH)

The National Longitudinal Study of Adolescent Health (Add Health) is a longitudinal study that collects individual, family, school, and community-level data pertaining to the health and well-being of adolescents and the influence of social networks (parents, friends, peers, and neighborhoods) on adolescent health and risk behaviors. The nationally representative sample includes more than 20,000 young people. Data collection began in 1994–1995, when the youth were in Grades 7 to 12, with subsequent waves occurring in 1995–1996, 2001–2002, and 2007– 2008. The study oversampled highly educated African Americans, Chinese, Cubans, Puerto Ricans, and disabled adolescents. There are also samples of adopted adolescents and, given that in some households more than one child was interviewed, samples exist for pairs of adolescents living in the same household.

Respondents were selected from 132 participating schools, 80 of which were high schools. One feeder school for each high school selected also participated. If a school declined, a new school was chosen. The data collection comprised a combination of in-school questionnaires and in-home interviews. The self-administered in-school student interviews took place in a 45- to 60-minute class period. The in-home adolescent questionnaires, administered using CAPI, took between 60 and 120 minutes, depending on the number of questions asked, a determination based on factors such as age, gender, and past experience. The parent questionnaire was a 40-minute, pencil-and-paper interview conducted by an interviewer. Data collection also included a 5-minute picture vocabulary test. For those who dropped out of school, in-home questionnaires were administered, with additional questions related to reasons for dropping out of school.

Wave 1 (1994–1995), when respondents were between Grades 7 and 12, consisted of adolescent in-school questionnaires (N=20,745) and school administrator self-administered questionnaires (N=164). Wave 2 (1995-1996) consisted of in-home interviews with the adolescent (N=14,738), with parents answering questions about their children (N=17,713) and about themselves as parents (N=17,699). School administrators were interviewed by phone. Some Wave 1 participants were ineligible to participate again in Wave 2, so 65 new participants were added to the sample. Wave 3 (2001–2002), when respondents were between the ages of 18 and 26 years old, consisted of in-home interviews with Wave 1 respondents and their partners (N=15,170). Wave 4 (2007–2008), when respondents were between the ages of 23 and 32 years old, aims to re-interview 85% of the original sample from Wave 1 (approximately N=17,000).

Data and variables vary across waves, and not all variables are included in all waves. As a whole, Add Health contains variables such as those pertaining to sexual activity, sexual preference, pregnancy, contraception use, and sexually transmitted diseases; drug and alcohol use; accessibility to a gun at home; suicide, including thoughts, attempts, and friends and family members who have committed or attempted suicide; violent victimization; physical assaults; weapons-carrying; delinquent behavior; crime involvement, such as the adolescents' involvement in and interaction with crime including age of first encounter, number of arrests before the age of 18 and charges, cases in a juvenile delinquent court, probation, length of probation, and time in jail; and satisfaction with one's neighborhood, its perceived safety, and whether the neighborhood includes physical fitness or recreation centers.

Early health measures include nutrition and diet, and disability and illness. The health measures regarding disability and diet contain information on physical disabilities that limit everyday activities, antibiotics for disabilities, diagnoses of cancer, asthma, depression, diabetes (age at diagnosis), seizures in the past 12 months, high blood pressure, and hypertension. Wave 3 also provides information on retrospective attention deficit hyperactivity disorder (ADHD) and inheritable health conditions.

Other measures cover gambling, and, for example, whether gambling caused problems with friends and family; intimate relationships, such as the ideal relationships and how the respondents met their significant others; and education and school-based experiences, such as happiness at school, post-secondary institution attended, degree received, and field studied. Wave 4 focuses on how biology relates to social, behavioral, psychological, and environmental processes of human development, and includes more information pertaining to young adult life. For instance, data include financial support from parents, siblings, and friends; romantic relationships; marital history; childbearing and health conditions of children; self-esteem, loneliness, and depression; civic participation and citizenship; obstacles to educational goals; interpersonal and occupational stressors; and balance between work and family. Biological data, collected noninvasively, include DNA, height, weight, saliva samples, and various cardiovascular measures.

Add Health contains an extensive list of variables that provide information on adolescent knowledge of pregnancy and sexually transmitted diseases, particularly AIDS, genital herpes, and gonorrhea. Wave 3 contains information on sexual experiences, including age of first act of vaginal intercourse; number of partners in your life and in the past 12 months; use of contraception, particularly condoms and birth control pills; perception of your partners' STD status; attraction to females and males; self-proclaimed sexual preference; parent's knowledge of child's sexual preferences; paying another for sex and vice versa; and partners' needle use. There is also information on whether the respondent has particular STDs, including HIV infection or AIDS.

The National Longitudinal Study of Adolescent Health data has been used in numerous ways and seen in many recent publications, such as to examine sex outcomes, such as the effect of gender and acculturation on adolescents' first sexual experience (Hahm & Lahiff, 2006), the effect of television on teenage sexual initiation (Ashby, Edmonson, & Arcari, 2006), the effects of partner discussions of contraception and STDs (Ryan, Franzetta, Manlove, & Holcombe, 2007), and the influence of religion on premarital pregnancies (Adamczyk & Felson, 2008). Add Health data have also been used to study topics involving drug abuse, such as the effects of cigarette smoking on adolescent depression (Munafò, Hitsman, Rende, Metcalfe, & Niaura, 2008), the result of religion on substance abuse (Rostosky, Danner, & Riggle, 2007), the correlation between access to alcohol, drugs, and guns at home to health-risk behavior (Swahn & Hammig, 2000), and the consequences of using illegal drugs, such as marijuana (Timberlake et al., 2007) and crystal methamphetamine

(Iritani, Hallfors, & Bauer, 2007) faced by young people. Health out-comes have also been researched, including the effects of rurality and ethnicity on child physical illness (Wickrama, Elder, & Abraham, 2007); self-esteem in Chinese, Filipino, and European-American adolescents (Russell, Crockett, Shen, & Lee, 2008); the risk of suicide because of sexual orientation (Silenzio, Pena, Duberstein, Cerel, & Know, 2007); and the relationship between obesity and immigrants (Popkin & Udry, 1998). Add Health data have been used to study the effects of race, such as the multiracial adolescent's choice of friends (Doyle & Kao, 2007) and interracial and intraracial relationships (Wang, Kao, & Joyner, 2006), and issues of violence, such as the effect of sports and peers on young male violence (Kreager, 2007), the connection between same-sex orien-tation and violence (Russell, Franz, & Driscoll, 2001), and child maltreat-ment and domestic partner violence (Fang & Corso, 2007). Other topics studied include the relationships among sports, gender, and academic achievement (Videon, 2002), research on twins (Horwitz, Videon, Schmitz, & Davis, 2003), the correlation between incarceration and intergenerational social exclusion (Foster & Hagan, 2007) and the con-tribution of environment to child ADHD (Haberstick et al., 2007).

Select Add Health data are available for public use, while other data are restricted to protect the safety and privacy of the respondents. The public-use data contain a random selection of half of the core sample and half of the oversampled African Americans who have a parent with a college degree. These public-use datasets are available on CD-Rom in ASCII format and are distributed by Sociometrics. The codebooks for the Add Health data are available at http://www.cpc.unc.edu/projects/addhealth/codebooks.

NATIONAL LONGITUDINAL SURVEYS (NLS)

The National Longitudinal Surveys (NLS) consists of a series of five cohorts, selected by age group, who are followed over a period of decades. Data collection on first cohort (NLS of Older Men) began in 1966 and ended in 1990. Data collection on the most recent cohort (NLSY97) began in 1997 and continues today. The NLS collects information about participants' labor market experiences as well as the factors that influ-ence those experiences, such as assets and income, education, training, family demographics and composition, attitudes and aspirations, and health conditions and behaviors. The NLS makes it possible to look at economic, familial, personal, and social changes over a lifetime. The NLS was originally funded by the U.S. Bureau of Labor Statistics to collect information on labor market experiences of different groups of people.

Each of the NLS cohorts, when weighted, is nationally representative of the population born between the years specified by each cohort and living in the United States when interviews started for that cohort. Each cohort has additional specific issues pertaining to representativeness. The NLS Older and Young Men and NLS Mature and Young Women are representative only of the civilian and noninstitutionalized population. Researchers also oversampled Black men and women. The NLSY79 includes three subsamples, the first of which is a cross-sectional sample representative for the civilian, noninstituionalized population. The second subsample consists of civilian Black and Hispanic youths and low-income youths, while the third includes a sample of military youths. The Children of the NLSY79 is representative of children born to parents who themselves were born between 1957 and 1964 and who were living in the United States in 1978. The NLSY97 includes a cross-sectional sample of youth, including those in institutions, as well as an additional sample of Black and Hispanic youths.

Researchers collected data from each cohort using a mixture of mail, in-person and, by 2002, mostly telephone interviews. These interviews collected core data from each cohort as well as topical data from select cohorts in select years. The *NLS Handbook* (http://www.bls.gov/nls/handbook/nlshndbk.htm) provides details about which cohorts and years were asked in which questions.

The cohorts include NLS of Older and Young Men, NLS of Mature and Young Women, NLS Youth of 79, Children of the NLSY79, and NLS Youth of 97. Sample sizes vary across cohorts. Researchers used a multi-stage, stratified probability sampling methodology to create the sample for each of the cohorts. The cohorts are not mutually exclusive, and a household could have more than one respondent in each cohort or have respondents in different cohorts. These sibling and partner pairs are not nationally representative, however.

The NLS of Older and Young Men, one of the original cohorts, consisted of two cohorts surveys. The first sampled men aged 45 to 59 years who were beginning to leave, or think about leaving, the work force and enter retirement (original N=5,020). Twelve surveys were conducted between 1966 and 1983. The National Institute of Aging conducted another survey in 1990 that consisted of interviews with the widows or living relatives of the deceased sample members and a record check of causes of death. The second survey, of younger men, included men aged 14 to 24 years who were finishing school and making decisions or entering the work force, military, or further education (original N=5,225). Twelve surveys were conducted between 1966 and 1981.

The NLS of Mature and Young Women, the other of the original cohorts, comprises two cohorts. The first consists of women aged 30 to 44 who were returning to the work force after raising their children (original N=5,083). Twenty-one surveys were conducted between 1967 and 2003. The second cohort includes young women aged 14 to 24 who were finishing school; entering the military, the work force or further education; and starting their own families. Twenty-two interviews were conducted between 1968 and 2003.

The NLS Youth of 79 (NLSY79) consists of a cohort of youths aged 14 to 22, born between 1957 and 1964 (original N=5,159). At this age, the youths are transitioning from school to work, the military, or further education and starting their own families. Annual surveys began in 1979 and, in 1994, changed to biennial surveys, which continue to the present, for a total of 22 surveys to date. The cohort includes two additional supplemental samples. The first includes youths who are Black or Hispanic and those of low income. Surveys with these supplemental samples ended after 1990. The second include military youths who were interviewed through the 1984 surveys.

The Children and Young Adults of NLSY79 is a supplemental data file of the NLSY79 that consists of interviews with the mothers in NLS79 and their children. When the children become 15 years old, they take a survey similar to that which their mothers take. Biennial data collection began in 1986 (children) and 1994 (young adults) and continues today for a total of 11 and seven surveys to date, respectively.

The NLSY97 is a cohort of youths aged 12 to 16, born between 1980 and 1984. Like the youths in the other NLS surveys, they are moving from school to work, the military, or further education and starting their own families. This cohort includes an oversampling of Black and Hispanic youth. Annual surveys began in 1997 and continue today, with a total of 11 surveys to date (1997–2007). In these interviews, some questions were asked of parents if the child was relatively young.

It is difficult to discuss the variables in the many National Longitudinal Surveys because there are so many versions of the data. I write about them in mostly general terms here. The core variables include labor market experiences, training, schooling, physical and mental health, household composition, marital histories, children/dependents, family assets and income from particular sources, geographic residence, and receipt of government assistance. Some important childhood variables include school records/behaviors/aptitude/intelligence scores, participation in Head Start or other preschool programs, and attitudes/aspirations/psychological well-being. For workers, content includes work-related discrimination, week-by-week work histories, retirement plans, pension eligibility, and pension plans. Other variables include adverse life events, volunteer and leisure activities, sexual activity, alcohol/cigarette/substance abuse, delinquency, criminal activities and arrest records, household chores, child care, and care of the ill and disabled. Some cohort datasets include additional variables or supplemental datasets with information about adoption, foster care and living arrangements, crime and violence, quality of the home environment, histories of public assistance, child development and prenatal care, and support network information for women. Children of the NLSY79 includes child development variables to assess vocabulary, verbal skills, reading, math, memory, behavior problems, temperament, self-perception, and motor and social development. NLSY97 includes information about how respondents spend their time each day, such as doing homework, reading, or lessons.

Health variables include health status and change over time; types of health problems and conditions; hospitalization and care received; height and weight; whether health problems resulted from injuries (on or off the job); assistance with daily living activities; use and frequency of emergency medical assistance; hospitalization; death information; work information as it relates to health (e.g., environment, satisfaction, conditions); health of respondents' parents; and, for women, whether discrimination based on health was experienced at work, information about menopause and hormone treatment, driving habits, and pregnancy and child information. NLSY97 also includes variables about respondents' perceptions of their weight and and how they manage any perceived weight problems, and experience with events such as violent victimization, homelessness, hospitalization of a household member, incarceration or unemployment of an adult, and use of medication. In addition to many of the above variables, Children of the NLSY79 includes information about the number and type of accidents/injuries/illnesses; timing of health and dental check ups; assistance with behavioral, emotional or mental problems; visits to psychiatrist/psychologist/counselor; and use of medications to control behavior.

Geographic and environmental data include current region of residence, location of job and birthplace; environmental characteristics such as labor force size and unemployment rate, relocation dates and reasons, and length of time at residences; perceptions about quality of neighborhood; and presence of neighborhood problems such as crime and violence.

Geocode information, down to the census tract level, is available for some of the NLS data (NLSY79 (1979-2002), NLSY97 Young Adult (1994–2002) and NLS97 (Rounds 1–7)). For NLSY97, information is available for each college that the person attended, along with the location of the school. Special contracts must be approved and signed in order to use such data. Information on obtaining the geocoded data can be found at http://www.bls.gov/nls/nlsfaqs.htm#anch2.

NLSY79 includes information about involvement and income from activities such as truancy, drug use and dealing, vandalism, shoplifting, and robbery, and involvement in the criminal justice system (arrest, police contact). NLS provides data about experience with events such as violent victimization, homelessness, hospitalization of a household member, adult in jail or unemployed, and parental divorce

One precaution about the NLS is that income data for the NLS are sometimes difficult to use. According to Moore, Pedlow, Krishnamurty, & Wolter (2000) (http://www.nlsinfo.org/ordering/display_db.php3), 22 percent of the data in the 1997 NLS of Youth is either missing or 0, with 0 indicating missing values. Other NLS datasets also have large proportions of cases with missing values. Unlike some other datasets, the NLS does not impute income data. It is possible to use components of income information to determine income for those with missing data, but imputation will be needed to do this because some or many of the components of income have missing information.

Researchers have used the NLS to do sibling studies, and they use fixed effect with sibling techniques in these studies (Ashenfelter & Zimmerman, 1997; Fletcher and Wolfe, 2008; Ven Den Oord & Rowe, 1998).

Researchers have used NLS cohorts to study a variety of questions related to employment and income. For instance, studies examine earning, skill, and market differences for men of different races (Gabriel, 2004), the relationship between cognitive skills and wages (Mitra, 2000), job satisfaction and gender (Donohue & Heywood, 2004) and racial discrimination and wages (Eckstein & Wolpin, 1999). Others study the relationships between poverty and math and reading achievement (Eamon, 2002), school and earnings (Ginther, 2000), and childhood neighborhood poverty and adult employment (Holloway & Mulherin, 2004). Researchers have also studied health-related factors such as the relationship between obesity and wages (Cawley, 2004) and predictors of work-related injuries and illnesses (Dembe, Erickson, & Delbos, 2004). One researcher looked at volunteerism across cohorts (Rotolo & Wilson, 2004).

Researchers have also used the NLS cohorts to study a variety of health-related variables. Some studies look at substance abuse, such as the consequences of binge drinking (Jennison, 2004) and the relationship between alcohol and work-related injuries (Veazie & Smith, 2000). Another researcher looked at the influence of childhood conditions on mortality (Hayward & Gorman, 2004). Other researchers examined child health and well-being through studies looking at the impact of absentee parents (Lang & Zagorsky, 2001), spanking (Slade & Wissow, 2004), television watching (Christakis, Zimmerman, Digiuseppe, & McCarty, 2004) and obesity (Strauss, 2000).

Further studies examine factors related to crime and imprisonment, such as the relationships between crime and the market (Gould, Weinberg, & Mustard, 2002), father absence and youth incarceration (Harper & McLanahan, 2004), and race, class and incarceration (Pettit & Western, 2004).

Data are collected on both adults and children, and there are several Bureau of Labor Statistics websites that give good listings of the variables available for each of the datasets (for example, for NLS of older men, see http://www.bls.gov/nls/handbook/2005/selvarom.pdf; for the NLS for younger men, see http://www.bls.gov/nls/handbook/2005/selvarym.pdf;

for the NLS for mature women, see http://www.bls.gov/nls/handbook/ 2005/selvarmw.pdf; for the NLS for young women, see http://www.bls. gov/nls/handbook/2005/selvarmw.pdf; for the NLS for youth, 1979, see http://www.bls.gov/nls/handbook/2005/selvary79.pdf; for the NLS for youth, 1997, see http://www.bls.gov/nls/nlsy97.htm). The codebook for the NLS of Youth, 1997 cohort is available at http://www.nlsinfo.org/ nlsy97/nlsdocs/nlsy97/questionnaires/R1Youth-final.pdf.

Public data for the 1997 NLSY are available online for downloading of specific variables for all 11 waves of the data. This site can be found at https://www.nlsinfo.org/investigator/pages/search.jsp.

Detailed information about the NLS is available through the Bureau of Labor Statistics (http://www.bls.gov/nls). Data for the many NLS versions are available at SODA POP, at The Pennsylvania State University, http://sodapop.pop.psu.edu/data-collections/nls. Permission must be granted from the Population Research Institute at Penn State to download these data. Data are also downloadable from the NLS Product Availability Center (http://www.nlsinfo.org).

NATIONAL MEDICAL EXPENDITURE SURVEY (NMES)/MEDICAL EXPENDITURE PANEL SURVEY (MEPS)

The National Medical Expenditure Survey consists of a series of surveys that collect information on medical expenditures and health insurance costs. The surveys, some of which contain a series of surveys within them, include the National Medical Care Expenditure Survey (NMCES, also known as NMES-1, 1977), the National Medical Care Utilization and Expenditure Survey (NMCUES, 1980), the National Medical Expenditure Survey (1987), and the Medical Expenditure Panel Survey (1996-2008).

The NMCES was conducted in 1977 by the National Center for Health Services Research, which is now called the Agency for Health Care Policy and Research. This study consists of three surveys. The Household Survey includes 13,500 randomly selected households and collected data pertaining to demographics, medical use, and expenditures in six rounds during1977 and 1978. The Health Insurance/Employer Survey supplemented and verified the Household Survey by surveying the individuals and organizations identified as private insurance providers in the Household Survey. The Medical Provider Survey collected data from

13,500 medical care providers, identified in the Household Survey, pertaining to patient visits, diagnoses, expenditures, and payments.

The National Medical Care Utilization and Expenditure Survey (NMCUES), conducted in 1980 by the National Center for Health Statistics and the Health Care Financing Administration, gathered information on health, access to and use of medical services, health insurance coverage, and charges and payments. The sample is representative of noninstitutionalized civilians in the United States in 1980. The NMCUES consists of three surveys. The National Household Component sampled 6,000 randomly selected households. The State Medicaid Household Component sampled 4,000 households from the Medicaid eligibility files from California, Michigan, New York, and Texas, containing 1,000 households from each state. Both surveys included five rounds of interviews in 14 months during 1980 and 1981. The Administrative Records Component gathered information on program eligibility and Medicare and Medicaid payments. The NMCUES collects information on variables such as annual number of bed and work-loss days, medical and emergency room visits, hospital overnights, and prescription medicines; types of medical services received; charges and out-of-pocket costs for a variety of medical services and prescription medicines; medical conditions; dental services and costs; insurance type; and work and income characteristics.

The National Medical Expenditure Survey of 1987, conducted by the Agency for Health Services and Research, included three surveys. The Household Survey, sampled with a stratified multistage area probability design, includes 35,000 individual in 14,000 households and is representative of the civilian noninstitutionalized population of the United States. Researchers oversampled poor and low-income families, the elderly, the functionally impaired, and Black and Hispanic individuals. Participants participated in four personal and telephone interviews and provided information pertaining to employment, health insurance, and medical expenditures.

The 1996–2008 Medical Expenditure Panel Survey includes anywhere from 9,000 to 14,600 households, and 21,000 to more than 37,000 individuals, in any year in the sample. Each group of respondents is surveyed for two years, with 12 panels through 2007. Thus, in any given year, two panels are being surveyed, one in its first year and another in its second year.

Part of the 1987 NMES is the Institutionalized Population Survey, which gathered information on nursing and personal care facilities, including those for the mentally retarded, and the people admitted to them. The sample includes 810 nursing and personal care homes and 691 facilities for the mentally retarded, sampled from the Inventory of Long-Term Care Places (1986) using specific criteria. Data was collected from facility administrators, caregivers, next of kin or other knowledge-able respondents, and Medicare claims information. The survey includes variables relating to medical, residence and institutional history, insur-ance coverage, institutional characteristics (e.g., size, type, ownership, and certification status) and expenditures for services rendered.

Another part of the 1987 NMES is the Survey of American Indians and Alaskan Natives (SAIAN), conducted in collaboration with Indian Health Service (IHS), which used a stratified area probability sampling process to create a sample of 7,071 individuals residing in households eligible to receive HIS services. The SAIAN uses the same data collection tools and procedures as the Household Survey, except that there were only three waves of data interviews, questions involving long-term care were omitted, and questions involving IHS facilities and traditional med-icine were added. Approximately 40% of interviews occurred entirely in the respondent's native language.

The longitudinal MEPS data are used to estimate health care usage and expenditures for individuals over a two-year period, using five or six rounds of interviews. The data track health care coverage, usage (includ-ing homeopathic and acupuncture treatments), behaviors, and expendi-tures; those using public health insurance; and employment, income, and assets. Respondents are asked when and where they went to receive care, such as hospitals, physicians, and pharmacies. The data contain information from those providers that indicate what procedures were performed, what conditions were treated, how much was spent, and who paid (Were procedures paid for by the patient or by insurance, and how much did each pay?). Confidential data files are also available for use with the public-use MEPS files. Some of these confidential data files include household-insurance linked files for 1996–1999 and 2001; a nursing home component for 1996; a medical provider component, in which detailed charges and payments from hospitals, physicians, home health agencies, and pharmacies are included; an area resource file, with variables for the county of residence of the household, that includes indicators of health facilities and health status; and tax simulations using the National Bureau of Economic Research's TAXSIM to estimate taxes paid by households.

Online data queries are available for the MEPS for the years 1996–2007. These queries can give simple statistics for such variables as perceived overall and mental health, poverty status, and health insurance status, as well as medical utilization and expenditures. Go to http://www.meps.ahrq.gov/mepsweb/data_stats/MEPSnetHC.jsp to use this data tool.

Researchers have used NMES/MEPS to explore treatment trends for anxiety disorders (Olfson, Marcus, Wan, & Geissler, 2004), attention deficit hyperactivity disorder (Olfson, Gameroff, Marcus, & Jensen, 2003), and psychotherapy (Olfson, Marcus, Druss, & Pincus, 2002). Others have explored medical expenses among the elderly (Selden & Banthin, 2003), expenses related to physical activity (Wang & Brown, 2004), and smoking (Johnson, Dominici, Griswold, & Zeger, 2003), as well as changes in health care utilization and expenditures for children and youth over a period of time (Simpson et al., 2004). Researchers have used NMES to study employment distortions resulting from the underwriting behavior of health insurance companies (Kapur, 2004) and the relationship between health insurance and employee commitment (Crocker & Moran, 2003). Others have explored the impact of tax policy on health insurance purchases (Ketsche, 2004) and the use of home health care and associated costs after the Balanced Budget Act of 1997 (Spector, Cohen, & Pesis-Katz, 2004).

NMES/MEPS data are available through the Inter-University Consortium for Political and Social Research (www.icpsr.umich.edu). The NMES surveys are relatively old now, but they have been have been publically released with projections from the data to years 1996 and 2005 (Moeller et al., 2002) (see http://www.meps.ahrq.gov/mepsweb/data_files/publications/mr13/mr13.pdf for a full explanation of the updates). The MEPS is current (through 2008 at the time of this writing) and can be found at http://www.meps.ahrq.gov/mepsweb.

NATIONAL SURVEY OF AMERICAN FAMILIES (NSAF)

The National Survey of American Families (NSAF) is a collection of three cross-sectional household surveys focusing on the economic, social, and health well-being of low-income children, adults, and families. Researchers collected data in 1997, 1999, and 2002 from more than 40,000 randomly selected respondents in each year. The respondents ranged in age from 16 to 64 years old. The NSAF includes in family responses unmarried partners, their respective children, and the relatives by blood, marriage, and adoption of each of the partners and their children. Designed as part of larger study by The Urban Institute, the NSAF gathers information useful in exploring the impact of devolution of social programs, especially Temporary Assistance for Needy Families (TANF) programs, on the economic, social, and health well-being of children, adults and families.

The sample was drawn from two sources: over-sampled data from 13 focus states and supplemental data from the rest of the country. The 13 focus states are Alabama, California, Colorado, Florida, Massachusetts, Michigan, Minnesota, Mississippi, New Jersey, New York, Texas, Washington, and Wisconsin. These states were chosen because they varied among themselves on different characteristics such as size, location, fiscal capacity, population needs, and government service delivery while at the same time closely resembling the national population. The NSAF is nationally representative of noninstitutionalized civilian individuals who are under 65 years of age. It is also representative at the state level for the focus states. Weights are provided to make the sample representative for different units of analysis (child, adult, and family).

Respondents participated in a telephone interview, answering questions on a variety of well-being measures. While some specific questions have been added, edited, or deleted across the survey years, all three surveys contain the same variables categorized into 16 sections: (a) student status of respondent; (b) health status (including physical, mental and learning health conditions and impairments and disability status); (c) education, educational expectation, and performance of focal child (including participation in special education and summer school); (d) household roster (including foster care information); (e) health care coverage (including SCHIP and other publicly funded insurance programs); (f) health care use and access for respondent and focal child; (g) child care arrangements (including participation in Head Start); (h) nonresidential parent information; (i) employment and earnings; (j) family income outside of employment income; (k) welfare program participation; (l) education and training of respondent and spouse/

partner; (m) housing and economic hardship; (n) issues, problems, and social services; (o) race, ethnicity and nativity; and (p) respondent opinions about welfare, working, and raising children.

Researchers used two sampling frames to select households. The first involved random digit dialing to screen out and select eligible households. The second involved area sampling for those households that did not have telephones and in-person screening for eligibility. These samples were then combined and additional within-household random sampling followed to create two groups of respondents: adults with children under 18 years old living with them (Option A) and adults who were not living with children under 18 years old (Option B). Within Option A, two focal children were randomly selected from all the children under 18 in the household. The researcher then found the most knowledgeable adult (MKA), who could answer questions about him/herself and his/her spouse/partner, if applicable, and the identified child. Each focal child could have a different MKA. With Option B, researchers sampled in two categories: households in which adults are childless and households in which adults do not have children under 18 years old living with them. From each group, researchers randomly selected up to two adults between 18 and 64 years old who were not spouses/partners of each other. These respondents participated in the interview and answered questions about him/herself and his/her spouse/partner, if applicable. Due to this methodology, each household could potentially have from one to four respondents. Households without telephones participated in the study through the use of cell phones provided by on-site research assistants.

The Urban Institute publishes a series of reports, *Snapshots of America's Families* that summarize the institute's analysis of key measures and trends. Given the wide array of well-being measures and different units of analysis contained in the NSAF data, researchers can use the dataset to examine the relationships and trends among different forms of well-being and different types of people. Additionally, the data can be coupled with national and state policy information to examine impacts of policy on quality of life for those same people or groups of people. The Urban Institute provides information on state welfare rules with its Welfare Rules Database. In this, researchers can examine how welfare rules have changed within and among states since 1996 (http://anfdata.urban.org/wrd/WRDWelcome.cfm). Researchers use this database even if not working with the NSAF data because it provides information that can be examined on its own or used with other databases, with data merges by county or state.

NSAF provides data on welfare program participation, such as receipt, spells, and characteristics of AFDC/TANF, food stamp (FS), and Supplemental Security Income (SSI); receipt, reductions, and why left welfare (welfare cut off because: earnings increased, assets were too high, did not follow program rules, reached end of time limit, not a U.S. citizen, or other); inquiries for government assistance such as TANF, food stamps, child care subsidies, and Medicaid; the completion of tax returns and the receipt of the Earned Income Tax Credit; and receipt of child support payments and free or reduced-cost breakfast or lunch programs. It also includes variables with respondent opinions about welfare. In addition, NSAF provides information on the education and training of the respondent and his or her spouse/partner, including unpaid work for the government under public assistance programs, receipt of education vouchers, and participation in job training.

Variables also provide information on respondent's attitudes and feelings (such as nervousness or peacefulness), as well as feelings toward children (such as caring for them or anger towards them) and children's activities and problems (such as getting along with others, concentrating and feeling unhappy, worthless or nervous, trouble sleeping, and cheating); parental behaviors (such as reading to children or taking them on outings); and degree to which the respondent is a risk taker.

Researchers have used NSAF to examine a variety of influences on different well-being outcomes. Some studies explore the relationship between family structure and the well-being of children and adults. These studies look at well-being as influenced by parental marriage and cohabitation (Brown, 2004; Manning & Brown 2006; Willetts & Maroules, 2005), kin and nonkin foster care (Ehrle & Geen, 2002), nonresidential fathers (Garasky & Stewart, 2007) and grandmothers who are child care givers (Mills, Gomez-Smith, & De Leon, 2005; Park, 2006).

Other studies focus on health-related outcomes. One such study focuses on trends in health care (Sturm, Andreyeva, Pincus, & Tanielian, 2005), while another looks at trends in employer-provided insurance (Shen & Long, 2006). Other studies examine the relationships between health insurance and Medicaid, and health care access and use (Busch & Horwitz, 2004; Garrett & Zuckerman, 2005; Long, Coughlin, &

King, 2005; Long, King, & Coughlin, 2006; Shen & Zuckerman, 2005) and out-of-pocket costs (Shen & McFeeters, 2006). Several studies examine the relationship of family characteristics, family health, and health care access and use. This set of research studies well-being as it relates to stressful family environments (Fairbrother, Kenney, Hanson, & Dubay, 2005) and immigrant families (Huang, Yu, & Ledsky, 2006; Yu, Huang, Schwalberg, & Kogan, 2005; Potocky-Tripodi, 2006).

Additional studies examine the relationship between family and personal characteristics and child care (Parish & Cloud, 2006), as well as the relationship between policy, especially welfare policy, and well-being (Zimmerman, 2003), and policy and household economics and housing (Robbins & Barcus, 2004; Heintze, Berger, Naidich, & Meyers, 2006).

Data are available through The Urban Institute (www.urban.org/center/anf/nsaf.cfm) for all three data collection years and for all three levels of analysis: child, adult and family. The specific number of observations varies based on the unit of analysis. The user guide provides detailed low-income observation data by the 13 focus states and the balance of the nation. Some survey questions are asked only of randomly selected adults from the sampled adult pool, and therefore researchers cannot create valid household aggregates. Through the ICPSR, online analysis of the data is available for the focal child, parents, and other adults, by year, through the Survey Documentation and Analysis (SDA), developed by the computer-assisted Survey Methods Program (CSM) at the University of California, Berkeley.

NATIONAL SURVEY OF CHILD AND ADOLESCENT WELL-BEING (NSCAW)

The National Survey of Child and Adolescent Well-Being (NSCAW), sponsored by the Administration of Children, Youth, and Families of the Department of Health and Human Services, is a study of children in the child welfare system who are at risk of abuse and neglect. The study collects data from more than 5,000 children who come in contact with child welfare systems, the pathways and services in the systems, and the short- and long-term effects of system involvement. The NSCAW covers a wide range of topics, such as neighborhoods, cognitive achievement, social functioning, delinquency, and sexual behavior. The study collects data from children, parents and caregivers, teachers, and caseworkers, in addition to administrative records. Baseline data collection occurred from the fall of 1999 through April 2001. Follow-up data was collected 12 months, 18 months, and 36 months after April 2001, with a fourth follow-up in 2005. The data is nationally representative for those who enter the child welfare system and who are white, African American, or Hispanic.

The sample was selected using composite sampling. The sample includes more than 5,501 children from infancy to age 14 who entered the child welfare system between October 1999 and December 2000. They came from 97 child welfare agencies across the country and represent both open and unopened cases investigated by local child protective services agencies. The core sample is supplemented by 727 children who have been in foster care for a longer period of time. The study oversampled for infants, victims of sexual abuse, and children receiving foster care. The study attempted to evenly sample for age, gender, and ethnicity, and it includes data about the severity of abuse. Severity of abuse is measured by the type of abuse rather than the effect of the abuse. Race and ethnicity is limited to white, Black and Hispanic.

Data were collected by computer-assisted personal interviews (CAPI) for the children, parents, caregivers, and caseworkers. Teachers were surveyed by mail, with computer-assisted phone interviews to follow-up on nonrespondents. The children were selected by computer-assisted programs, which also helped to collect data from administrative records.

The child interviews inquired about school achievement, behavior problems, relationships with parents and peers, cognitive skills, and exposure to violence. Children 11 years and older also were asked about delinquent behavior, exposure to sexual behavior, substance abuse, and maltreatment history. The caregiver survey collects data on children, the caregiver, and the family and community. Child variables include health and disabilities, social skills, temperament, and disruptions in living environment. Caregiver information includes mental health and substance use, relationship with the child, disciplinary actions, and physical health. Family and community information concerns the neighborhood environment, domestic violence, and parental criminal involvement.

The local and state child welfare agency survey inquired about such topics as agency services and staff. The state survey also collected data on local-state agency collaboration. The caseworker survey, at baseline, collected data about the risk assessment of children and families, case-worker characteristics, and services for children and their families. Follow-up interviews collected information pertaining to the history before and since the case report and the caseworker involvement with the child and family. The teacher survey included topics such as school socialization, interpersonal aggression, school absences, home-teachers contacts, and special education needs.

The National Survey of Child and Adolescent Well-being data has been used to explore topics such as mental health (Burns et al., 2004), chronic conditions (Jee et al., 2006), and behavioral problems (Barth, Lloyd, Green, James, Leslie, & Landsverk, 2007; Grogan-Kaylo, Ruffolo, Ortega, & Clarke, 2008), with a particular look at behavioral issues following reunification after foster care (Bellamy, 2008), and the interplay between urbanicity, child behavior problems, and poverty (Barth, Wildfire, & Green, 2006). The data have been used to study maltreatment and abuse, particularly sexual abuse (McCrae, Chapman, & Christ, 2006), the correlation between maltreatment and aggressiveness, and delinquent behavior in adolescents (Wall & Barth, 2005), and the relationship between intimate partner violence and child injury/use of emergency room (Casanueva, Foshee, & Barth, 2005). Other focus areas include parental incarceration (Hayward & DePanfilis, 2007; Phillips, Burns, Wagner, & Barth, 2004); alcohol, drug, and mental health treatment and race/ethnicity (Libby et al., 2006); social, emotional, and academic competence (Jaffee & Gallop, 2007); police involvement in child protective service investigation (Cross, Finkelhor, & Ormrod, 2005); and evaluating substance abuse services for child welfare clients (Guo, Barth, & Gibbons, 2006).

Data have been separated into general-use data, stripped of identifying information and geographic detail, and restricted-use data. To obtain any of the NSCAW data, researchers must fill out and agree to the data licensing agreement. The people eligible for the agreement are faculty and nonstudent research personnel at institutions with an Institutional Review Board/Human Subjects Review Committee (IRB). For non-U.S. residents or organizations wishing to obtain the data, applications will be handled on a case-to-case basis, and it may be more costly to obtain a licensing agreement. Using restricted-use data, in addition to the licensing agreement, requires an application, a data protection plan, and unannounced on-site inspections of the research facility. More information about data availability and access is available through the National Data Archive on Child Abuse and Neglect, www.ndacan.cornell.edu. The codebook for the data is available at http://www.ndacan.cornell. edu/NDACAN/Datasets/UserGuidePDFs/092_Intro_to_NSCAW_ Wave_1.pdf.

NICHD STUDY OF EARLY CHILD CARE AND YOUTH DEVELOPMENT (SECCYD)

The Study of Early Child Care and Youth Development (SECCYD), supported by the National Institute of Child Health and Human Development, is a longitudinal study examining the relationship between child care and child development. Started in 1991, the study follows a starting sample of 1,364 children, from 10 different locations in the United States, as they develop to age 14 and 15 years old. The study uses multiple methods, including interviews, questionnaires, testing, and trained observers, to collect data on various aspects of child development, including language, social, emotional, and intellectual development, behavioral problems and physical health.

The original sample children were selected through a conditionally random sampling process, in order to obtain demographic diversity. Of the mothers in the original sample, 60% planned on going back to work or school full-time in the child's first year, 20% planned on part-time work or going to school part time, and 20% planned on staying home. Excluded from the sample were children with mothers under 18 years of age, families who planned on moving out of the area within the first three years of the child's birth, children with disabilities at birth, and children with mothers who were not sufficiently conversant in English.

The study is conducted in four phases. Phase I (1991–1994) assessed the original sample, aged birth to three years (N=1,364) and focused on observing child care and child development in the first three years of life. Data collection instruments include a child behavior checklist, a family finance interview, a home inventory and a love-and-relationship questionnaire. Data was collected at 1, 6, 15, 24, and 36 months of age. Phase II (1994–2000) assessed the children from 54 months to first grade (N=1,100), continuing the child care and development observations as well as the transition into elementary school. Data collection instruments include a child-parent relationship scale completed at home when the child was in kindergarten, and in the lab when in first grade; parent involvement and physical environment checklist completed at 54 months in child care; and friendship-interaction coding done at 54 months in child care and in school in first grade. Phase III (2000 and 2005) assesses the children from second to sixth grades (N=1,100), focusing on experiences in early and middle childhood and how those affect development. Data collection instruments included child questionnaire, completed at home in fifth grade; and a mother questionnaire, one completed in the lab in third and in fifth grade. A depression inventory is done in the home by the child in fifth grade and again by the child and a friend in the lab in sixth grade, and family emotional expressiveness is done at home by the mother and father. Phase IV (current) assesses the children at the ages of 14 and 15 (N=1,000 plus) and concentrates on how early experiences combined with maturational factors in adolescence affect health, intellectual achievement, social relationships, and transitions. A list of instruments used and reliability scores are given at these web sites: https://secc.rti.org/Phase2InstrumentDoc.pdf, https://secc.rti.org/Phase3InstrumentDoc.pdf, https://secc.rti.org/Phase4InstrumentDoc.pdf, and https://secc.rti.org/MeasuresPhase1_4Chart.pdf.

The data collected in the NICHD Study of Early Childcare and Youth Development have been used in numerous other studies and publications. These data have been used to examine the reasons for choosing child care (Peyton, Jacobs, O'Brien, & Roy, 2001), the traits of infants with and without special needs (Booth & Kelly, 1998), the correlation between child care and accidental injury (Schwebel, Brezausek, & Belsky, 2006), the difference between United States and Korean child care programs (Clarke-Stewart, Lee, Allhusen, Kim, & McDowell, 2006), and the effects of child care by grandparents in the first few years after birth (Vandell, McCartney, Owen, Booth, & Clarke-Stewart, 2003). The data have also been used to study certain health outcomes, such as the correlation between neighborhoods and weight issues (Lumeng, Appugliese, Cabral, Bradley, & Zuckerman, 2006) and infant sleeping disorders due to attachment to mother (McNamara, Belsky, & Fearon, 2002). Other attachment issues have been studied, including maternal caution upon their children entering kindergarten (Early et al., 2002) and how maternal attachment affects children's friend-making abilities (Lucas-Thompson & Clarke-Stewart, 2007). Studies examine behavioral issues, such as the association between teacher's relationships with children and behavioral issues (Stuhlman & Pianta, 2002). Others explore the involvement of parents (Whiteside-Mansell, Bradley, & Rakow, 2000), effects of divorce (Clarke-Stewart, Vandell, McCartney, Owen, & Booth, 2000) and the effects of marital intimacy (O'Brien & Peyton, 2002). NICHD data have been used to study family income-to-needs and how changes affect children (Dearing, McCartney, & Taylor, 2001) and depressive symptoms in women (Dearing, Taylor, & McCartney, 2004). Other research includes the study of the effect of welfare on good child care (Wolfe, & Vandell, 2002), the correlation between gender and cognition in 3-year olds (O'Brien et al., 2000), and the association between socioeconomic status and language ability in 3-year-olds (Raviv, Kessenich, & Morrison, 2004).

Data and variable descriptions are available through the SECCYD website, http://secc.rti.org. The data can only be obtained by filling out an application, in order to protect the privacy and rights of the respondents. Once the requests are completed, the Research Triangle Institute (RTI) decides whether the person who requested is a qualified user. After data are provided, the RTI monitors the use of the data.

THE PANEL STUDY OF INCOME DYNAMICS (PSID)

The PSID is a longitudinal dataset that currently covers the years 1968 to 2007. At the time of this writing, the 2009 version of the PSID is available for only a few variables, such as measures of mortgage distress (see http://simba.isr.umich.edu/Zips/zipSupp.aspx#MW), with the rest of the 2009 data to be released later. It is nationally representative of the nonimmigrant, U.S. population for men, women, children, and the families in which they live. It allows researchers to examine intergenerational aspects of economic, health, and family life.

The PSID comes from two samples: a cross-sectional sample assembled by the Survey Research Center (SRC) at the University of Michigan, a nationally representative sample drawn from the 48 contiguous United States, which yielded roughly 3,000 families; and the second, which comes from the Survey of Economic Opportunity (SEO), a sample of around 2,000 low-income families, with heads of households who were under 60 years old in Standard Metropolitan Statistical Areas (SMSAs) in the North and non-SMSAs in the South. These core families have been followed since 1968, with additional children and families forming that are now new respondents in the PSID. Thus, when a marriage splits up, and both members of the marriage were part of the original PSID, both partners are followed. As children grow up and have their own children, these children are followed as well. Anyone who was an original PSID member will always be a PSID member (although they may become a nonrespondent), and their offspring will also be PSID members. Nonrespondents can come back to the sample after they have left, and the PSID attempts to contact members who have not responded. Thus, one can look at the data and see that some members leave the sample for some years but then return. It is possible to be a non-sample member and be interviewed. Generally, anyone who is not in the bloodline of an original sample member is not considered to be a sample member. Those who are not sample members are given person numbers that differ from sample-member person numbers (they are 170 or above, while sample-member person numbers are below 170). In 1997, changes were made to the PSID, such that a "refresher" sample was generated in order to better reflect immigration to the United States since 1968. Also, instead of being an annual survey (which it was from 1968 to 1996), it moved to a biennial survey. Numerous questions were asked about the previous year after the move to the biennial survey.

Response rates for the PSID are relatively high since its inception. According to the Survey Research Center, response rates were around 76% in 1968, the initial year of the PSID, but grew to 88.5% in 1969, when those who did not respond to the 1968 interview were recontacted. Since 1969, annual response rates have been between 96.9%–98.5%. Obviously, even with low attrition rates, these rates accumulate over time, and by 1988, roughly 56.1% of the original individuals in the PSID were still in the sample. Fitzgerald, Gottschalk, and Moffit (1998) find that even though attrition rates by 1989 were at roughly 50 percent, they found no strong evidence that this attrition has distorted the representativeness of the PSID. Response and attrition rates for the more recent PSID waves were not found.

From 1968 to 1972, interviews were either face-to-face or mailed. From 1973 to 1993, interviews were done by telephone or through mailings.

Since 1993, all interviews have been done by computer-assisted telephone interviews. Before 1997, interviews lasted around 30 minutes; after this time, interviews last around 70–80 minutes.

The PSID has both a family file and an individual file for those who are aged 16 and above. For the family file, questions are generally asked of the person deemed head of household or the wife of the head of household. In a man-woman relationship, the head is generally deemed the man, except in special cases, in order to conform to the U.S. Census definition of the head of household. It is possible for a female to be a head of household, but this is generally when there is no man in the family. Thus, a female-headed household, with an unmarried woman and no boyfriend who has been in the family unit for a year, is headed by the woman. For women who are not married but have a boyfriend for more than a year, the boyfriend is considered to be the head of household. There is only one head of household per family, and he can have only one wife. Starting in 1984, "wife" was also used, to designate heads (men) and women who were living together but not married. Generally, more extensive information is available for the head of household or the wife in the family files of the PSID than for other individuals in the family. Family earnings, for example, are generally given for the head of household, the wife, and for "others." Thus, it is difficult to determine how much is earned by which others (children, other adults in the family) from these families files. Some of this is given in the individual files, but these individual files, for each sample member who is over the age of 16 in the family unit, are very limited for each year.

All families have a 1968 family ID number that identifies which original family that person came from. For every following year, the person will have a new family ID number, depending on the family with whom he or she resides. The person number uniquely identifies the person within the family. If you are interested in merging variables from a particular year for families, you use the family ID number from the particular year. Generally, what you want to do to use the longitudinal nature of the PSID is sort the data by 1968 interview number and person number (v30001 and v30002 for years prior to 1994 and er30001 and er30002 for subsequent years). You can then merge all years of the data together by these two variables. If you would like only to examine heads of household (given that there is only one of these per family), you can subset the data by head of household (by use of the relationship to head variable in the individual file for any particular year). If you are only interested in wives, you can subset by wives from the relationship to head variable in the individual year files.

The PSID continues to follow all blood relatives (or adoptive children) of those born to original PSID members. Thus, if a child were born into an original PSID family in 1971, and becomes a head of household or a "wife" in 1991, and has children in 1995, you can examine how parental and grandparent outcomes affect this child, especially if you use the Child Development Supplement to the PSID, or if you follow this child until s/he becomes a head of household or a wife.

Because the PSID is based on the population of the United States in 1968, some groups are underrepresented in the data in later years. While sampling weights can make the data nationally representative, sample sizes for certain groups may be small. The Survey Research Center attempted to increase the number of Latino observations in the data by adding 2,000 Latino observations in 1990 (which they called the Latino Supplemental Sample), consisting of families from Mexico, Puerto Rico, and Mexico. While the sample did increase the number of Latinos in the sample, it did not increase the number of other groups, such as Asians, who are also underrepresented in the data. The Latino sample was dropped in 1995, while 511 immigrant families were added by 1999.

As mentioned above, the PSID needs to be weighted in order to be nationally representative. These family or individual weights are used to take into account both differential rates of selection into the sample as well as differential rates of attrition from the sample. The best advice for using weights is to use the most current family weight when examining families and the most recent individual weight when examining individuals.

The PSID collects a wide range of data, and the data that have been collected have changed over the years. Most of the variables described below are available in the family files for particular years of the PSID. Some variables include employment; detailed income data, often by month since 1984; program participation for numerous forms of government assistance including AFDC/TANF, Medicaid, Medicare, SSI, SS, and Food Stamps, again, by month starting in 1984; housing, including whether living in public housing; marriage and fertility histories; food expenditures for some years; education level; education expenses; utility expenses; and wealth variables, covering savings, stock and bond holdings, and total wealth including or excluding housing values for PSID years 1984, 1989, 1994, and 1999–2007. Variables on health include information on height and weight for both the head of household and the wife for 1999–2005 (and from which body mass indices can be calculated); general health status for 1984–2005 for heads of household and wives; a vast array of particular diseases for the head or wife, including diabetes, cardiovascular disease, heart attack, heart disease, and memory loss, for PSID years 1999–2007; depression and anxiety in 2001–2003; health behaviors such as smoking in 1986 and 1999–2007; alcohol consumption in 1999–2007; and physical activity in 1999–2007. There is extensive information on expenditures, such as child care, housing, health care, transportation, clothing, recreation, home repair and maintenance, and trips and vacations.

The PSID also collects some retrospective variables, mostly from the head of household but some from the wife as well. Some of these are the economic standing of the family while growing up, the educational level of the head of household's father and mother, the occupation of the head of household's parents, and, in later versions of the PSID, the health status of the head and wife for ages 0 to 16. New to the PSID in 2007 are retrospective questions on illegal drug use as a child and adolescent.

There are a large number of supplements to the PSID, including the Geocode identifier supplement to the PSID. In these files, PSID respondents are identified by their state and county, down to their census tract and census block number. Census and other information can then be merged with the PSID for examination of area and neighborhood characteristics. Restrictive contracts must signed by the researcher and the researcher's institution and be approved by the Survey Research Center to receive these data. Other supplements include family history files, which include relatively easy ways to get information on marriage, childbirth, and adoptions for the family/individual.

Most of the PSID information is available from the PSID web page. This data center page makes it relatively easy to find and download variables. The data center organizes the data by family and individual data and then by variable type, such as health, income, education, and wealth variables. Once you click on the variable type, you are given the years in which the variables are available, and you can click on those years for the variable you would like. You can save these variables for checkout and then go to the individual variables desired. Once you choose the individual variables, the data center will automatically create identifier variables, such as family ID for the years you have chosen, as well as the 1968 family ID and person number. You can download these variables in an SAS export, in Excel, or as ASCII data, with SAS, SPSS, or Stata programs to read the data. If you forget some data on your first try, you can merge data by using the 1968 ID and person number for this merge. The data center also makes whole year datasets available. Thus, if you are only interest in the 2005 PSID and would like all of the variables for this year, you can download the entire family dataset and the entire individual file without having to choose variables. If you then want to merge these two files, you will need to use the 2005 family ID, along with the 2005 family ID on the individual file, to merge these data.

The Survey Research Center recently made a file available that allows you to determine whether people in the PSID are siblings or have some other relationship (https://simba.isr.umich.edu/FIMS/). This linking of people with their relatives makes the examination of intergenerational outcomes much easier than having to do all of this programming yourself. The PSID is thus one of the few datasets you can use to examine factors relating to how grandparents may affect grandchildren without using only retrospective data. This data file, known as the family identification and mapping system (FIMS), can be downloaded in SAS, Excel, or in ASCII with SAS, SPSS, or Stata statements. You can thus look at either intergenerational mapping (which they call GID) or intragenerational mapping (SID) for siblings. They provide a SAS macro program for doing this determination of the siblings or other intergenerational relationships within the data and merging it with other PSID data. The program determines whether the siblings are full, half, or other types of siblings. Determining sibling relationships can be useful for using sibling fixed effects models, when examining how childhood circumstances may affect adult outcomes. By using the sibling fixed effects method for your analysis, unobserved but permanent features of the family can be controlled even when these variables are not present in the data.

You can use fixed effects models in any of the mainstream statistical programs (SAS, SPSS, or Stata) but the ease of use in Stata is especially appealing, and that is the program that I use for such models. To use sibling fixed effects models in Stata, you will need a sibling identifier for each set of siblings. Once you have this, and have only those families that have more than a single sibling in the data, you can run the Stata code for determining fixed effects. In the example below, I use fixed effects to determine hours of work as an adult, using childhood variable as predictors.

```
xtreg Hours AFDC FS marriedmom, fe i(id)
```

The "fe" indicates a fixed effects model (you can also run random effect models or between effect models); "i" (newid) indicates the sibling ID number that must be used to identify which of the observations are siblings. This method determines a sibling family mean for each set of siblings and subtracts this sibling family mean from the individual mean. Thus, if there is only a single individual in the family, all of their mean values go to zero, and you do not want to include a child with no siblings in these models.

PSID data are used by many researchers on a wide variety of studies. Research dealing with welfare and government assistance include studies on the relationship teenage out-of-wedlock births and welfare receipt (An, Haveman, & Wolfe, 1993), single-parent families and the effect of welfare benefit levels (Butler, 1996), the long-term effects of poverty and welfare receipt on young single mothers (Vartanian & McNamara, 2004), and worker's compensation, looking particularly at data on individuals (Leigh, 1985). Also frequently studied using PSID data are health topics, such as the time and quantity of sleep (Adam, Snell, & Pendry, 2007), the contribution of neighborhood environment to overweight children (Grafova, 2008), and the correlation between food insecurity and weight gain in women (Jones & Frongillo, 2007). Studies involving education topics include higher education and mate selection (Arum, Roksa, & Budig, 2008), correlations between neighboring children and their educational attainment (Solon, Page, & Duncan, 2000), long-term effects of Head Start (Garces, Thomas, & Currie, 2002), and the effect of neighborhood conditions on high school drop-out and graduation rates (Vartanian & Gleason, 1999). Studies on employment and income include occupational injuries and diseases and compensating wages (Leigh, 1981), income tax policy and charitable giving (Brooks, 2007), young women heading households and the relationships among race, industry restructuring, and employment (Browne, 2000), the correlations among race and sex and on-the-job earnings differences (Duncan & Hoffman, 1979), union membership and wages (Cunningham & Donovan, 1986), and child and adolescent neighborhood effects on adult

income (Vartanian & Buck, 2005). Other studies include the relationships among race and sex and intergenerational poverty (Corcoran &
Adams, 1997), delayed fatherhood (Weinshenker, 2006), the influence
of household poverty spells on mortality risk (Oh, 2001), philanthropy
in the United States after September 11 (Steinburg & Rooney, 2005),
poverty among the recently widowed (Smith & Zick, 1986), and the
intergenerational differences between whites and African Americans in
neighborhood mobility (Vartanian, Buck, & Gleason, 2007).

Additional publication lists are available at http://psidonline.isr.
umich.edu/Publications/Bibliography/default.aspx.

Data and codebooks for the PSID can be obtained at http://simba.isr.
umich.edu/Zips/ZipMain.aspx. An index of the variables, both person
and family level, can be viewed at http://simba.isr.umich.edu/VS/i.aspx.

PANEL STUDY OF INCOME DYNAMICS, CHILD DEVELOPMENT SUPPLEMENT

The Child Development Supplement CDS) is a supplement to the Panel
Study on Income Dynamics (PSID) that consists of a sample of children
from families in the PSID. This supplement was created to gather specific
information on the children within the PSID families and to create the
ability to examine the relationships between economic and social factors
and child development. The CDS collects data on the health, education,
employment, relationships, time use, social and psychological well-
being, and development of children and young adults, as well as information about the home, school, and neighborhood contexts in which
they live. The CDS followed the children from 1997 to 2008, collecting
data in three waves (1997, 2002–2003, and 2007–2008). The Transition
to Adulthood Supplement 2005 and 2007 gathered information on CDS
youths who were 18 years or older at that time in order to understand
their experiences as they moved from their parents' homes to indepen-
dence. With sampling weights, the CDS is nationally representative.

The CDS-I sample is the original CDS sample about which data were
collected in 1997. To create this sample, families with children under the
age of 13 years were identified, and then researchers randomly sampled
up to two children from these families. The final sample consists of
3,563 children from 2,394 families. The CDS-II, or second wave of data
collection in 2002, collected data on these same children when they were

5 through 18 years old, half of whom were in adolescence. This sample includes 2,907 children from 2,019 families. The CDS-III was collected in 2007 and includes approximately the 1,677 children who were 10 to 18 years old at that time. Interviews were conducted with primary caregivers (PCG), the children (ages 3 and above), other caregivers, absent fathers, and preschool/daycare/elementary/middle school teachers and administrators,

The CDS-I, CDS-II, and CDS-III contain similar data using similar procedures, with modifications based on the development stage of the child at each data collection point. Data collection included interviews with the child, primary caregiver, other caregivers, and school teachers as well as educational achievement assessments, course and grade reports, and data from external school databases (CDS-II gathered data from Common Core of Data). CDS-I focused on developmental issues from infancy through middle childhood, while CDS-II focused more on issues of adolescence and psychological and school data. The Transition to Adulthood 2005 and 2007 (TA) collects data on CDS sample youths who were 18 years old or older in 2005 and 2007, respectively, and information related to their transition into adulthood. Data collection occurred in 2005 and 2007, with 745 young adults participating in interviews (87% of those eligible to participate) in 2005 and 1,115 young adults participating in 2007 (85% of those eligible to participate). Fewer than half of adults become heads of household or wives in the PSID from ages 18 to 24, and thus less information is collected for them relative to those who are heads of household or wives. This transition to adulthood data thus gives more detailed information on the period of time when the person is no longer a child but has not started his/her own household. The TA interviews the young adults on a variety of issues specific to this period of transition, such as their own employment, income and wealth, educational achievements, current relationships and children, and experiences with discrimination.

The CDS contains a variety of information pertaining to the well-being, education, health, economics and employment, time use and family, and home and neighborhood environments of children and young adults. Well-being and behavioral variables include anti- and pro-social behaviors, social competence, and self-esteem, as well as experiences with bullying, victimization, and incarceration. Additional variables include sexual activity, such as experiences with sexual intercourse, pregnancy and the use of condoms; experiences with discrimination; and expectations for the future. Education variables include school status and achievement (elementary, secondary, post-secondary, including grades and reading and math assessments using the Woodcock-Johnson Revised Tests of Achievement), educational expectations and aspirations of both parents and children, school district characteristics, type and cost of school, attendance, participation in special education or gifted programs, enrollment in federal lunch and breakfast programs, and courses taken in school. Health variables include chronic conditions, eating and exercising behaviors, obesity, smoking, alcohol and drug use, and health care utilization. Time use variables include the types and frequencies of various activities in which respondents participate (and with whom) and electronic media use. Family data include information such as parental monitoring, attitudes toward parenting, relationships between absent parents and their children, social support, child care characteristics, family conflict and closeness, cognitive and emotional stimulation, and sibling interactions. Other relationship variables include dating behaviors, peer relationships, and familial expectations. Numerous scales are available for self-esteem, self-efficacy, psychological distress, and many other variables. Variables for perceived neighborhood conditions include residential stability, social cohesion, and neighborhood safety. Time diaries are kept for some of the CDS respondents, with overall time diaries, as well as school-based diaries. To see all of the variables in the CDS and TA files, see http://psidonline.isr.umich.edu/CDS/wavesdoc.html.

The CDS data can be linked to PSID data, making it possible to examine the relationship between child-related outcomes and family demographic and economic data (including intergenerational data). Information about years prior to 1997, when the CDS started, can be determined for those in the CDS sample. Thus, researchers may be interested in circumstances of the family throughout the life of the children or in the years before the birth of the child. Through the 1968 family ID and the person number, such information can be determined for CDS/PSID respondents. Thus, the average income over the life of the child can be determined even though it is not given in the CDS data. The CDS and the PSID can be linked by using the 1968 family ID (er30001) and the person number (er30002) for the individual.

Like the PSID, the CDS can be linked to Census tract and other census information in order to ascertain neighborhood conditions.

Special contracts must be obtained in order to get this link to census information. Note that the Survey Research Center does not provide the Census information, but it does provide the census identifiers (such as census tract, county and city, and other census identifiers).

Researchers have used CDS data to explore the predictors of media use (Bickman et al., 2003) and the relationships between television watching and social isolation (Bickham & Rich, 2006), anti-social behavior (Christakis & Zimmerman, 2007), and obesity (Vandewater, Shim, & Caplovitz, 2004). Other have studied the relationships between time use and weight (Curtin & Hofferth, 2003), and physical activity and outcomes such as depression (Desha, Ziviani, Nicholson, & Martin, 2007). Researchers also have studied the relationships between parental characteristics and child outcomes such as parental education and income on child achievement (Davis-Kean, 2005), ideologies on after-school activities (Dunn, Kinney & Hofferth, 2003), the timing of childbearing and child achievement and behavior (Hofferth & Reid, 2002), family income and behavior (Hofferth et al., 2000), mental health on behavior and well-being (Kahn, Brandt, & Whitaker, 2004), and fathers' school involvement and student achievement (McBride, Schoppe-Sullivan & Ho, 2005).

Other researchers have explored the relationships between economic factors and child health and development (Condliffe & Link, 2008; Shanks & Williams, 2007), and program participation and outcomes such as school lunch programs and child well-being (Dunifon & Kowaleski-Jones, 2003), food stamps and obesity (Gibson, 2004; Hofferth & Curtin, 2005), and mother's work and welfare use and child well-being (Neblett, 2007)

Researchers have also studied the relationships between neighborhood characteristics and a variety of child outcomes (Jackson & Mare, 2007; López Turley, 2002), including obesity (Grafova, 2008) and school achievement (Kowaleski-Jones, Dunifon, & Ream, 2006).

There are several ways to select variables for the CDS. One of the easier ways is to use the index system to select variables. To do this, go to http://simba.isr.umich.edu/VS/f.aspx, then click on the "+" sign for CDS and TA (including time diary aggregates). You will see all of the different files to choose from, including the demographic file, the primary caregiver child file, the child file, and other files. You can click on any of the

+ signs, choose the variables of interest, and put them into your data cart. For example, you may wish to put the variables child's race from the demographic file and emotional and physical condition of the child from the child file. Do this by clicking on these variables and clicking on "Add to Cart." You can then click on "Variables Added" to your cart. It will look like this:

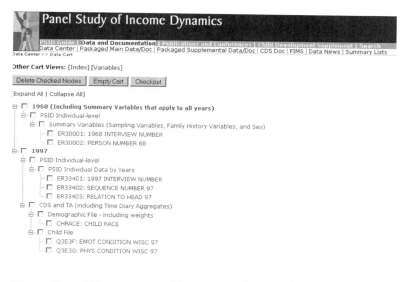

Note that the file automatically creates the 1968 interview number and the person number, which are the unique identifiers for the person. You can then download this page and use it, or create more variables, both from the PSID and from the CDS. You can then check out and download the data, with a codebook for the variables you have chosen, in ASCII format with SAS, SPSS, Stata statements, as an SAS transport file, or in dBase or Excel. You can then send the files to your e-mail address or create the files and download them on the web page. You must create a login account to get any of the data.

CDS-I, CDS-II, CDS-III, and TA data are available through the PSID Data Center at http://simba.isr.umich.edu.

PROJECT ON HUMAN DEVELOPMENT IN CHICAGO
NEIGHBORHOODS (PHDCN)

The Project on Human Development in Chicago Neighborhoods (PHDCN) is a large, interdisciplinary study that collected cross-sectional neighborhood data and longitudinal cross-sectional individual data over a period of seven years. This dataset makes it possible to look at how environmental factors such as neighborhood, family, and school features shape an individual's behavior and personal development, especially as it relates to antisocial behaviors such as juvenile delinquency, adult crime, violence, and substance abuse. The data consists of two studies within one design, resulting in both neighborhood and individual level data. These two data types exist independently from each other, allowing researchers to study the way in which neighborhood type and conditions predict future behavior by coupling the neighborhood information with the individual and behavioral data. This study is representative only of Chicago and the ages used to define the cohorts in the Longitudinal Cohort Study (birth/0, 3, 6, 9, 12, 15, and 18).

Researchers collected neighborhood level data from 343 neighborhood clusters, with 8,000 individuals each, created by combining Chicago's 825 census tracks into ecologically meaningful, demographically similar (stratified by seven racial/ethnic groups and three socioeconomic groups) and geographically contiguous groups. Neighborhood data gathered include information about the social, economic, organizational, structural, political, and cultural life of the community. The neighborhood aspect of the study consisted of a Community Survey and Systematic Social Observations (SSO).

The Community Survey includes household interviews with 8,782 randomly selected household members over 18 years of age from the neighborhood clusters. Data were collected only in 1994–1995 and 2001–2002. The survey asked participants a variety of questions about their perspectives on and experiences in their neighborhoods, including the neighborhood social organization, services and activities, neighbor relationships, social cohesion, crime and violence, political structure, cultural values, and informal and formal social control. The survey also inquires about participants' normative values on a variety of issues and behaviors and their experiences as victims of crime and with violence. The Community Survey collects data about residents' perceptions on the best and worst parts of living in Chicago; their definition of neighborhood; their length of residence in neighborhood; whether they would consider moving; neighborhood characteristics; perceived neighborhood danger; availability of social service agencies; and neighbor relationships, recognition, and socialization and how often neighbors participated in activities together. Social order and disorder measures include perceptions about neighborhood conditions, such as fear of crime, drugs, gangs, sexual assault, robbery, theft, and excessive force by law enforcement agencies. The PHDCN has one of the most extensive measures on neighborhood characteristics. Thus, if your research is neighborhood related and you are interested in childhood outcomes, this is an excellent dataset for such studies. The data does not contain adult variables for the children in the study.

The Systematic Social Observations (SSO) consisted of both person and videotaped standardized observations of 80 Chicago neighborhoods (27,734 blocks), selected through stratified random sampling, in which researchers recorded data about physical, social, and economic neighborhood characteristics relating to security, physical and social disorder, and decay and land use. Data was collected in 1995 and in approximately 2000–2002. Observation occurred as two observers and one videographer were slowly driven through each of the 80 selected neighborhoods. The systematic social observations recorded information about neighborhood characteristics, such as the visible presence of children and teens, graffiti, drug dealing, gang indicators, adult loitering and drunkenness, fights, and prostitution. In addition, observations noted land use, the condition of buildings, residential housing, commercial buildings, street conditions, and recreational facilities.

The individual level data includes a Longitudinal Cohort Study and an Infant Assessment Unit. The Longitudinal Cohort Study followed 6,226 children, adolescents, young adults, and their primary caregivers over a period of eight years. Participants came from seven age cohorts (birth (0), 3, 6, 9, 12, 15 and 18 years of age) and were randomly selected from the 80 neighborhood clusters. Researchers collected data in three waves: 1994–1997, 1997–1999, and 2000–2002. The overall response rate for Wave 1 was 75%; for Wave 2, the overall response rate was 86%; and for Wave 3, the overall response rate was 78%.

Individual variables include assessments of mental health, antisocial behavior, internalizing problems, emotional and attention behaviors, suicidal ideation and attempts, and classifications with mental health problems, substance abuse, self-efficacy, view of the future, health service utilization, and social networks and support. Other individual level variables include indicators of verbal, cognitive, and motor skills; sexual activity and attitudes toward sex; personality and attitude information including temperament; educational expectations; and discrimination. Environmental variables include data about climate and safety of the school environment, the quality of education, funding of the day care, characteristics of the day care and provider, and the physical home environment.

Family variables provide family health history, including mental health and specific medical problems such as depression, substance abuse, suicide (relationship to child, method and care received), therapy treatment, and exposure to violence. Parental warmth/involvement is measured, as is social support; community involvement; structure; involvement of the mother and father; supervision; conflict; encouragement for intellectual, social, and physical growth; and religiosity.

The Infant Assessment Unit studied 412 infants from the birth cohort in Wave 1 (1994–1997) and their primary caregivers to investigate how pre- and postnatal conditions affect the infant's health and development during the infant's first year of life. The assessment is also designed to connect this early development to the existence of later antisocial actions behaviors. Survey and observational data of both infant and primary caregiver were collected when infants were between 5 and 7 months of age. This assessment was conducted in addition to the protocol administered in the longitudinal cohort study. The assessment measured infants' temperament, physical growth and development, cognition, and pregnancy conditions. The assessment also studied the primary caregivers, measuring the developmental and physical environment in which the child is raised; child care situation; social support and relationship with the father; caregivers' psychological, emotional, and behavioral health and quality of life; and the prenatal and delivery conditions of the infant's biological mother.

Because of the neighborhood clustering and the ability to examine more than a single child within a family, many people have used hierarchical linear modeling (HLM) with the PHDCN. This allows, for example, for the nesting of individuals within families, within neighborhoods.

This allows for fixed and random effects at each level of the nesting (Buka, Brennan, Rich-Edwards, Raudenbush, & Earls, 2003; Kuo, Mohler, Raudenbush, & Earls Raudenbush, & Bryk, 2001; Raudenbush & Bryk, 2001).

Both community and individual level data have been used to study a variety of outcomes. In addition to investigating the relationship between the neighborhood environment and general health outcomes (Browning & Cagney, 2002, 2003; Cohen, Farley, & Mason, 2003; Wen, Browning, & Cagney,2003), other health-related outcomes include differences across sociocultural settings (Drukker, Buka, Kaplan, McKenzie, & Van Os, 2005), respiratory disease (Cagney & Browning, 2004), physical activity (Molnar, Gortmaker, & Buka, 2004), birth weight (Buka, Brennan, Rich-Edwards, Raudenbush, & Earls, 2003; Morenoff, 2003), mortality (Browning, Wallace, Feinberg, & Cagney, 2006; Lochner, Kawachi, Brennan, & Buka, 2003; Wen, Cagney, & Christakis, 2005), health among older adults (Cagney, Browning, & Wen, 2005; Wen, Hawkley, & Cacioppo, 2006) and sexual activity and attitudes (Browning & Burrington, 2006; Browning, Leventhal, & Brooks-Gunn, 2004; Browning & Olinger-Wilbon, 2003). Published studies also test the relationships between social bonds and elderly migration (Oh, 2003) and homeowner-ship among the poor (Brisson & Usher, 2007).

Additional, researchers have examined the relationships between the environment and child maltreatment (Molnar, Buka, Brennan, Holton, & Earls, 2003), substance use (Novak, Reardon, & Buka, 2002; Reardon, Brennan, & Buka, 2002), including differences in substance use across races (Reardon & Buka, 2002), and crime and violence (Browning, Feinberg, & Dietz, 2004; Kirk, 2008; Kirk, 2006; Morenoff, Sampson, & Raudenbush, 2001; Obeidallah, Brennan, Brooks-Gunn, & Earls, 2004; Sampson, Morenoff, & Raudenbush, 2005), as well as the relationship between exposure to violence and violent or other antisocial behavior (Bingenheimer, Brennan, & Earls, 2005; Molnar, Browne, Cerda, & Buka, 2005; Molnar, Miller, Azrael, & Buka, 2004).

The National Archive of Criminal Justice Data that is included in the PHDCN is restricted to users who are willing and able to sign contracts indicating that they will use the data only for statistical analyses and not for identifying users. This generally means that you must use the data at a stand-alone computer (with no network connections) with password

protection and often, encrypted data. See the website http://www.icpsr.
umich.edu/NACJD/private/ for a full explanation of how to gain access
to these restricted files.

A list of all of the instruments and scales used in the data are located
at http://www.icpsr.umich.edu/PHDCN/instruments.html. Codebooks
for the data are available at http://dvn.iq.harvard.edu/dvn/dv/mra/faces/
study/StudyPage.xhtml?studyId=431&tab=files&studyListingIndex=
0_73cb0790aba235a8a5812876af39.

Data are available at the ICPSR website, www.icpsr.umich.edu/
PHDCN. Data currently are available only for the first wave of the
Community Survey and Systematic Social Observation. Longitudinal
Cohort Study Data for all three waves are available. The dataset is set up
in many different files which will need to be merged, depending on the
needs of your research. For example, at the ICPSR the Wave 3 data are
available for primary caregivers, young adults, youth self-reports, school
screening, and substance use follow-up. All of these files, plus many,
many more are available in the first waves of the study as well (for 172
publicly available files). To merge these files by neighborhood characteristics, you will need the neighborhood link variable, linc_nc, or the link
for the neighborhood cluster. To link the different cohort files together,
you will need the respondent link, or rc_num.

PUBLIC-USE MICRODATA SAMPLES

The Public-Use Microdata Samples (PUMS) consists of sample data
from the U.S. decennial census, sampled from the "long form" or the
American Community Survey, which is replacing the long form in the
2010 census. These data are collected to provide information about
the social, economic, and financial characteristics of the population to
assist in the determination of federal spending and service provision.
PUMS includes both individual and household level data pertaining to
demographics and economic, social, housing, and financial characteristics of the population. Household level data include data pertaining to
individual housing units and group housing units, such as nursing
homes, military barracks, school dormitories, and correctional facilities.

The long form and its replacement, the American Community Survey
(ACS), collect similar data pertaining to the demographic, economic,

social, housing, and financial characteristics of the population. The long form data, however, was collected decennially for a point-in-time estimate, whereas the ACS is a nationwide, annual, continuous survey providing yearlong averages. PUMS is a subsample of the ACS dataset that allows researchers to select individual and household level variables of interest and create their own tables and statistics on those variables, a feature the ACS summary data does not allow.

PUMS includes all variables collected by the ACS, with some modifications to protect identities, but for a limited group of observations based on geographic population size. Data for PUMS is sampled using a stratified sampling procedure that sampled data address-by-address and, for group quarters, person-by-person. Two independent samples are drawn: 5% of which includes approximately 14 million people and 5 million housing units (2000), and 1% of which includes approximately 2.8 million people and 1 million housing units (2000). The records in each sample are different. PUMS data are provided for census-created geographic regions called Public Use Microdata Areas (PUMAs), derived from the 1% or 5% data files. Each PUMA has a minimum census population of 100,000 and consists of entire communities or combinations of contiguous counties or census tracts that have similar characteristics but do not cross state lines. Each PUMA is derived from the 5% sample file. Super-PUMAs, with a minimum of 400,000 census population, are aggregates of PUMAs and are derived from the 1% sample data.

The ACS PUMS files, starting in 2006, are released in one-, three- and five-year estimates. One-year estimates are only for those areas with a population of 65,000 or more and contain data on 1% of the population. Three-year estimates are for those with a population of 20,000 or more and contain data on approximately 3% of the population. Five-year estimates include all areas. With each estimate, the sample size grows while the minimum population threshold decreases. One-year estimates have been released since 2006, three-year estimates since 2008, and the first five-year estimates were released in 2010. In 2000, the ACS conducted over half a million interviews, while in years 2005 to 2008, close to two million interviews were conducted.

Because of these geographic limitations, data cannot be summarized for individual cities, counties, or other small areas. Because PUMS is a subsample of the census data, the estimates differ from population estimate provided by the Census Bureau. Weights are subsequently provided to correct this.

The PUMS dataset includes individual and household level information. Individual level data include information such as demographics, English proficiency and language spoken at home, citizenship, disability status, education attainment and enrollment, military and work status, occupation and industry, income and poverty status, work-related modes of transportation and commuting time, fertility, and personal care and work limitations. Household level information includes variables relating to housing, such as mortgage, property value, and taxes; linguistic isolation; rooms, utilities and facilities (e.g., kitchen and plumbing) within the living unit; costs (e.g., mortgage, rent, utilities); children and subfamilies within the unit; length of time in unit; household income and Food Stamps; and vehicles associated with the unit. For a fuller list of variables, see http://www.census.gov/acs/www/Products/PUMS/PUMS3.htm or http://www.census.gov/prod/cen2000/doc/pums.pdf.

PUMS data allow researchers to explore the relationships among demographic, social, economic, financial, and housing variables. Researchers have studied health issues such as the prevalence of disabilities among particular ethnic groups (Dallo et al., 2009; Goins et al., 2007), education issues such as mortality and its relationship to educational attainment (Hadden & Rockswold, 2008) and the relationship between education and household location (Sander & Testa, 2009). Researchers have used PUMS to examine family relationships, such as changing fertility among ethnic groups (Ren, 2009), marriage migration (Hidalgo & Bankston, 2008), and interracial marriage and socioeconomic well-being (Fu, 2008). Researchers have also studied economic issues, such as the market labor costs and earnings as they relate to particular ethnic groups (Takei, Saenz, & Li, 2009; Wang, 2008), spousal mobility and earnings (McKinnish, 2008), and the impact of residential segregation on self-employment (Fairchild, 2008).

PUMS data, and additional resources for using the data and the ACS, are available through the U.S. Census through both the Census 2000 page (www.census.gov/main/www/cen2000.html) and the PUMS page (www.census.gov/acs/www/Products/PUMS). Use the Data Ferret from the Census Bureau to access a number of these files, including ACS for 2004 –2007, and some three-year averages. Files from 1996–2007 are available on the PUMS web page (http://www.census.gov/acs/www/Products/PUMS/acspums_archived.html). To get the files in the Data Ferret, the program must be downloaded(http://dataferrett.census.gov/TheDataWeb/launchDFA.html). Once you have downloaded the Data Ferret, you can begin to choose datasets and variables you would like to examine. The Data Ferret looks like this:

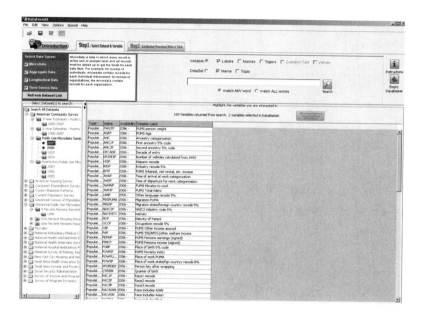

Once you choose a dataset to work with, you click on the + sign to open up which of the datasets to work with, then click on variables you would like to put into your data basket. Here, when you choose the Decennial Public Use Microdata, only the 1990 data are available. If you choose the American Community Survey, years 2004–2007 are available. Let's choose the 2007 Public Use Microsample, as show above. Click on whichever variables you would like to use, using the control button to click on a number of variables to be selected at the same time. Next, click on "Browse/Select Highlighted Variables." You will be taken to a code-book for all of the variables you have selected. You can then choose the variables to go into your data basket by clicking on the box for "Select All Variables," and then clicking on "OK."

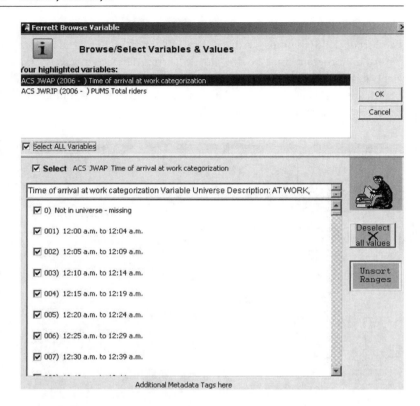

Once you are done selecting variables, you will go to Step 2 at the top of the page. Here, you can either make a table and save it in a number of formats, or you can download the data in a great number of formats, including SAS, SPSS, Stata, or Excel. This is shown in the figure in the following page.

The Integrated Public Use Microdata Series (IPUMS) is where the PUMS data are stored, preserved, documented, and "harmonized." There is also an international IPUMS. These files can be found at http:// usa.ipums.org/usa/. Samples for the IPUMS go back to 1850 and up to the current ACS sample.

SCHOOL DATA DIRECT

School Data Direct (SDD) is an online source for state educational data and analytical tools (http://www.schooldatadirect.org). The SDD is part

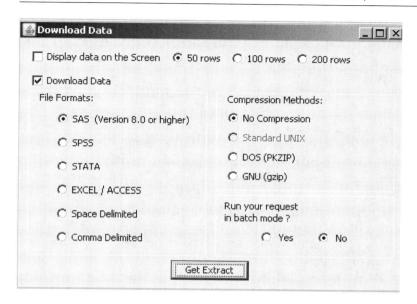

of the State Education Data Center, which is in turn a part of the Council of Chief State School Officers' National Education Data Partnership. In addition to the website with publicly available data, SDD serves as a leading advocate for quality educational data collection, standard, and use.

The SDD provides information about public schools and public school districts. It includes the full universe of public primary and secondary schools. The SDD provides information about student proficiency on statewide reading and math tests, financial data (including spending per student, staff compensation, and long-term debt), whether the school is making adequate yearly progress toward No Child Left Behind targets, teacher qualifications and certifications, class size, school safety (e.g., presence of physical assaults, firearms and nonfirearm weapons, violence against staff, and disciplinary sanctions), student performance, and student and community demographic data, such as ethnicity, gender, disabilities, income levels, property values, educational level, and population information. Math proficiency data are available from third to 11th grades, as are college entrance exams; for lower elementary grades, participation in math and reading is measured. SDD provides data on the community in which the school or district exists. These variables include adult education level, household characteristics such as income and single-parent-headed households, population distribution by age, and labor statistics. Data are currently available from 2002–2007. In the early years of the sample, many schools had missing data for many of the variables.

Researchers can search and download data by state, district, or school. Data are available in Excel tables, researcher-created tables (including a maximum of 100 schools or districts), or through the data directory using the data download tool. The website provides guides for the download and interpretation of data, data definitions, abbreviations and sources, and other relevant information. Given that states may collect data differently, researchers should view state-specific information before accessing and using the data. Additionally, urban status data reflect metro-centric data rather than urban-centric data, and state payments on behalf of the district have been excluded from district level financial data.

Data are collected through a variety of sources, coordinated by EDFacts, a project of the U.S. Department of Education. Student proficiency data come from state departments of education, the National Center for Education Statistics, and test vendors. The financial data come from the National Center for Education Statistics National Public Education Finance Survey, state departments of education, and U.S. Census Form F-33. The community demographic data come from the 2000 Census of Population and Housing. The Coordinated Data, an effort by the Data Quality Campaign and the Department of Education, offers a unified data collection template for researchers.

To download data for an aggregate of the schools in a state, you would first need to sign agreements on the web page, and then go to http://download.schooldatadirect.org/DataDownloadFileLister.html. Next, click on your state of interest—here, Pennsylvania is chosen—then State, to obtain information at the state level. Please see the figure given in the following page.

From here, you can choose which year you would like to open, from 2002 to 2008. You can see that the 2008 file is small and contains little information. I click on the 2007 file and open the dataset after it has been decompressed. Next, open the file in Excel, with Delimited formatting, other delimiters (use the | symbol as the other delimiter) and text columns. (See http://download.schooldatadirect.org/_ddtv/DataDownload GuideFiles/SDD_How_to_Download_Data.pdf for a step-by-step method

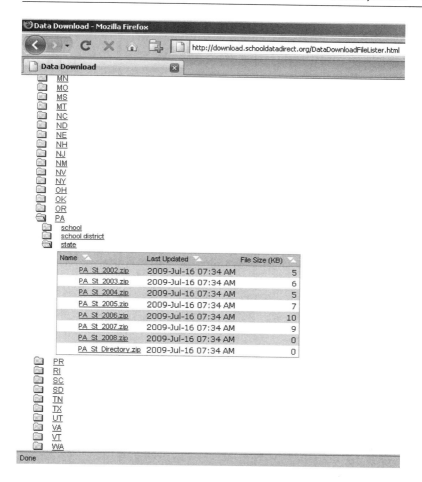

of getting the data into Excel.) The Excel page will look like the figure shown at the top of the following page, with information on reading and math proficiency and information on average yearly progress for the No Child Left Behind law for each school district.

You can also use pivot tables in Excel to view the variables across the top of the screen, but these are limited to tables with 256 rows or fewer. The data will look something like the figure shown at the bottom of the following page once you are able to pivot the data (http://download. schooldatadirect.org/_ddtv/DataDownloadGuideFiles/SDD_How_to_ Download_Data.pdf).

	4205400	Central Dauphin School District	2007	Analytics	RaMP Reading Proficiency EconDis (%)	47	
59201	4205400	Central Dauphin School District	2007	Analytics	RaMP Reading Proficiency Female (%)	72.2	
59202	4205400	Central Dauphin School District	2007	Analytics	RaMP Reading Proficiency Hispanic (%)	53.1	
59203	4205400	Central Dauphin School District	2007	Analytics	RaMP Reading Proficiency LEP (%)	25.9	
59204	4205400	Central Dauphin School District	2007	Analytics	RaMP Reading Proficiency Male (%)	63.7	
59205	4205400	Central Dauphin School District	2007	Analytics	RaMP Reading Proficiency StudwDis (%)	24.1	
59206	4205400	Central Dauphin School District	2007	Analytics	RaMP Reading Proficiency Total (%)	67.9	
59207	4205400	Central Dauphin School District	2007	Analytics	RaMP Reading Proficiency White (%)	76.1	
59208	4205400	Central Dauphin School District	2007	Analytics	RaMP Score (%)	70.4	
59209	4205400	Central Dauphin School District	2007	Analytics	RaMP Scores - Asian/PI	81.6	
59210	4205400	Central Dauphin School District	2007	Analytics	RaMP Scores - Black	48.7	
59211	4205400	Central Dauphin School District	2007	Analytics	RaMP Scores - EconDis	51.2	
59212	4205400	Central Dauphin School District	2007	Analytics	RaMP Scores - Female	72.3	
59213	4205400	Central Dauphin School District	2007	Analytics	RaMP Scores - Hispanic	56.7	
59214	4205400	Central Dauphin School District	2007	Analytics	RaMP Scores - LEP	33.6	
59215	4205400	Central Dauphin School District	2007	Analytics	RaMP Scores - Male	66.7	
59216	4205400	Central Dauphin School District	2007	Analytics	RaMP Scores - StudwDis	28.2	
59217	4205400	Central Dauphin School District	2007	Analytics	RaMP Scores - White	78.3	
59218	4205400	Central Dauphin School District	2007	Analytics	RaMP Up Target	4.2	
59219	4205400	Central Dauphin School District	2007	Analytics	Return on Spending Index (RoSI) - Adjusted for Geographic Costs	10.5	
59220	4205400	Central Dauphin School District	2007	Analytics	Return on Spending Index (RoSI) - Adjusted for Geographic Costs & Stude	13.2	
59221	4205400	Central Dauphin School District	2007	Analytics	Return on Spending Index (RoSI) - Adjusted for Student Needs	10.8	
59222	4205400	Central Dauphin School District	2007	Analytics	Return on Spending Index (RoSI) - Unadjusted	8.6	
59223	4205400	Central Dauphin School District	2007	Analytics	Students with Special Needs Index	20.4	
59224	4205400	Central Dauphin School District	2007	Community Di	County Labor Statistics - Employment Labor Force	134,853	
59225	4205400	Central Dauphin School District	2007	Community Di	County Labor Statistics - Employment Total	129,648	
59226	4205400	Central Dauphin School District	2007	Community Di	County Labor Statistics - Employment Unemployment Rate	3.9	
59227	4205400	Central Dauphin School District	2007	NCLB	AYP Attendance Total (%)	95.7	
59228	4205400	Central Dauphin School District	2007	NCLB	AYP Elementary Math Participation Target Status Asian (y/n)	Yes	
59229	4205400	Central Dauphin School District	2007	NCLB	AYP Elementary Math Participation Target Status Black (y/n)	Yes	
59230	4205400	Central Dauphin School District	2007	NCLB	AYP Elementary Math Participation Target Status EconDis (y/n)	Yes	
59231	4205400	Central Dauphin School District	2007	NCLB	AYP Elementary Math Participation Target Status Hispanic (y/n)	Yes	
59232	4205400	Central Dauphin School District	2007	NCLB	AYP Elementary Math Participation Target Status LEP (y/n)	Yes	
59233	4205400	Central Dauphin School District	2007	NCLB	AYP Elementary Math Participation Target Status Multi (y/n)	n.a.	
59234	4205400	Central Dauphin School District	2007	NCLB	AYP Elementary Math Participation Target Status NatAm (y/n)	n.a.	
59235	4205400	Central Dauphin School District	2007	NCLB	AYP Elementary Math Participation Target Status StudwDis (y/n)	Yes	
59236	4205400	Central Dauphin School District	2007	NCLB	AYP Elementary Math Participation Target Status Total (y/n)	Yes	
59237	4205400	Central Dauphin School District	2007	NCLB	AYP Elementary Math Participation Target Status White (y/n)	Yes	
59238	4205400	Central Dauphin School District	2007	NCLB	AYP Elementary Math Proficiency Target Status Asian (y/n)	Yes	
59239	4205400	Central Dauphin School District	2007	NCLB	AYP Elementary Math Proficiency Target Status Black (y/n)	Yes	
59240	4205400	Central Dauphin School District	2007	NCLB	AYP Elementary Math Proficiency Target Status EconDis (y/n)	Yes	
59241	4205400	Central Dauphin School District	2007	NCLB	AYP Elementary Math Proficiency Target Status LEP (y/n)	Yes	
59242	4205400	Central Dauphin School District	2007	NCLB	AYP Elementary Math Proficiency Target Status Multi (y/n)	n.a.	
59243	4205400	Central Dauphin School District	2007	NCLB	AYP Elementary Math Proficiency Target Status NatAm (y/n)	n.a.	
59245	4205400	Central Dauphin School District	2007	NCLB	AYP Elementary Math Proficiency Target Status StudwDis (y/n)	Yes	

Once you have pivoted the table, you can continue to work in Excel, or export the data into SAS, SPSS, or Stata to more easily program the data.

School Data Direct can be used with the PSID Child Development Supplement through a special contract with the Survey Research Center at the University of Michigan. It can also be merged onto many other data files that have identifiers at the school, school district, or state level.

Name	RaMP Reading Proficiency Asian/PI (%)	RaMP Reading Proficiency Black (%)	RaMP Reading Proficiency EconDis (%)	RaMP Reading Proficiency Female (%)	RaMP Reading Proficiency Hispanic (%)	RaM Profic
Appoquinimink School District	90.3	78	76.1	89.7	84.5	
Brandywine School District	92.3	63.8	64	83.1	66.7	
Caesar Rodney School District	93.2	79.3	79	89.8	88.8	
Cape Henlopen School District		68.3	75	87.9	71	
Capital School District	75	69	68.6	79.8	79.8	
Christina School District	87.5	64.6	64.8	78.6	66.9	
Colonial School District	94.2	71.6	71.9	83.5	80.6	
Delmar School District		67.7	74.6	86.4		
Indian River School District		78.3	82.9	90.7	85.5	
Lake Forest School District		68.7	73.8	86.5		
Laurel School District		59.2	66.2	77		
Milford School District		78.1	81.1	89.3	82.3	
Red Clay Consolidated School District	94.9	66.6	67.9	84.8	70.1	
Seaford School District		63.2	68.9	78.8	85.7	
Smyrna School District		79.2	79.2	88.6		
Woodbridge School District		71.6	72.8	81.6	75	
Grand Total	89.62857143	70.44375	72.925	84.70625	78.075	

SURVEY OF INCOME AND PROGRAM PARTICIPATION (SIPP)

The Survey of Income and Program Participation is a longitudinal study that contains person and household information about income and program participation for people aged 15 to 64 years old living in the United States. The datasets include such information as program participation, employment, government and other income sources and amounts, and details about employers, unemployment and job searches, health insurance, child care, education, and other factors relating to economic and social well-being. SIPP also contains information about children under 15 years old through proxy interviews with other adults in the household. Panels began in 1984 (when this first sample started), with the most recent panels in 2001, 2004, and a new 2008 panel (with only a few waves available at the time of this writing), and members are interviewed every four months (each of these periods is a wave of data), and generally, with information regarding each of the previous four months. Sample members in a given SIPP panel are typically followed for two to three years (eight to 12 waves), although some panels were shorter than this (such as the 1988 and 1989 panels).

SIPP is nationally representative of U.S.-based, noninstitutionalized individuals aged 15 –to 64 years. Starting in 1990, low-income households were oversampled. Sampling weights are available to make the sample nationally representative. The dataset is not representative at the state level.

The SIPP uses a two-stage sampling design: (a) select primary sampling units (PSUs), and (b) select address units within those sample PSUs, which have been clustered based on Census Bureau sampling frames. Researchers then visit each address to verify that it exists and has occupants and to record the number of units at each address. Following SIPP membership rules, they identify and create a roster of the household members, aged 15 through 64 years, who live in each of the units. Researchers determine the reference person (owner or renter), and then identify the others by their relationships to that person. All these individuals are the original sample members and those whom researchers follow over the course of the panel, even as they move to new locations. Should a panel member live with other people, in the original household or because they moved to another household, those new individuals also become panel members for as long as they live with the original member. Interviews stop if a panel member moves to military barracks, is institutionalized, or moves outside the United States. Interviews also stop if a household no longer has an original member living within it.

Sample size varies across SIPP panels. The 1984 panel's sample included 19,878 households, while the 2004 sample included 43,711 households. In Wave 1, researchers conducted interviews with all original sample members within the household who were 15 through 64 years old. Proxy interviews gather data on those who are not present in future waves, children under 15 years of age, and those within the household who are unable to respond for themselves.

Researchers gather two types of data, core content and topical content. Core content was gathered in each wave, and each question has the same four-month reference period. Labor force participation is recorded on both a weekly and a monthly time frame. Given the different reference periods for the core and topical contents (described below), the dataset uses a person-month structure in which all data are coded at the monthly level. Data are aggregated or disaggregated based on the reference period to that monthly level. Each set of wave data includes one record for each person for each month in the wave.

Following a 1996 redesign, core content included three categories: (a) employment and earnings such as employment status (week by week), employer characteristics, self-employment, earnings (including from unemployment), and time spent job seeking; (b) program, general, and asset income such as Social Security, Food Stamps, disability, workers compensation, child support and alimony, and other assets such as bonds, stocks, and retirement accounts; and (c) other information such as health insurance ownership and coverage, education, energy assistance, and school lunch program participation.

Different topical modules are generally included with the core questions at each four-month interview. Each topical content question has a different reference period, ranging from the time at the interview to one's whole life. The topical content questions revolve around a variety of topical modules: adult well-being, annual earnings and benefits, annual income and retirement accounts, assets, liabilities and eligibility, child care, child support agreements, child support paid, children's well-being, employment history, extended well-being measures (household and neighborhood), fertility history, functional limitation and disability, housing costs, long-term care, marital history, migration history, reasons for not working/reservation wage, recipient history (of government programs), retirement expectations and pension plan coverage, selected financial assets, taxes, time spent outside work force, welfare history and child support, public assistance eligibility and recipiency, and work-related expenses.

SIPP provides health variables that provide information about adult and child physical and mental disabilities and limitations that affect daily living and work; special education services; need for personal assistance; hospital, facility, and psychiatric institution stays; illnesses/injuries that lead to bedrest; use of home health care and caregiver type; long-term health conditions and care that impact daily living and who provides such care; whether respondent provides home or long-term health care to someone else; and types of professionals who delivered health care.

The SIPP data make it possible for researchers to look at income, program participation, and other economic and social variables across individuals, families, and households over time as well as across different subgroups or demographics. The data can also be linked with policies in order to examine how policy relates to a variety of individual, family, or household outcomes. Because SIPP also provides information about how family and household composition changes over time, researchers can also examine factors that are influenced by or predict those changes. Data can also be used cross-sectionally.

As an example of using the SIPP, variables from the 2004 panel are shown below. The panel has 12 waves, with each wave covering four months of information, so that the information provided in the dataset is given on a monthly basis. Each of the first eight waves also has topical modules that cover such areas as employment history and recipiency history in Wave 1; marital history, migration history, and fertility history in Wave 2; and child well-being, child care, and welfare reform variables in Wave 8.

In Data Ferret, the screen for the topical modual for Wave 2 looks like the figure given in the next page.

You can then choose your variables or search for variables. You can next choose variables from any of the waves and any of the topical modules and put them into your data basket for downloading.

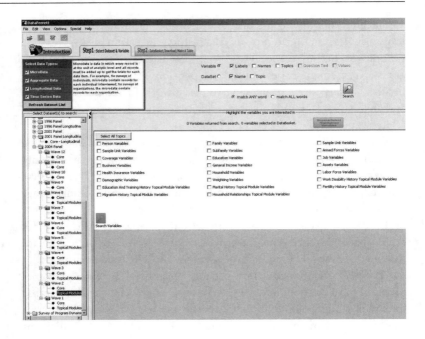

Sample attrition in the SIPP has been around 35% by the end of the sampling period, according to the Census Bureau (http://www.acf. hhs.gov/programs/opre/other_resrch/eval_data/reports/common_ constructs/com_appb_sipp.html).

Researchers have used SIPP to study demographics such as the number of deaf individuals in the United States (Mitchell, 2006). Others have examined the relationship between family structure or living arrangements on the well-being of children (Hynes & Dunifon, 2007; Manning, 2006) and among immigrants (Van Hook & Glick, 2007). Researchers also have studied the relationships between educational returns among those who are disabled (Hollenbeck & Kimmel, 2008), and marital dissolution and women's education (Martin, 2006).

Researchers also have extensively studied the relationships between income and economic factors and a variety of outcomes. One study looks at pathways out of poverty (Pandey & Kim, 2008) and others look at the relationship between maternal employment and child care (Lopoo, 2007; Isaacs, 2006; Kimmel & Powell, 2006). Others look at income trends (Copeland, 2007) and economic factors or conditions across different demographics (Cobb-Clark & Hildebrand, 2006; Grinstein-Weiss, Yeo, Zhan, & Charles, 2008; She & Livermore, 2007; Wu & Eamon, 2007). Several studies focus specifically on income and the elderly (Rupp, Strand, Davies, & Sears, 2007; Copeland, 2006; Elder & Powers, 2006).

SIPP makes it possible to study the linkages between policy and various outcomes such as psychological well-being (Cheng, 2007), mothers' well-being (Boushey, 2008), household outcomes (Duggan & Kearney, 2007), and home ownership (Herbert & Tsen, 2007). Other studies look at the impact of welfare policy on different economic conditions such as unemployment insurance eligibility (Boushey & Wenger, 2006), Food Stamp accessibility (Hanratty, 2006), work disability and migration (Graefe, De Jong, & May, 2006) and scar effects of unemployment (Gangl, 2006).

Researchers also can study the characteristics of different income or employment types, such as self-employment (Lofstrom & Wang, 2007), the dynamics of participation in the Food Stamp Program (Gleason, Schochet, & Moffitt 1998), spells on welfare and income after welfare (Vartanian & Gleason, 1999) and the relationship between labor market dynamics and employment (Mazumder, 2007).

Data are available through the Census Bureau website, www.census. gov/sipp and also http://dataferrett.census.gov/TheDataWeb/launch DFA.html. Codebooks for the SIPP can be found at http://www.census. gov/apsd/techdoc/sipp/sipp.html.

SURVEY OF PROGRAM DYNAMICS

The Survey of Program Dynamics (SPD), a longitudinal and demographic study, was created after Congress passed the Personal Responsibility and Work Opportunity Reconciliation Act of 1996, as an extension of the Survey of Income and Program Participation (SIPP). The Survey of Program Dynamics studied the SIPP participants, originally interviewed in 1992–1993, and continued to survey them until 2002. The survey aimed to observe the impact of the act, the long-term effects of welfare reforms on recipients and their families, and the interaction of welfare reforms with each other and employment, income, and family circumstances. The SPD collected data on economic, household and social characteristics in three waves: 1992–1993, 1997, and 1998–2002. The sample is nationally representative.

The SPD population consists of adults and children, including those in group-living situations, such as dormitories or religious dwellings. It does not include people in nursing homes, institutionalized people, or entire military families. The study also excludes U.S. citizens living abroad and foreigner visitors to the United States. The original SIPP 1992–1993 sample includes 35,291 households, and the 1997 wave includes 30,125 households. The household sample sizes for the 1998–2002 wave differs for each year: 16,395 (1998), 16,659 (1999), 18,716 (2000), 22,340 (2001), and 12,496 (2002) (http://www.census.gov/spd/pubs/spdug_01.pdf).

Sample attrition rates for the SPD were initially high because of a 26.6% sample attrition in the SIPP, where the sample was started. In 1998, after two years of the SPD, sample attrition was up to 50%. By 2000, the sample attrition rate had slowed, and recontacting those who had dropped out has increased the response rate to 53% in 2002. See http://www.census.gov/spd/design/sample.html for a full report on response rates for the SPD.

The first wave, 1992–1993, collected core and topical data using the SIPP instruments. The SIPP collected data from households once every four months and followed respondents when they moved. Core data, collected at every interview and generally measured on a monthly basis, included such variables as demographics, labor force participation, program participation, and private health insurance. Topical data, collected less frequently, gathered more in-depth information, such as marital history, school enrollment, disability, and work history.

The second wave, 1997, used a modified version of the March annual income supplement to the Current Population Survey to collect demographic and income information.

The third wave, 1998–2002, used the SPD instrument to collect economic, demographic, and social data once a year about the previous year. A self-administered CAPI questionnaire collected more sensitive data, such as marital conflict and parental depression. In 1998 and 2001, respondents completed a self-administered paper questionnaire completed by adolescents on subjects such as the presence of violence among family members, substance abuse, sexual activity, and vocational goals. In 2000, the SPD included a Children's Residential History Calendar to monitor the frequency and timing of children's moves. In 1999 and 2002, additional questions were collected on children's well-being, positive behavior, and conflict between parents. The drug and alcohol sections of the data include questions on irresponsible drinking, alcohol leading to emotional/psychological problems, addiction tendencies, alcohol and drug use affecting home life and work, frequency of times drank more than intended, spending the majority of daily life drinking or getting over the effects of drinking, and dealing with drinking more alcohol than previously needed to achieve a desired effect. SPD also inquires about specific drugs, including tranquilizers or nerve pills, amphetamines or other stimulants, analgesics or other prescription painkillers, inhalants, marijuana, cocaine, LSD and other hallucinogens, and heroin. Questions are asked regarding treatment for drug and alcohol problems. SPD also provides information on whether mental health problems limit work, everyday activities, or schoolwork.

The SPD collected core data for adults on employment, income, program participation, health insurance and utilization, child well-being, marital relationships, parents' depression, vehicle expenses, and food security. The core data questions for children included topics such as school enrollment, enrichment activities, disability, health care utilization, and mother's work schedule.

Researchers have used SPD to study welfare reform, earnings, and income (Connolly & Marston, 2005) and the impact of welfare reform on adolescent outcomes (Trzcinski & Brandell, 2002; Trzcinski, Brandell, Ferro, & Smith, 2005), as well as to evaluate welfare reform (Hisnanick, 2004). Other studies have looked at the impact of legislation on parental leave (Han & Waldfogel, 2003); the relationship among welfare reform, food assistance programs, and the labor supply (Huffman & Jensen, 2005); food assistance programs and household food security (Huffman & Jensen, 2003); the length of welfare spells for female-headed households in rural areas (Porterfield, 1998); and the correlation between poverty and food sufficiency (Ribar & Hamrick, 2003).

Data are publicly available through ICPSR for each wave of the data collection and as a longitudinal file. The codebooks are available through the ICPSR at http://www.icpsr.umich.edu/cgi-bin/bob/archive2?study= 3594&path=ICPSR&docsonly=yes and other information, including information on merging SPD files, is available at http://www.census.gov/ spd/pubs/spdug_01.pdf. The data are accessible at http://www.icpsr. umich.edu/cocoon/ICPSR/SERIES/00136.xml. The U.S. Census Bureau web page provides additional information about the SPD (http:://www. sipp.census.gov/spd/ and http://www.census.gov/spd/survey.html). The 1999 to 2002 cross-sectional and the longitudinal file of the SPD data are also available from the Data Ferret. If you use the Data Ferret, there are 2,982 variables in the longitudinal file, and you can choose among these variables.

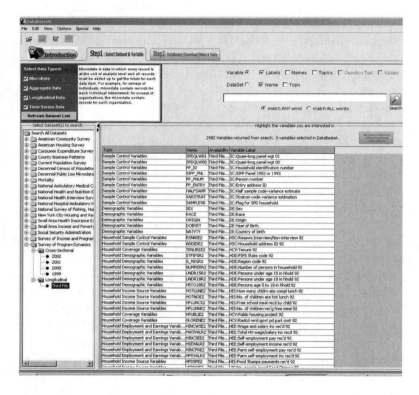

Click on the variable of interest, hold down the control button, and then pick other variables. You would then click on Browse/Select Highlighted Variables, click on Select All Variables, and click on OK. To download the variables, go to Step 2 at the top of the page and click on download. From there you will have a variety of formats to download the data (including SAS, SPSS, Stata, and Excel).

The data and codebooks are available at http://www.census.gov/spd/ spdmrg.html, or through Data Ferret.

UNITED STATES CENSUS

The United States Census is a decennial count of the population residing in the United States, Puerto Rico, and the Island Areas on April 1 every 10 years. As required by the Constitution (Article 1, Section 2), Congress took the first census in 1790. Short forms collect count information from everyone in the country while long forms, collecting social, economical and housing information, are sent to approximately 17% of the population. With the 2010 Census, the American Community Survey, an annual continuous survey, replaces the decennial long form.

The Census Bureau works with the United States Postal Service and local government officials to create the distribution list for the forms. Forms are mailed out in March, with follow-up postcards sent to non-responders mailed on April 1. The 2000 Census had a response rate of 67%, an increase from the 1990 rate of 65%.

Questions on both the short and the long form may be revised, deleted, or added to take into account shifting conventions or the need for new types of information. For instance, the 2000 Census included a new question about grandparents as caregivers and created the opportunity for respondents to identify with multiple race categories.

The Census data are analyzed at various levels, summarized into two categories: legal and administrative entities and statistical entities. The legal and administrative entities include congressional districts, counties, incorporated places such as cities and towns, minor civil divisions (e.g., District of Columbia, Puerto Rico, and the Island Areas), states, and voting districts. Statistical entities include block groups; Census-determined areas (e.g., blocks, county divisions, designated places, regions, and tracts); metropolitan, rural, urban and urbanized areas; zip code tabulation areas; and public use microdata areas, which are areas created for use with Public Use Microdata Samples. Data are also available for American Indian, Alaska native and native Hawaiian entities and areas.

Census data are available on the Census website, with the primary distribution tool being the American Fact Finder (AFF). The AFF, which originated with the 2000 Census, also includes information and data from others surveys conducted by the U.S. Census, including the 1990 census, the American Community Survey and the Economic Census. Data from the long form and American Community Survey are available through the Public Use Microdata Samples, data extracts that researchers may use to conduct their own statistical analyses with variables of interest. The Census Bureau also releases summary files and other data and tables useful for a variety of research. Researchers may also request special tabulations, for a fee, from the Census Bureau for a variety of their surveys.

Data from the Census are also available on DVD for the 2000 Census and on CD for some previous decennial censuses. Note that you can also do this same type of work by using the Census Bureau's Data Ferret (http://dataferrett.census.gov/TheDataWeb/launchDFA.html) to download data for the 1990 and 2000 Censuses. The 2000 Census can also be downloaded as an SAS export file at http://www.ssc.wisc.edu/cde/library/cdeftp.htm, where many other data files are located, including the 1970 Census, and the County and City Data books for many years. While general Census Bureau's website (http://www.Census.gov) may be a convenient way to access the decennial census, the DVDs are probably a much easier way of getting information at small area levels for the nation. For example, many of the datasets described in this book provide geocode information at the Census tract level. To use the web page to download all of that tract information would be very time consuming. One can get data at any level of Census aggregation (Census tract, Primary Metropolitan Statistical Area [PMSA]), on the DVD. For example, to get Census tract information, you need to first install the DVD. Let's say that you would like to get information at the Census tract level on the number of people at particular levels of income and numbers of people by race. You can determine percentages of people in these conditions by dividing by the population in the area you are examining. Your first step is knowing which data files to use. For Census tract information, you would use Census SF3 US 2000 US_2 Data on the DVD for workspace, as shown in the following page.

You next need to click on the second tab, pick geography, and choose State (40), County (50), and Census Tract by County (140). This is the way to uniquely identify census tract information. If you wanted to get information at the zip code level, you would use the US_3 file, with geographic identifiers 40, 50, and 871. For Metropolitan Statistical Areas (MSAs), use file US_2, with geographic identifiers 30, 390, and 395. And for Census place, use file US_2, with geographic identifiers as 40 and 160.

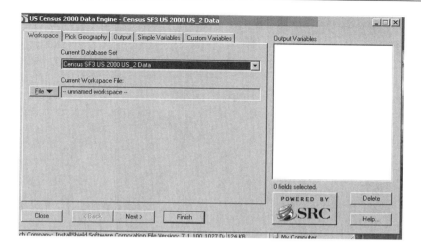

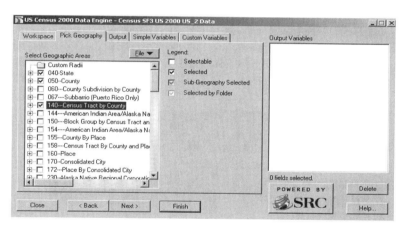

Next, go to "output," where you will give the file a name and save it to a location on your disk (please see the first figure shown in the following page).

If you are merging this data onto another dataset, you do not want to create the data as a summary. If you would simply like the information as it is, you can create the data as a summary.

You will next go to simple variables and add on all the variables that you would like, including the geographic identifier variables (which is in

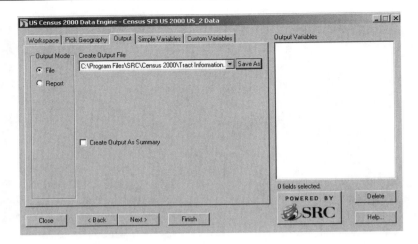

a separate folder), state (G11), county (G12), and tract (G21). These variables are given by housing and person variables. Choose whichever variables you would like, and click on "select" to move them over to the output variables. Chosen here are simple variables by person for family income, population, and race.

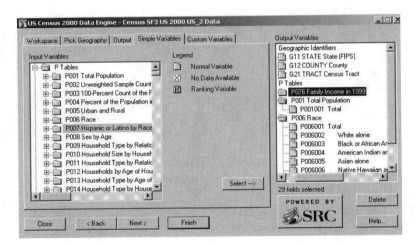

You can then choose to customize your variables in this program if you would like by going to "Custom Variables," where you can add, subtract, divide, or use other formulas to come up with new variables.

I prefer to use SAS or some other statistical program to do this work after I have outputted the data.

Click on "Finished," and you should get your variables in an .CSV file, which you can open in Excel. You can then use Stata Transfer to transfer the data into SAS, Stata, or SPSS to more easily use the data.

Thus, in SAS, you could write a file that looks something like the following to get the percentage of people of a particular race, or the percentage of people in a particular income group. You will want to delete records that do not have census tract information so, here, there is an "if" statement indicating that the record should be deleted unless tract information is available. The file will contain information on states, which you will not want in your file. Note that the memory in your Excel file may not be able to open this large dataset. You can either increase the memory on Excel, or simply go right to transferring the data to SAS, SPSS, or Stata, which will contain all of the information that was created in the Census file.

data in5.tract4a;set out1.tract;

```
t101=p001001;*population in the area;
if p006001>0 then t151=p006002/p006001;*% white;
if p006001>0 then t152=p006003/p006001;*% black;
if p006001>0 then tAsian=p006005/p006001;*% Asian;
if p006001>0 then t2race=p006008/p006001;*% 2 or
more races;
if p007001>0 then t155=p007010/p007001;*% Latino;

if p076001>0 then t800=p076002/p076001;*% of
families with income under $10,000;
if p076001>0 then t801=p076003/p076001;*% of
families with income $10,000-14;
if p076001>0 then t802=p076004/p076001;*% of
families with income $14,000-19999;
if p076001>0 then t803=p076005/p076001;*% of
families with income $20,000-24,999;
if p076001>0 then t804=p076006/p076001;*% of
families with income $25,000-29,999;
if p076001>0 then t805=p076007/p076001;*% of
families with income $30,000-34,999;
```

```
if p076001>0 then t806=p076008/p076001;*% of
families with income $35,000-39,999;
if p076001>0 then t807=p076009/p076001;*% of
families with income $40,000-44,999;
if p076001>0 then t808=p076010/p076001;*% of
families with income $50,000-59,999;
if p076001>0 then t809=p076011/p076001;*% of
families with income $60,000-74,999;
if p076001>0 then t810=p076012/p076001;*% of
families with income $75,000-99,999;
if p076001>0 then t811=p076013/p076001;*% of
families with income $100,000-124,999;
if p076001>0 then t812=p076014/p076001;*% of
families with income $125,000-149,999;
if p076001>0 then t813=p076015/p076001;*% of
families with income $150,000-199,999;
if p076001>0 then t814=p076016/p076001;*% of
families with income $200,000+;

if tract>0;
proc sort; by state county tract;
run;
```

If you were to then merge the Census file for Census tract data onto another dataset, you would use the census identifiers, state, county, and tract, to do this merge. This will involve sorting the data by these three variables (in the order given above), for both files (Census file and the file you are merging to, such as the PSID, or another dataset that has census identifiers).

WELFARE, CHILDREN, AND FAMILIES: A THREE CITY STUDY

Welfare, Children, and Families: A Three City Study (http://web.jhu. edu/threecitystudy) collects data, post-welfare reform, on the well-being of low-income children and families and the strategies families have used to respond to welfare reform, such as employment, education and training, residential mobility, and fertility, and the effect of those strategies on children's health, development, and use of social services. Data were collected from families in low-income neighborhoods in Boston, Chicago, and San Antonio in three waves: 1999, 2000–2001, and 2005–2006. This study utilizes three interrelated components: longitudinal surveys, embedded development studies, and contextual, comparative ethnographic studies.

Wave 1 (March–December 1999) includes a random sample of approximately 2,400 low-income households with children between the ages of 0 to 4 or 10 to 14 years. In Wave 2 (September 2000–July 2001) 80 percent of children in Wave 1 were re-interviewed; these children were then between the ages of 1 and 6 and 11 and 16 years. In those cases in which the caregiver was no longer the same as in Wave 1, a modified instrument was used to incorporate the new caregiver into the new study (e.g., asking when the child came to reside with her and reasons for no longer living with previous caregiver). The original caregiver continued to be interviewed, but child information was gathered from the new caregiver. The Wave 2 sample includes 2,158 focal children, 2,187 new and original caregivers and 63 separated caregivers (the category given to caregivers when an older child is living independently). In Wave 3 (February 2005 and February 2006), focal children were re-interviewed, as were continuing, new, and separated caregivers, representing 79.7% of the original Wave 1 sample. Focal children were between the ages of 5 and 10 or 15 and 20 years. In this wave, new caregivers were those who were new to Wave 3; new caregivers in Wave 2 were listed as continuing caregivers and interviewed only if they continued as caregivers into Wave 3. Wave 3 included 114 independent youths and 229 separated caregivers. Approximately 75% and 90% of Wave 3 agreed to participate in the administrative records and school studies, respectively.

The longitudinal study collected data from female caregivers and a focal child. Caregivers and older children participated in in-person interviews using a computerized instrument. Researchers collected data from younger children through tests and assessments. Caregivers provided information such as demographics, education, welfare participation, father involvement, positive behaviors, neighborhoods, financial strain, domestic violence, illegal activities, income, and health. The older children's interviews were used to collect data on schooling, physical measurements, mother-child relationships and activities, father-child relationships, parental monitoring, delinquency, and sex and pregnancy. The assessment of the younger children looked at physical measurements, and ages and stages. The third wave of data collection also included an administrative records study and a school study, collecting agency and school/teacher based data on employment-, service-, and school-related variables, going back to 1997. Wave 3 youths living independently from caregivers provided additional information relating to their income, union history, household membership, and work and welfare experience.

The embedded development study collected data through interviews with maternal caregivers, nonmaterial primary caregivers, and biological fathers, as well as observational data within the home. Researchers conducted this study, with a sample of 737 children, only in Wave 1, when the children were between the ages of 2 and 4 years old, and Wave 2, when the children were between the ages of 3 and 6 years old. This study involved a home visit with the female caregiver and child that included videotaping caregiver-child interactions and a caregiver interview, collecting data on social networks and relationships, child temperament, and the mothers' ability to balance work and family life. Researchers interviewed the child's nonmaternal primary caregiver, collecting data on the number of hours per week the child is in care, fees, and child-staff ratio. Researchers also interviewed the biological father, gathering information including demographic information, psychological functioning and involvement in illegal activities, involvement with child and parenting practices, and ratings of the child. Time diary studies were also used.

The ethnography study collected data on an additional 256 nonrandomly chosen children and families who resided in the same neighborhoods as the respondents. Researchers interviewed or observed the families once or twice a month for 12 to 18 months, and then every 6 months until 2003. Two hundred and twelve of these families were chosen because they had a child aged 2 to 4 years old during the study recruitment period (June 1999–December 2000). The other 44 were chosen because they had a disabled child between the ages of 0 and 8. This sample was recruited from Head Start; Women, Infants, and Children (WIC); neighborhood community centers; and churches.

This study includes variables for child abuse/neglect, such as whether parental absence is due to abuse or neglect; child emotional well-being; development; mental, emotional, and behavioral problems and whether any of these types of problems caused them to seek professional services; caregiver mental health; foster care; school status, involvement and atmosphere, including information on current level, grades, self-assessed current academic status, and overall safety and atmosphere; father, caregiver, and child health information, including insurance coverage, disability status and diseases, whether the child and caretaker have insurance, general health and disability information about the primary adult, whether health issues are causing absences from school, and whether health was a reason for separation between children and adults; neighborhood information collected from the child and adult; food insecurity; participation in government programs; child and adult illegal drug use; child and adult sexual activity; and dating and domestic violence, including rape and child physical/sexual abuse.

The data include an assortment of welfare variables such as time limits of benefits received and what affects those time limits, if the rules of welfare were not being followed and the reasons and repercussions for not following these rules, and if the family has tried to manipulate the system to its advantage. Teachers are asked whether the children she teaches receive welfare.

The data also include extensive information on diseases in the context of whether they prevent individuals from activities or require that they need special help at home. Diseases included are numerous, including anemia, epilepsy or seizures, asthma, food or digestive allergy, arthritis, diabetes, and sickle cell anemia. Information is also provided on presence of a sexually transmitted disease in the focal child, including genital herpes, HPV, HIV infection, and AIDS.

Neighborhood information in the study includes neighborhood friends of the child and the life goals of these friends, their popularity among people in their neighborhood, and neighborhood kids' thoughts about school and grades. Neighborhood information is also provided in the adult questionnaire and separated, continuing, and new caregiver questionnaires; information includes whether or not a bad neighborhood is the reason why a child does not live with his or her biological mother, and whether the child's father lives in the main adult's neighborhood. There is also a section of the main adult questionnaire dedicated to neighborhoods. Topics include the level of responsibility of the neighborhood, for example whether neighbors would take action if children were seen skipping school, painting graffiti, being disrespectful, or getting into fights. Other topics include trustworthiness of neighbors, and overall atmosphere and safety of the local school (for example, information on whether it is close-knit, the presence of assaults, open drug deals, burglaries, gangs, and the lack of police). Some economic topics, like ability and amount main adult takes out in loans at the neighborhood "money store," are also included.

Questions about food insecurity are included in the data, such as whether there was food insecurity in the last 12 months, with questions involving lack of necessary amount of food, need to cut the size of meals or skip meals for children and adults, weight loss associated with lack of food, and receipt of food from a church or a food bank within the past 30 days. Wave 3 also includes a Food Insecurity Total Score for continuing, new, and separated caregivers

The study provides information on illegal drugs, such as child's use of hard drugs in the past 12 months; amount of child's friends who use or sell drugs; presence of drugs in the home environment; drugs such as marijuana, cocaine, and heroin sold by father; drug use by the main adult, separated, new, and continuing caregivers in general or in exchange for prostitution; and likelihood that the child will engage in drug use, from the main adult's perspective.

The data provide information on sexual activity, such as the child's view of his or her peers' sexual activity, age during first act of sexual intercourse, age of partner during first act of sexual intercourse, and trading sex for drugs and issues of sexual abuse.

Data from the Three City Study have been used to study various aspects of welfare and poverty. Some research has looked into the issue of violence and abuse, such as the correlation between violence and psychological distress in low-income urban women (Hill, Mossakowski, & Angel, 2007), partner violence with particular interest in Hispanic subgroups (Frias & Angel, 2005), the effect of physical and sexual abuse on marriage and cohabitation (Cherlin, Burton, Hurt, & Purvin, 2004), and the relationships among domestic violence, welfare, and low-wage work (Bell, 2003). The Three City Study data have also been used to study family- and neighborhood-related topics, such as father involvement from both the father's and mother's perspective in low-income minority families (Coley & Morris, 2002), grandmother's involvement in young adolescents (Pittman, 2007), creating family time in low-income communities (Tubbs, Roy, & Burton, 2005), the connections among neighborhood disorder, psychological distress, and abuse of alcohol (Hill & Angel, 2005), the relationship between out of school care and problem behavior (Coley, Morris, & Hernandez, 2004), and the correlations among welfare, work, and changes in mothers' living arrangements in low-income families (Cherlin & Fomby, 2004). Studies have also examined issues involving public assistance, like use among U.S.-born children of immigrants (Fomby & Cherlin, 2004); the advantages and disadvantages to shifting from welfare to work (Moffitt & Winder, 2005); household insurance coverage among low-income families (Angel, Frias, & Hill, 2005); the relationship between nonfinancial factors and entry and exit in the TANF program (Moffitt, 2003); and experiences with sanctions and case closings for noncompliance among welfare recipients (Cherlin, Bogen, Quane, & Burton, 2002). Other research study topics that use Three City data include child development (Votruba-Drzal, Coley, & Chase-Lansdale, 2004) and the social capital of low-income African-American and Latin-American mothers (Dominguez & Watkins, 2003).

All of the public and restricted-release data for the three waves of the longitudinal study are available through the Inter-University Consortium for Political and Social Research. The public data and the embedded development study data are also available through Sociometrics, Inc. Data from the ethnography study is not currently available. Through the ICPSR and through the Survey Documentation and Analysis (SDA), developed by the computer-assisted Survey Methods Program (CSM) at the University of California, Berkeley, you can also run simple statistics online http://www.icpsr.umich.edu/cgi-bin/SDA/ICPSR/hsda?dsdr +04701-0004, in a page that looks like the figure shown at the top of the following page.

You can either run these cross tabulations or examine variable frequencies, for example, to see if there is a large sample size for particular variables of interest to you. Here, I show the frequencies for whether the respondent believes that she or he will still be alive at age 35. Please see the second figure shown in the next page.

To download all or some of the different data sets in SAS transport, SPSS, or Stata formats, go to downloads (see figure 4.25, at the top of the page), then choose the types of formats and the data sets you would like. Download page looks like the figure given in page 143.

The picture shows all of the data sets available for public use.

SDA [Use classic interface]   Selected Study: Welfare, Children, and Families: A Three-City Study, Dataset 0004

Analysis | Create Variables | Download | Codebook | Getting Started

Variable Selection: Help

Selected: ASC41A [View]

Copy to: Row | Col | Ctrl | Filter

Mode: ○ Append ● Replace

□ PEER VICTIMIZATION AND SCHOOL ENGAGEMENT
□ PEER VICTIMIZATION AND SCHOOL ENGAGEMENT RECODES
□ HOUSEHOLD MEMBER INFORMATION
□ MARRIAGE AND COHABITATION INFORMATION
□ HOUSEHOLD MEMBER RECODES
□ EDUCATION INFORMATION
□ EDUCATION RECODES
□ SCHOOL CONNECTEDNESS
□ SCHOOL CONNECTEDNESS RECODES
□ LOHMAN SCHOOL AUTONOMY
□ LOHMAN SCHOOL AUTONOMY RECODES
□ EXTRACURRICULAR INFORMATION
□ HEALTH EDUCATION INFORMATION
□ CARETAKER ACTIVITIES
□ CARETAKER ACTIVITIES RECODES
□ EXPECTATIONS FOR FUTURE
□ ETHNICITY INFORMATION
□ EDUCATION AND EXTRACURRICULAR RECODES
□ FRIENDS INFORMATION
□ FRIENDS INFORMATION RECODES
□ FEELINGS ABOUT CAREGIVER
□ FEELINGS ABOUT CAREGIVER RECODES
□ CAREGIVER INTERACTIONS
□ CAREGIVER INTERACTIONS RECODES
□ PARENTAL MONITORING DATA
□ PARENTAL MONITORING DATA RECODES
□ RELATIONSHIP WITH FATHER
□ RELATIONSHIP WITH FATHER RECODES
□ RELATIONSHIP INFORMATION
□ RELATIONSHIP RECODES
□ DELINQUENCY DATA
□ DELINQUENCY RECODES

SDA Frequencies/Crosstabulation Program
Help: General / Recoding Variables

REQUIRED Variable names to specify
Row: [   ]
OPTIONAL Variable names to specify
Column: [   ]
Control: [   ]
Selection Filter(s): [   ]   Example: age(18-50)
Weight: [No Weight   ]

TABLE OPTIONS

Percentaging:
☑ Column □ Row □ Total
with [1 ▼] decimal(s)

□ Confidence intervals Level: [95 percent ▼]
□ Standard error of each percent
Sample Design: ● Complex ○ SRS

□ Statistics with [2 ▼] decimal(s)

□ Question text □ Suppress table
☑ Color coding □ Show Z-statistic
□ Include missing-data values

Title: [   ]

[Run the Table] [Clear Fields]

CHART OPTIONS

Type of chart: [Stacked Bar Chart ▼]
Bar chart options:
Orientation: ● Vertical ○ Horizontal
Visual Effects: ● 2-D ○ 3-D
Show Percents: □ Yes
Palette: ● Color ○ Grayscale
Size - width: [600 ▼] height: [400 ▼]

ASC41A   Live to 35 chances

Description of the Variable

What do you think are the chances you will live to age 35?

Percent	N	Value	Label
1.0	9	1	No chance
3.9	36	2	Some chance
10.0	92	3	About 50-50
20.9	193	4	Pretty likely
64.2	593	5	It will happen
	7	-1	Don't know
	1,014	.	(No Data)
100.0	1,944		Total

Properties

Data type:	numeric
Missing-data codes:	-1,-2
Mean:	4.44
Std Dev:	.89
Record/columns:	1/1931-1932

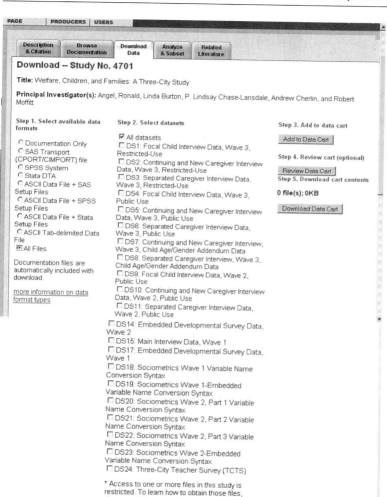

PAGE | PRODUCERS | USERS

| Description & Citation | Browse Documentation | Download Data | Analyze & Subset | Related Literature |

Download -- Study No. 4701

Title: Welfare, Children, and Families: A Three-City Study

Principal Investigator(s): Angel, Ronald, Linda Burton, P. Lindsay Chase-Lansdale, Andrew Cherlin, and Robert Moffitt

Step 1. Select available data formats

- ○ Documentation Only
- ○ SAS Transport (CPORT/CIMPORT) file
- ○ SPSS System
- ○ Stata DTA
- ○ ASCII Data File + SAS Setup Files
- ○ ASCII Data File + SPSS Setup Files
- ○ ASCII Data File + Stata Setup Files
- ○ ASCII Tab-delimited Data File
- ● All Files

Documentation files are automatically included with download.

more information on data format types

Step 2. Select datasets

- ☑ All datasets
- ☐ DS1: Focal Child Interview Data, Wave 3, Restricted-Use
- ☐ DS2: Continuing and New Caregiver Interview Data, Wave 3, Restricted-Use
- ☐ DS3: Separated Caregiver Interview Data, Wave 3, Restricted-Use
- ☐ DS4: Focal Child Interview Data, Wave 3, Public Use
- ☐ DS5: Continuing and New Caregiver Interview Data, Wave 3, Public Use
- ☐ DS6: Separated Caregiver Interview Data, Wave 3, Public Use
- ☐ DS7: Continuing and New Caregiver Interview, Wave 3, Child Age/Gender Addendum Data
- ☐ DS8: Separated Caregiver Interview, Wave 3, Child Age/Gender Addendum Data
- ☐ DS9: Focal Child Interview Data, Wave 2, Public Use
- ☐ DS10: Continuing and New Caregiver Interview Data, Wave 2, Public Use
- ☐ DS11: Separated Caregiver Interview Data, Wave 2, Public Use
- ☐ DS14: Embedded Developmental Survey Data, Wave 2
- ☐ DS15: Main Interview Data, Wave 1
- ☐ DS17: Embedded Developmental Survey Data, Wave 1
- ☐ DS18: Sociometrics Wave 1 Variable Name Conversion Syntax
- ☐ DS19: Sociometrics Wave 1-Embedded Variable Name Conversion Syntax
- ☐ DS20: Sociometrics Wave 2, Part 1 Variable Name Conversion Syntax
- ☐ DS21: Sociometrics Wave 2, Part 2 Variable Name Conversion Syntax
- ☐ DS22: Sociometrics Wave 2, Part 3 Variable Name Conversion Syntax
- ☐ DS23: Sociometrics Wave 2-Embedded Variable Name Conversion Syntax
- ☐ DS24: Three-City Teacher Survey (TCTS)

* Access to one or more files in this study is restricted. To learn how to obtain those files, please read the restrictions listed on the description page.

Step 3. Add to data cart

Add to Data Cart

Step 4. Review cart (optional)

Review Data Cart

Step 5. Download cart contents

0 file(s): 0KB

Download Data Cart

Even though the files are compressed, they are still very large, in part because of the large PDF files that document the data. I downloaded these files in SAS, which then gives you the input statements, variable formats, and missing value codes. For the focal child interview for Wave 3, the SAS code looks like this:

```
* SAS DATA, INFILE, INPUT STATEMENTS;

DATA a;
INFILE "Z:\DATA\Three City Study\10322479\ICPSR_04701\DS0004\04701-0004-Data.txt" LRECL=3862;
INPUT
        CASEID 1-4              SCRID $5-12             SEGID 13-16
        PU 17-19                HHID $20-27             SITE 28
        R3CHT5WT 29-34 .2       R3LCT5WT 35-40 .2       R3CHE5WT 41-44 .2
        R3LCE5WT 45-48 .2       STR 49-50               ZRID $51-58
        COMPDATE $59-66         COMPTIME $67-74         CAPIMODE 75
        CCHAIN 76               INDEP 77                FCSEX 78
        FCRREL 79-80            RFCREL 81-82            RSEX 83
        IWDATE $84-91           INCENT 92               SCENARIO 93
        RESERVE1 94             DADDEAD 95              PRLFCSEX 96
        PRLRSEX 97              PRLIDATE $98-105        PRLRPAGE 106-107
        PRLRFCRL 108-109        PRLFCAGE 110-111        PRLFCREL 112-113
        PRLRSPID 114            PRLRCIT 115             PRLDEGRE 116-117
        PRLRGRDE 118-119        PRLRGED 120-121         PRLFCCIT 122
        PRLLEGAG 123            PRLPENAG 124            PRLAGREE 125
        PRLCHDSA 126-129        PRLCHDSF 130            PRLDED 131
        TMRIVS $132-139         TMRIVE $140-147         TMRIVC 148
```

Note that the infile statement is blank upon receipt of the file and must be filled in with the proper file and file location. The logical record length information is given in the file. Above these statements are the variable formats and below are the missing value codes. All of this information is extremely valuable in saving coding time. The "caseid" is the unique identifier for the child, and you can merge all data sets for the focal child by sorting and merging by caseid.

Appendix Tables

Appendix Tables 1 and 2 give summaries of the data sets presented in this book. Appendix Table 1 shows the sample size, whether the data set is longitudinal or cross-sectional, the representativeness of the data, age of the primary respondents, the persons interviewed and records available. In Appendix Table 2, a general summary of variable types available (not specific variables) in each of the data sets is presented. I do not specify which years the particular variables are available, only that they are available in some of the years. Appendix Table 3 gives websites for the codebooks for each of the data sets. Some codebooks are not available on the web and I make note of that as well.

Appendix Table 1 Summary Tables

Data Sets	Sample Size	CS or LG	Years Available
Adoption and Foster Care Analysis and Reporting System (AFCARS)	Adoptions – 2005:51,485; 2004: 52,468; 2003:50,342; 2002:52,881; 2001:50,599; 2000:51,050; 1999:46,772; 1998:36,694; 1997:22,678; 1996:16,010; 1995:14,786 Foster Care – 2005:801,200; 2004:800,128; 2003:801,018; 2002:814,428; 2001:813,817; 2000:811,855; 1999:814,360; 1998:724,601; 1997:390,481; 1996:335,836; 1995:280,691	CS but data can be used longitudinally for some states	1995-2005
Child Neglect: Cross Sector Service Paths and Outcomes (CSSPO)	10,187 children	LG	1993-2001
Common Core of Data (CCD)	97,000 public schools and 18,000 public school districts in the 50 states, District of Columbia, Department of Defense schools, and outlying areas	LG	Data is collected annually beginning in 1986 until present; different data began being collected a different times, but 1986 was the earliest
Continuing Survey of Food Intake by Individuals (CSFII)	1994-96: 16,103 individuals; Supplemental Children's Survey 1998: 5,559 children added to data from 4,253 children from 1994-96	CS	1989-91; 1994-96; 1998 (Supplemental Children's Survey)

Representativeness	Ages of respondents	Persons interviewed
Representative of cases of foster care and adoption that occur through public welfare agencies	Less than one to 20 years of age	States send data to the Children's Census Bureau concerning each child in foster care and each child that is adopted
Nationally representative of children receiving AFDC	Children ages 18 and under	No interviews; data was only administrative and census
Nationally representative and data is comparable across states	Not applicable	Public schools (elementary and secondary), school districts, education agencies (local and state)
Nationally representative	All ages; Supplemental Children's Survey 1998: 0 to 9	Respondents

Continued

Appendix Table 1 Summary Tables *(Continued)*

Data Sets	Sample Size	CS or LG	Years Available
Current Population Survey (CPS)	About 50,000 to 100,000 households	CS	Data is collected on a monthly basis for over 50 years
Development Victimization Survey (DVS)	Phase 1: 2,030 children; Phase 2: 1,467 children	LG	2002-03; 2003-04
Early Childhood Longitudinal Survey (ECLS)	birth cohort: 14,000 children;In total: 19,173 children	LG	Birth cohort: 2001-02, 2003-04, 2005-6, 2006, 2007-08; Kindergarten cohort: 1998-99, 1999-2000, 2002, 2004, 2007
Fragile Family and Child Wellbeing Study (FFCWS)	Wave I:4,898 families (including 3,712 unwed couples and 1,186 married couples); Wave II (after 1 year): 4270 mothers of whom 1029 were married and 3241 were unmarried at the time of birth; Wave III (after 3 years): 4140 mothers of whom 1012 were married and 3128 were unmarried; Wave IV: 4055 mothers of whom 975 were married and 3080 were unmarried (after five years).	LG	Initial interviews took place between February 1998 and September 2000, each respondent had a one-year, three-year, and five- year follow-up, then a nine year follow-up in 2007-09
General Social Survey (GSS)	Around 1,500 each year	CS	Every year since 1972 (excluding 1979, 1981, 1992) and every two years beginning in 1994

Representativeness	Ages of respondents	Persons interviewed
Nationally representative of the civilian noninstitutionalized population	Data focuses on ages 16 and over	Respondents
Nationally representative	Ages 2 to 17	Children and caregivers
Nationally representative	Birth cohort: 9 months to kindergarten or higher; kindergarten cohort: kindergarten to eighth grade	Parents, children, teachers, school administrators
Nationally representative of cities with populations over 200,000	Birth to 9 years old	Mothers, fathers, children
Nationally representative	Adults and young adults	Respondents

Continued

Appendix Table 1 Summary Tables *(Continued)*

Data Sets	Sample Size	CS or LG	Years Available
Health and Retirement Study (HRS)	Wave 1 (1992): 12,654; Wave 2 (1994): 11,597; Wave 3 (1996): 11,199; Wave 4 (1998): 10,857; Wave 5 (2000): 10,377; Wave 6 (2002): 10,142; Wave 7 (2004): 9,759	LG	Biennial surveys beginning in 1992
Longitudinal Studies of Child Abuse and Neglect (LONGSCAN)	1354 children and their caregivers	LG	1991-2004
National Child Abuse and Neglect Data System (NCANDS)	Child file data – 2006 :3,477,988; 2005: 3,461,872; 2004: 3,134,026; 2003: 1,216,626; 2002: 1,216,626; 2001: 1,216,626; 2000: 1,032,362 - DCDC J/K files – 1999: 783,467/227, 064; 1998: 660, 081/221,967; 1997: 376,919/167,738; 1996: 383,275/157, 962; 1995: 630, 594/258,206	CS	State-level data began in 1990; Case-level data began in 1995; Puerto Rica began submitting in 2005
National Educational Longitudinal Survey (NELS)	1,000 schools, almost 25,000 students, 5,000 teachers; 2nd follow-up included 15,000 parents; by year 2000, 12,144 observations	LG	1988, 1990, 1992, 1994, 2000

Representativeness	Ages of respondents	Persons interviewed
Nationally representative of Americans over the age of 50	Ages 50 and over	Respondents and spouses
Nationally representative of children who have suffered maltreatment	Ages 4 or less through 18 years old	Children and caregivers
Nationally representative of children whose alleged and victimization were reported to child and protective services	Data discusses children under 18 years of age	Child and protective agencies
Te sample of schools represents the 40,000 public and private schools in the U.S.; the sample of students represents the 3,000,000 eighth graders attending schools in 1988	13 or 14(eighth grade) to 25 or 26(eighth years out of high school)	Parents, students, teachers, school administrators

Continued

Appendix Table 1 Summary Tables *(Continued)*

Data Sets	Sample Size	CS or LG	Years Available
National Health and Nutrition Examination Survey (NHANES)	NHANES I: 31,973; NHANES II: 27,801; NHANES III: 33,994; HHANES: 16,000; NHANES 1999-00: 9,965; NHANES 01-02: 11,039	CS	NHANES I: 1971-75; NHANES II: 1976-80; NHANES III: 1988-94; 1999-2000, 2001-02, 2003-04, 2005-06, 2007-08
National Longitudinal Study of Adolescent Health (Add Health)	Wave I: over 20,000 young people; Wave II: about 14,000 young people; Wave III: eligible people for Wave I and 1,500 of their sexual partners	LG	1994-1995, 1995-1996, 2001-2002
National Longitudinal Surveys (NLS)	NLS of Older Men: 5,020; NLS of Mature Women: 5,083; NLS of Young Men: 5,225; NLS of Young Women: 5,159; NLSY79: 12,686; Children and Young Adults of NLSY79: 5,255; NLSY97: 8,984	LG	NLS of Older Men: 1966-1990; NLS of Mature Women: 1967-2003; NLS of Young Men: 1966-1981; NLS of Young Women: 1968-2003; NLSY79: 1979-ongoing; Children and Young Adults of NLSY79: 1986-ongoing; NLSY97: 1997-ongoing

Representativeness	Ages of respondents	Persons interviewed
Nationally representative of all noninstitutionalized persons	Birth to age 74	Respondents, family
Nationally representative of adolescents	Respondents were first interviewed between the grades of 7-12, then the final wave of interviews was between the ages of 18 and 26	Parents, children, school administrators, romantic/sexual partners
Nationally representative of the population born in the years specified by the cohort, but each cohort has specific issues pertaining to representativeness. E.g. Children of the NYLS79 is representative of children born to parents who themselves were born between 1957 and 1964 and were living in the U.S. in 1978	NLS of Older Men: Ages 45 to 59; NLS of Mature Women: Ages 30 to 44; NLS of Young Men: Ages 14 to 24; NLS of Young Women: Ages 14 to 24; NLSY79: Ages 14 to 21; Children and Young Adults of NLSY79: Birth to age 14 for children and 15 and older for young adults; NLSY97: Ages 12 to 16	Respondents and children of respondents for Children and Young Adults of NLSY79

Continued

Appendix Table 1 Summary Tables *(Continued)*

Data Sets	Sample Size	CS or LG	Years Available
National Medical Expenditure Survey (NMES)	NMES-1: 13,500 households; NMES-2's Household Survey: 14,000 households, NMES-2's Survey of American Indians and Alaskan Natives: 2,000 individuals, NMES-2's Institutional Population Component:11,000 individuals and 2,000 institutions; MEPS (Medical Expenditure Panel Survey)'s Household Component: 10,500 households, MEPS's Medical Provider Component: 22,000 health care providers, MEPS's Insurance Component: 10,000 employers, insurers, and unions, MEPS's Nursing Home Component: not listed	CS	NMES-1: 1977; NMES-2: 1987; MEPS: 1996-2008
National Survey of American Families (NSAF)	40,000 respondents	CS	1997, 1999, 2002
National Survey of Child and Adolescent Wellbeing (NSCAW)	5,501 children	LG	1999-2005

Representativeness	Ages of respondents	Persons interviewed
Nationally representative of the civilian population		NMES-1 and NMES-2: respondents and nursing homes; MEPS: respondents, insurers, medical providers, and nursing homes
Nationally representative of the noninstitutionalized population under 65 years of age	16 to 64 years old	Respondents
Nationally representative of children in contact with the welfare system	Ages 0 to 14 years old	Children, parents, caregivers, caseworkers

Continued

Appendix Table 1 Summary Tables *(Continued)*

Data Sets	Sample Size	CS or LG	Years Available
NICHD Study of Early Childcare and Youth Development	Phase 1: 1,364 children; Phase II & III: 1,100 of original children; Phase IV: 1,000 of original children	LG	1991-1994, 1994-2000, 2000-2005
Panel Study of Income Dynamics (PSID)	Original 1968 sample size: 4,802 families and 18,230 individuals; 8,289 families in 2007, and 23,508 individuals.	LG	1968 to present; PSID went from annual to biennial data collection in 1997
Panel Study of Income Dynamics, Child Development Supplement	3,653 children in 1997, 2,907 children in 2002.	LG	1997; 2002-03
Project on Human Development in Chicago Neighborhoods (PHDCN)	Neighborhood data: respondents; Individual data: respondents and their primary caregivers	LG	Neighborhood data: 1994-95, 2001-02; Individual data: 1994-97, 1997-99, 2000-02
Public-Use Microdata Samples (PUMS)	1% and 5% samples generally cover areas with 100,000 persons; 1 in 1000 samples are not listed	CS	1940 to present; data is collected every 10 years
School Data Direct	In 2007, there were 100,308 schools in 14,556 school districts in the 50 states. Example of available data: There are 48 variables for Grade 9 data in Alaska.	CS	Data is collected by state, by school district, and by school and is available online for about the last decade

Representativeness	Ages of respondents	Persons interviewed
Nationally representative of children ages 15 and younger	Phase I: birth - 3 years old; Phase II: 54 months - 1st grade; Phase III: 2nd grade - 6th grade; Phase IV: 14-15 years old	Children, mothers
Nationally representative of individuals and the family units they live in	All ages	Families and individuals
Nationally representative	Birth to 12 years of age in wave I, and 5 to 17 in wave 2.	Children, primary caregivers, other caregivers, school administrators, teachers.
Representative of Chicago and the ages used to define the cohorts	Neighborhood data: over 18 years of age; Individual data: 7 different cohorts (birth, 3, 6, 9, 12, 15, 18 years of age)	Neighborhood data: 8,782 respondents in 343 neighborhood clusters; Individual data: 6,226 children, adolescents, young adults, and their primary caregivers
Nationally representative	All ages	Respondents
Nationally representative	Not applicable	Schools, school districts, and states

Continued

Appendix Table 1 Summary Tables *(Continued)*

Data Sets	Sample Size	CS or LG	Years Available
Survey of Income and Program Participation (SIPP)	1984 Wave I: 19, 878 original households; 1985 Wave I: 13,349 original households; 1986 Wave I: 11,513 original households; 1987 Wave I: 11,689; 1988 Wave I: 11,774; 1989 Wave I: 11,892; 1990 Wave I: 18,363; 1991 Wave I: 14,316; 1992 Wave I: 19,582; 1993 Wave I: 19,583; 1996 Wave I: 36,805; 2001 Wave I: 35,102; 2004 Wave I: 43,711	LG	1984-1993, 1996, 2000, 2001, 2004, 2008
Survey of Program Dynamics (SPD)	1992-93 SIPP: 54,600 households; 1997 SPD: 34,609 households; 1998 SPD: 19,129; 1999 SPD: 19,303; 2000 SPD: 23,258; 2001 SPD: 29,341; 2002 SPD: 22,694	LG	1992-93, 1997-2002
U.S. Census	Size of the population	CS	Data is collected every 10 years. 1990 & 2000 available on-line. Some previous years available on CD.
Welfare, Children, and Families: A Three City Study	Wave I: 2,400 households; Wave II: 2,158 focal children with 2,187 continuing or new caregivers; Wave III: 79.9% of original sample children from Wave I	LG	Wave I: March-Dec 1999; Wave II: 2000-01; Wave III: 2005-06

Note: LG=longitudinal; CS=cross sectional

.

Representativeness	Ages of respondents	Persons interviewed
Nationally representative of noninstitutionalized individuals between the ages of 15 and 64	Ages 15 to 64	Respondents
Nationally representative	All ages	Respondents
Nationally representative	All ages	Respondents
Representative of low-income families and children in three observed cities (Boston, San Antonio, and Chicago)	Wave I: 0 to 4 and 10 to 14; Wave II: 1 to 6 or 11 to 16; Wave III: 5 to 10 or 15 to 20	Children, caregivers (particularly female)

Continued

Appendix Table 2

Data Set	Child Questions	Child Abuse & Neglect	Child Emotional Well Being	Mental Health
AFCARS		X	X	X
Child Neglect	X	X	X	X
CCD				
CSFII				
CPS				
DVS	X	X	X	X
ECLS	X			
FFCWS	X	X		X
GSS	X	X	X	X
HRS				X
LONGSCAN	X	X	X	X
NCANDS	X	X	X	X
NELS	X		X	X
Add Health	X	X	X	X
NLS	X		X	X
NMES/MEPS				
NSAF	X		X	X
NSCAW	X	X	X	X
NHANES	X			
NICHD	X			X
PSID	X		X	X
PSID, CDS	X	X	X	X
PHDCN	X		X	X
PUMS				
SDD	X			
SIPP	X		X	X
SPD	X			
U.S. Census				
A Three-City Study	X	X	X	X

Foster Care	Adoption	Education	School Test Scores	Overall Health	Health Coverage
X	X	X	-	X	-
X		X		X	X
		X	X		
		X		X	
		X			X
X	X	X	-	X	
	X	X	X	X	X
X	X	X		X	X
	X	X		X	X
		X		X	X
X	X	X		X	-
X				X	
X		X	X	X	
X	X	X		X	X
X	X	X	X	X	X
		X		X	X
X	-	X	-	X	X
X	X	X		X	
		X		X	X
		X	X	X	
	X	X		X	X
X	X	X	X	X	X
	X	X		X	X
		X			
		X	X		
X	X	X		X	X
		X		X	X
		X			
X	X	X	X	X	X

Continued

Appendix Table 2 *(Continued)*

Data Set	Disability status	Health Problems	Prescription Drug Use	Smoking	Physical activity/ weight
AFCARS		-			
Child Neglect	X	X			
CCD					
CSFII					
CPS	X			X	
DVS					
ECLS	X	X			
FFCWS	X	X	X	X	
GSS	X	X			
HRS	X	X	X	X	
LONGSCAN					
NCANDS		X			
NELS	X			X	
Add Health	X	X	X	X	X
NLS	X	X		X	
NMES/MEPS	X	X	X	X	
NSAF	X	X			
NSCAW	X			X	
NHANES		X		X	X
NICHD	X	X		X	X
PSID	X	X	X	X	X
PSID, CDS	X	X		X	X
PHDCN	X	X	X	X	X
PUMS	X				
SDD					
SIPP	X				
SPD	X	X			
U.S. Census					
A Three-City Study	X	X			

General well-being	Neighborhood Perception	Neighborhood Characteristics	Diet	Food Insecurity
	-	-		
		X		
		X		
		X	X	
				X
	X	X		
	X	X	X	X
	X	X	X	X
X	X			
X	X			
X	X			
X		X		
	X	X	X	
X	X	X	X	
	X			
			X	X
X	X			
	X	X		X
X	X	X	X	X
	X	X		
		X		
		X		
	X	X		X
X				X
	X	X		X

Continued

Appendix Table 2 *(Continued)*

Data Set	AFDC/ TANF	Food Stamps	SS, SSI	Medicaid	Medicare
AFCARS	X		X		
Child Neglect	X			X	X
CCD					
CSFII	X	X	X		
CPS	X	X	X	X	X
DVS	X		X		
ECLS	X	X	X	X	
FFCWS	X	X	X	X	X
CSS	X		X	X	X
HRS		X	X	X	X
LONGSCAN	-	X	X	X	
NCANDS	X	X	X		
NELS	X	X	X	X	
Add Health	X	X	X	X	
NLS	X	X	X	X	
NMES/MEPS	X	X	X	X	X
NSAF	X	X	X	X	X
NSCAW	X				
NHANES		X		X	X
NICHD	X	X	X	X	
PSID	X	X	X	X	X
PSID, CDS	X	X	X	X	X
PHDCN					
PUMS	X		X		
SDD					
SIPP	X	X	X	X	X
SPD	X	X	X	X	X
U.S. Census		X			
A Three-City Study	X	X	X	X	

Crime/violence	Alcohol	Illegal Drugs	Incarceration	Sexual Activity	Pregancy	STDS
X		X				
X	X	X	X	X		
X	X	X		X		
X	X	X			X	
X	X	X		X		
X		X		X		
X	X					
X		X		X		
X	X	X				
X	X	X		X	X	
X	X	X	X	X	X	X
X	X	X		X	X	
	X					
-						
X	X			X		
		X		X		
	X	X				
	X	X	X	X	X	
X	X	X	X	X	X	
X	X	X	X	X	X	X
X						
	X			X		
X		X		X	X	X

Continued

Appendix Table 2 *(Continued)*

Data Set	Dating violence	Domestic violence	Savings & Wealth	Home Environment	Emotional Support
AFCARS			-	X	-
Child Neglect					
CCD					
CSFII			X		
CPS					
DVS	X			X	
ECLS			X	X	
FFCWS	X	X		X	
GSS			X	X	X
HRS			X		
LONGSCAN				X	
NCANDS				X	
NELS				X	
Add Health	X			X	
NLS	X		X	X	
NMES/MEPS					
NSAF				X	
NSCAW		X		X	
NHANES				X	
NICHD				X	
PSID			X		
PSID CDS			X	X	X
PHDCN		X	X	X	X
PUMS					
SDD				X	
SIPP			X	X	
SPD			X	X	
U.S. Census					
A Three-City Study	X	X	X	X	X

Parental traits & behaviors	Family characteristics	General well-being	General behavior	Adverse experiences
X	X			
	X			
	X			
X				X
X	X		X	
X	X			
X	X	X		X
	X	X		
X		X		X
X				X
	X	X		
X	X			
X	X	X		X
X				
X	X			
	X			
X	X	X	X	
	X			
X	X	X	X	
X	X			X
	X			
X	X			
X	X	X	X	
	X			
X	X		X	

Continued

Appendix Table 2 *(Continued)*

Data Set	Service Utlization and characteristics	Child care	Employment/ job training	Housing	Military
AFCARS					
Child Neglect			X		
CCD					
CSFII		X	X		
CPS		X	X	X	X
DVS					
ECLS		X	X	X	
FFCWS		X	X	X	X
GSS	X	X	X	X	X
HRS			X	X	
LONGSCAN			X		
NCANDS	X				
NELS			X		X
Add Health		X	X	X	X
NLS	X	X	X	-	X
NMES/MEPS	X	X		X	
NSAF	X	X	X		
NSCAW	X	X			
NHANES			X		
NICHD		X	X		
PSID		X	X	X	X
PSID,CDS	X	X	X	X	X
PHDCN	X	X	X		
PUMS				X	X
SDD					
SIPP	X	X	X	X	X
SPD	X	X	X	X	X
U.S. Census			X	X	X
A Three-City Study	X	X	X	X	X

Internet Use	Religion	Expenditures	Attitudes	Suicide	State Identifiers
					X
X					X
					X
X	X	X			
	X				X
	X		X		
X					
					X
X			X		
	X			X	
X	X		X		
		X			X
					X
					X
X					
X	X	X			X
	X	X	X		X
X	X		X	X	-
					X
					X
	-				-
			X		
	X		X		X

Continued

Appendix Table 2 *(Continued)*

Data Set	Gambling	Relation-ships	Leisure	Physical activity/weight	Agency/staff Character-istics	Develop-ment
AFCARS						
Child Neglect						
CCD						
CSFII						
CPS						
DVS			X			
ECLS		X				X
FFCWS						
GSS			X			
HRS						
LONGSCAN						
NCANDS						
NELS		X	X			
Add Health	X	X		X		X
NLS			X			
NMES/MEPS					X	
NSAF			X			
NSCAW					X	
NHANES				X		
NICHD		X		X		X
PSID			X	X		
PSID,CDS		X	X	X		X
PHDCN			-	X		X
PUMS						
SDD						
SIPP						
SPD		X				
U.S. Census						
A Three-City Study		X	X			

Note: Relationships often include parent-child relationships. Development often includes child development.

Appendix Table 3 Codebooks

Adoption and Foster Care Analysis and Reporting System (AFCARS)
http://www.ndacan.cornell.edu/NDACAN/Datasets/UserGuidePDFs/AFCARS_
Guide_1995-1999.pdf

Child Neglect: Cross Sector Service Path and Outcomes
http://www.ndacan.cornell.edu/NDACAN/Datasets/UserGuidePDFs/116user.pdf

Common Core of Data (CCD)
http://sodapop.pop.psu.edu/data-collections/ccd/dnd

Continuing Survey of Food Intake by Individuals
http://sodapop.pop.psu.edu/data-collections/csfii/dnd

Current Population Survey
http://sodapop.pop.psu.edu/data-collections/cps/dnd

Developmental Victimization Survey
http://www.ndacan.cornell.edu/Ndacan/Datasets/UserGuidePDFs/126user.pdf

Early Childhood Longitudinal Survey
Codebook is on the CD from the NCES.

Fragile Family and Child Well-Being Study (FFCWS)
http://www.fragilefamilies.princeton.edu/documentation.asp
http://sodapop.pop.psu.edu/data-collections/ff

General Social Survey (GSS)
http://www.norc.org/GSS+Website/Download/ -- data
http://publicdata.norc.org:41000/gss/documents//BOOK/Main%20Body.pdf
-- codebook

Health and Retirement Survey
http://hrsonline.isr.umich.edu/index.php?p=showcbk

For Longitudinal Studies Of Child Abuse And Neglect (LONGSCAN)
http://www.ndacan.cornell.edu/Ndacan/Datasets/UserGuidePDFs/144.pdf
http://www.iprc.unc.edu/longscan/pages/measelect/Measure%20Table%20%
28up%20through%20Age%2018%20Interviews%29.pdf

National Educational Longitudinal Study
(http://search.icpsr.umich.edu/IAED/query.html?col=abstract&op0=%2B&tx0
=national+education+longitudinal+study+of+1988+(nels)+series&ty0=p&fl0=
series%3A&op1=-&tx1=restricted&ty1=w&fl1=availability%3A&op2=%2B&tx
2=IAED&ty2=w&fl2=archive%3A&nh=50&rf=3)

National Child Abuse and Neglect Data System (NCANDS)
http://www.ndacan.cornell.edu/NDACAN/Datasets/UserGuidePDFs/
NCANDS_MultiYear_Guide.pdf

National Health and Nutrition Examination Survey (NHANES)
http://www.cdc.gov/nchs/nhanes/nhanesi.htm
http://www.cdc.gov/nchs/nhanes/nhanesii.htm
http://www.cdc.gov/nchs/data/nhanes/nhanes3/ssnh3hrm.pdf

Continued

Appendix Table 3 Codebooks *(Continued)*

The National Longitudinal Study of Adolescent Health (Add Health)
http://www.cpc.unc.edu/projects/addhealth/codebooks

National Longitudinal Surveys (NLS)
http://www.bls.gov/nls/handbook/2005/selvarom.pdf
http://www.nlsinfo.org/nlsy97/nlsdocs/nlsy97/questionnaires/R1Youth-final.pdf
http://sodapop.pop.psu.edu/data-collections/nls

National Medical Expenditure Survey (NMES)/ Medical Expenditure Panel Survey
http://www.icpsr.umich.edu/cgi-bin/bob/newark?study=6371&path=ICPSR
http://www.meps.ahrq.gov/mepsweb/survey_comp/survey.jsp

National Survey of Child and Adolescent Well-Being (NSCAW)
http://www.ndacan.cornell.edu/NDACAN/Datasets/UserGuidePDFs/092_
Intro_to_NSCAW_Wave_1.pdf

NICHD Study of Early Child Care and Youth Development (SECCYD)
https://secc.rti.org/

The Panel Study of Income Dynamics (PSID)
http://simba.isr.umich.edu/Zips/ZipMain.aspx
https://simba.isr.umich.edu/Zips/ZipSupp.aspx#ACTSAV

Panel Study of Income Dynamics, Child Development Supplement
http://psidonline.isr.umich.edu/CDS/wavesdoc.html

Project on Human Development in Chicago Neighborhoods (PHDCN)
www.icpsr.umich.edu/PHDCN

Public-Use Microdata Samples
http://www.census.gov/acs/www/Products/PUMS/PUMS3.htm
http://www.census.gov/prod/cen2000/doc/pums.pdf

School Data Direct
http://www.schooldatadirect.org/
As of this writing, this web site is being updated but should be up soon.

Survey of Income and Program Participation (SIPP)
http://www.census.gov/apsd/techdoc/sipp/sipp.html
http://www.bls.census.gov/sipp_ftp.html

Survey of Program Dynamics
http://www.icpsr.umich.edu/cgi-bin/bob/archive2?study=3594&path=ICPSR&
docsonly=yes

United States Census
http://usa.ipums.org/usa/volii/codebooks.shtml

Welfare, Children, and Families: A Three City Study
http://web.jhu.edu/threecitystudy/Public_Release/documentation.
html#Questionnaires

Glossary

American Standard Code for Information Interchange (ASCII) Data File This is data that are in "raw" form, or generally, variables that are listed in columns, with a different row for each observation. Some data may have many rows for each individual. You will need to transform these types of data into one of the main data software packages by using programming language within those packages. Often, data come with such programming so that the end user will not have to. One reason for using ASCII format to download data is that the size of the data is much smaller than if the data were in SAS, SPSS, or Stata format.

Computer-Assisted Personal Interview (CAPI) A means of interviewing the respondent, either by having an interviewer enter information into a computer during the interview, or having the respondent enter information directly.

Cross-Sectional Data These are data that are collected over one period of time. Cross-sectional data may be collected only once from one sample of people, or it may be collected many times, over many periods, from different samples.

Fixed Effects Models These are generally models that are used with longitudinal data, in which unobservable but permanent characteristics are controlled. For example, fixed effect models can be used with siblings: For each variable, the family mean is subtracted from the individual mean. In this way, variables in which there are no differences among family members that are permanent and unobserved (such as IQ level of the parent) are factored out of the model. These models are often seen as being able to control for more factors than models that do not used fixed effects. Unobserved variables that are not permanent over time are not controlled in these models.

Geocode Information This generally relates to the inclusion of information related to the place of residence or other such information relating to the survey member. Some data sets include only information such as the state, country, zip code, census tract, or census block, and it is then up to the researcher to link data (such as census data) with this link. Other data sets do not provide such links but provide specific information relating to the geography of the sample member, such as poverty rates, for specific geographical areas.

Identification Numbers Usually, each data set has a unique identification number for each respondent or other unit. Often, when merging data sets together, or when adding variables to your data file, you will need to sort, then merge, your data by this identification number.

Longitudinal Data These are data that follow the same set of people over an extended period of time. For example, people in the longitudinal data set may be asked questions at given intervals of time, such as on a yearly or monthly basis. These questions may be the same questions over time, or the researchers may ask a set of core questions for each survey and another set of questions that differ at each survey.

Oversampling A strategy to choose more than a representative number of people from a particular group to ensure that more precise measurement can be made for this group. For example, people with a particular mental disorder may be oversampled in a particular data set because so few people in the population have the disorder. If only a few people are chosen for the sample (as would most likely be the case if a random sampling design were used), then it would be difficult to examine relationships between this mental disorder and other factors. By oversampling, and using sampling weights, more precise measurement can be made and relationships can be more easily found. There is thus a lower likelihood of a Type II error when examining the relationships between those with the mental disorder and other factors.

Primary Data These are data that are collected by the investigator doing the research by methods such as questionnaires, interviews, focus groups, diaries, observation, or a variety of other methods.

Random Sampling This is a sampling method in which each individual in the population, group, or universe has an equal chance of being selected into the sample.

Response Rates The proportion of respondents who participate in the survey when asked to. Attrition rates refer to the proportion of sample respondents that leave the sample in a longitudinal design, due to refusal to partake in the sample, death, or any other reason.

SAS A statistical software package used to statistically analyze data. Often, researchers can download data in raw form form and use a SAS input statement that includes the columns where variable data are located. Or, users can use a SAS transport file, and proc copy to use the transport file.

Sampling Weights These are used to make samples representative of some group. Statistical programs will often allow you to weight the data by these sampling weights, and give higher weights to those who are undersampled (there are proportionately fewer of them in the sample than in the population), and lower weights to those who are oversampled (there are proportionately more of them in the sample than in the population).

Secondary Data These are data that are collected by someone other than the researcher conducting the research. Methods such as surveys, focus groups, questionnaires, and a variety of other methods may be used to collect the data.

Sibling Studies These are often used with fixed effects models. To use such models, more than a single sibling must be surveyed in the data. Those who do not have siblings, or who have all siblings with missing data for variables used in statistical models, cannot be used in such models.

SPSS A statistical software package used to statistically analyze data.

STATA A statistical software package used to statistically analyze data.

Stratified Sampling This is a method of sampling in which the population is divided into subgroups, and random samples are taken of each subgroup. This may be done if a goal is to make sure that certain subgroups are highly represented within the sample. For example, a number of samples stratify their sampling by poverty level, to make sure that a large number of sample members come from poor families. Sampling weights must then be used to make the sample representative of the population being examined.

References

Aaronson, D., & French, E. (2004). The effect of part-time work on wages: Evidence from the Social Security rules. *Journal of Labor Economics*, 22(2), 329–352.

Adam, E. K., Snell, E. K., & Pendry, P. (2007). Sleep timing and quantity in ecological and family context: A nationally representative time-diary study. *Journal of Family Psychology*, 21(1), 4–19.

Adamczyk, A., & Felson, J. (2008). Fetal positions: Unraveling the influence of religion on premarital pregnancy resolution. *Social Science Quarterly*, 89(1), 17–38.

Adamek, R. (1994). The Polls—A Review: Public opinion and Roe v. Wade: Measurement difficulties. *Public Opinion Quarterly*, 58(3), 409–418.

Agree, E. M. (1999). The influence of personal care and assistive technology on the measurement of disability. *Social Science & Medicine*, 48(4), 427–443.

Aidala, A. A. (1989). Communes and changing family norms. *Journal of Family Issues*, 10(3).

Ainsworth, J. W. (2002). Why does it take a village? The mediation of neighborhood effects on educational achievement. *Social Forces*, 81(1), 117–152.

Akamigbo, A. B., & Wolinsky, F. D. (2007). New evidence of racial differences in access and their effects on the use of nursing homes among older adults. *Medical Care*, 45(7).

Alba, R. D., & Chamlin, M. B. (1983). A preliminary examination of ethnic identification among whites. *American Sociological Review*, 48, 240–247.

Alston, J. P. (1973). Perceived strength of religious beliefs. *Journal for the Scientific Study of Religion*, 12, 109–111.

Alwin, D. F. (1989). Changes in qualities valued in children in the United States, 1964 to 1984. *Social Science Research*, 18(3), 195–236.

An, C.-B., Haveman, R., & Wolfe, B. (1993). Teen out-of-wedlock births and welfare receipt: The role of childhood events and economic circumstances. *Review of Economics and Statistics*, 75(2), 195–207.

Anderman, E. M., & Kimweli, D. M. S. (1997). Victimization and safety in schools serving early adolescents. *Journal of Early Adolescence*, 17(4), 408–438.

Anderson, J. E. (2003). Condom use and HIV risk among U.S. adults. *American Journal of Public Health*, 93(6), 912–914.

Angel, J. L., Jiménez, M. A., & Angel, R. J. (2007). The economic consequences of widowhood for older minority women. *The Gerontologist*, 47(2), 224–234.

Angel, R. J., Frias, S. M., & Hill, T. D. (2005). Determinants of household insurance coverage among low-income families from Boston, Chicago, and San Antonio: Evidence from the Three-City Study. *Social Science Quarterly*, 86, 1338–1353.

Anton, R. F., O'Malley, S. S., Ciraulo, D. A., Cisler, R. A., et al. (2006). Combined pharmacotherapies and behavioral interventions for alcohol dependence: The COMBINE study: A randomized controlled trial. *Journal of the American Medical Association*, 295(17), 2003–2017.

Arum, R., Roksa, J., & Budig, M. J. (2008). The romance of college attendance: Higher education stratification and mate selection. *Research in Social Stratifcation and Mobility*. 2008; 26(2), 107–121.

Ashby, S. L., Arcari, C. M., & Edmonson, M. B. (2006). Television viewing and risk of sexual initiation by young adolescents. *Archives of Pediatrics Adolescent Medicine*, 160(4), 375–380. Retrieved Apr, from

Ashenfelter, O., & Zimmerman, D. J. (1997). Estimates of the returns to schooling from sibling data: Fathers, sons, and brothers. *The Review of Economics and Statistics*, 79(1), 1–9.

Baker, D. W., Sudano, J. J., Albert, J. M., Borawski, E. A., & Dor, A. (2002). Loss of health insurance and the risk for a decline in self-reported health and physical functioning. *Medical Care* 40(11), 1126–1131.

Barth, R. P., Lloyd, E. C., Green, R. L., James, S., Leslie, L. K., & Landsverk, J. (2007). Predictors of placement moves among children with and without emotional and behavioral disorders. *Journal of Emotional and Behavioral Disorders* 15(1), 46–55.

Barth, R. P., Wildfire, J., & Green, R. L. (2006). Placement into foster care and the interplay of urbanicity, child behavior problems, and poverty. *American Journal of Orthopsychiatry* 76(3), 358–66.

Bartkowski, J. P., Xu, X., & Levin, M. L. (2008). Religion and child development: Evidence from the Early Childhood Longitudinal Study. *Social Science Research*, 37(1): 18–36.

Battle, J. J. (2002). Longitudinal analysis of academic achievement among a nationwide sample of Hispanic students in one- versus dual-parent households. *Hispanic Journal of Behavioral Sciences*, 24(4), 430–447.

Beaver, K. M., & Wright, J. P. (2005). Evaluating the effects of birth complications on low self-control in a sample of twins. *International Journal of Offender Therapy and Comparative Criminology*, 49(4), 450–471.

Beebout, H. S. (2006). Nutrition, food security, and obesity. *Gender Issues*, 23(3), 1245–1262.

Beets, M. W., & Foley, J. T. (2008). Association of father involvement and neighborhood quality to kindergarteners' physical activity: A multilevel structural equation model. *American Journal of Health Promotion*, 22(3), 195–203.

Bell, H. (2003). Cycles within cycles: Domestic violence, welfare, and low-wage work. *Violence Against Women*, 9(10).

Bellamy, J. L. (2008). Behavioral problems following reunification of children in long-term foster care. *Children and Youth Services Review* 30(2), 216–228.

Benjamin, M. R. (2006). Does religion influence patient satisfaction? *American Journal of Health Behavior*, 30(1), 85–91.

Bennett, P. R., & Xie, Y. (2003). Revisiting racial difference in college attendance: The role of historically Black colleges and universities. *American Sociological Review*, 68(4), 567–581.

Beydoun, M., Powell, L., & Wang, Y. (2009). Reduced away-from-home food expenditures and better nutrition knowledge and belief can improve quality of dietary intake among U.S. adults. *Public Health and Nutrition*, 12(3), 369–381.

Beydoun, M., & Wang, Y. (2008). How do socio-economic status, perceived economic barriers and nutritional benefits affect quality of dietary intake among U.S. adults? *European Journal of Clinical Nutrition*, 62(3), 303–313.

Bickham, D. S., & Rich, M. (2006). Is television viewing associated with social isolation? Roles of exposure time, viewing content, and violent content. *Archives of Pediatrics & Adolescent Medicine*, 160(4), 387–393.

Bickham, D. S., Vandewater, E. A., Huston, A. C., Lee, J. H., Gillman Caplovitz, A., & Wright, J. C. (2003). Predictors of children's media use: An examination of three ethnic groups. *Media Psychology*, 5(2), 107–137.

Bielinski, J., & Davison, M. L. (2001). A sex difference by item difficulty interaction in multiple-choice mathematics items administered to national probability samples. *Journal of Educational Measurement*, 38(1), 57–77.

Bingenheimer, J. B., Brennan, R. T., & Earls, F. J. (2005). Firearm violence exposure and serious violent behavior. *Science*, 308(5726), 1323–1326.

Blau, D. M. (1998). Labor force dynamics of older married couples, 595–629. *Journal of Labor Economics*, 16(3).

Bodine, A. (2003). School uniforms, academic achievement, and uses of research. *Journal of Educational Research*, 97(2), 67–71.

Booth, C. L., & Kelly, J. F. (1998). Child-care characteristics of infants with and without special needs: Comparisons and concerns. *Early Childhood Research Quarterly*, 13(4), 603–621.

Boslaugh, S. (2007). *Secondary Data Sources for Public Health: A Practical Guide*. Cambridge: Cambridge University Press.

Boushey, H. (2008). Family friendly policies: Helping mothers make ends meet. *Review of Social Economy*, 66(1), 51–70.

Boushey, H., & Wenger, J. B. (2006). Unemployment insurance eligibility before and after welfare reform. *Journal of Poverty*, 10(3), 1–23.

Bright, C., Jonson-Reid, M., & Williams, J. (2008). Onset of juvenile court involvement: Exploring gender-specific influences of maltreatment and poverty. *Children and Youth Services Review*, 30(8), 914–927.

Brisson, D., & Usher, C. L. (2007). The effects of informal neighborhood bonding social capital and neighborhood context on homeownership for families living in poverty. *Journal of Urban Affairs*, 29(1), 65–75.

Brodowski, M. L., Nolan, C.M., Gaudiosi, J. A., Yuan, Y.Y., Zikratova, L., Ortiz, M.J., et al. (2008). Nonfatal Maltreatment of Infants—United States, October 2005-September 2006. *Morbidity and Mortality Weekly Report*, 57(13), 336–339.

Brooks, A. C. (2007). Income tax policy and charitable giving. *Journal of Policy Analysis and Management*, 26(3), 599–612.

Brown, S. L. (2004). Family structure and child well-being: The significance of parental cohabitation. *Journal of Marriage and Family*, 66(2), 351–367.

Brown, S. L., Bulanda, J. R., & Lee, G. R. (2005). The significance of nonmarital cohabitation: Marital status and mental health benefits among middle-aged and older adults. *The Journals of Gerontology*, 60B(1), S21–S29.

Browne, I. (2002). Opportunities lost? Race, industrial restructuring, and employment among young women heading households. *Social Forces*,78(3), 907–929.

Browning, C. R., & Burrington, L. A. (2006). Racial differences in sexual and fertility attitudes in an urban setting. *Journal of Marriage and Family*, 68(1), 236–251.

Browning, C. R., & Cagney, K. A. (2002). Neighborhood structural disadvantage, collective efficacy, and self-rated physical health in an urban setting. *Journal of Health and Social Behavior*, 43(4), 383–399.

Browning, C. R., & Cagney, K. A. (2003). Moving beyond poverty: Neighborhood structure, social processes, and health. *Journal of Health and Social Behavior*, 44(4), 552–571.

Browning, C. R., Feinberg, S. L., & Dietz, R. D. (2004). The paradox of social organization: Networks, collective efficacy, and violent crime in urban neighborhoods. *Social Forces*, 83(2), 503–534.

Browning, C. R., Feinberg, S. L., Wallace, D., & Cagney, K. A. (2006). Neighborhood social processes, physical conditions, and disaster-related mortality: The case of the 1995 Chicago heat wave. *American Sociological Review*, 71(4), 661–678.

Browning, C. R., Leventhal, T., & Brooks-Gunn, J. (2004). Neighborhood context and racial differences in early adolescent sexual activity. *Demography*, 41(4), 697–720.

Browning, C. R., & Olinger-Wilbon, M. (2003). Neighborhood structural disadvantage, social organization, and number of short-term sexual partnerships. *Journal of Marriage and the Family*, 65(3), 730–745.

Brunsma, D. L. (2005). Interracial families and the racial identification of mixed-race children: Evidence from the Early Childhood Longitudinal Study. *Social Forces*, 84(2), 1131–1157.

Buka, S. L., Brennan, R. T., Rich-Edwards, J. W., Raudenbush, S. W., & Earls, F. (2003). Neighborhood support and the birth weight of urban infants. *American Journal of Epidemiology*, 157(1), 1–8.

Burdette, H. L., Wadden, T. A., & Whitaker, R. C. (2006). Neighborhood safety, collective efficacy, and obesity in women with young children. *Obesity*, 14(3), 518–525.

Burdette, H. L., & Whitaker, R. C. (2005). A national study of neighborhood safety, outdoor play, television viewing, and obesity in preschool children. *Pediatrics*, 116(3), 657–662.

Burke, J., Lee, L.-C., & O'Campo, P. (2008). An exploration of maternal intimate partner violence experiences and infant general health and temperament. Maternal and Child Health, 12, 172–179.

Burkhauser, R. V., Couch, K. A., & Wittenburg, D. C. (2000). A reassessment of the new economics of the minimum wage literature with monthly data from the current population survey. *Journal of Labor Economics*, 18(4), 653–680.

Burkhauser, R. V., Daly, M. C., Larrimore, J., & Kwok, J. (2008). The transformation in who is expected to work in the United States and how it changed the lives of single mothers and people with disabilities. University of Michigan Retirement Research Center. Unpublished manuscript. Retrieved from http://www.mrrc.isr.umich.edu/publications/papers/pdf/wp187.pdf. Retrieved May, 2010.

Burkhauser, R. V., Feng, S., & Larrimore, J. (2008). Measuring labor earnings inequality using public-use March current population survey data: The value of including variance and cell means when imputing topcoded values. National Bureau of Economic Research Working Paper No. 14458. http://www.nber.org/papers/w14458. Retrieved May, 2010.

Burns, B. J., Phillips, S. D., Wagner, H. R., Barth, R. P., Kolko, D. J., Campbell, Y., et al. (2004). Mental health need and access to mental health services by youths involved with child welfare: A National Survey. *Journal of the American Academy of Child and Adolescent Psychiatry* 43(8), 960–70.

Busch, S. H., & Horwitz, S. M. (2004). Access to mental health services: Are uninsured children falling behind? *Mental Health Services Research*, 6(2), 109–116.

Butler, A. C. (1996). The effect of welfare benefit levels on poverty among single-parent families. *Social Problems*, 43(1), 91–115.

Cagney, K. A., & Browning, C. R. (2004). Exploring neighborhood-level variation in asthma and other respiratory diseases. *Journal of General Internal Medicine*, 19(3), 229–236.

Cagney, K. A., Browning, C. R., & Wen, M. (2005). Racial disparities in self-rated health at older ages: What difference does the neighborhood make? *The Journals of Gerontology. Series B, Psychological Sciences and Social Sciences 2005*, 60(4), S181–190.

Calafat, A. M., Ye, X., Wong, L.-Y., Reidy, J. A., & Needham, L. L. (2008). Urinary concentrations of triclosan in the U.S. population: 2003–2004. *Environmental Health Perspectives*, 116(3), 303–307.

Campbell, J. R., & Auinger, P. (2007). The association between blood lead levels and osteoporosis among adults: Results from the Third National Health and Nutrition Examination Survey (NHANES III). *Environmental Health Perspectives*, 115(7), 1018.

Carlson, M. J., McLanahan, S. S., & Brooks-Gunn, J. (2008). Coparenting and nonresident fathers' involvement with young children after a nonmarital birth. *Demography*, 45(2), 461–488.

Carlson, S. A., Fulton, J. E., Lee, S. M., Maynard, L. M., Brown, D. R., Kohl, H. W., III, et al. (2008). Physical education and academic achievement in elementary school: Data from the Early Childhood Longitudinal Study. *American Journal of Public Health*, 98(4), 721–727.

Casanueva, C., Foshee, V., & Barth, R. (2005). Intimate partner violence as a risk factor for children's use of the emergency room and injuries. *Children and Youth Services Review*, 27(11), 1223–1242.

Casciano, R. (2007). Political and civic participation among disadvantaged urban mothers: The role of neighborhood poverty. *Social Science Quarterly*, 88(5), 1124–1151.

Casciano, R., & Massey, D. S. (2008). Neighborhoods, employment, and welfare use: Assessing the influence of neighborhood socioeconomic composition. *Social Science Research*, 37(2), 544–558.

Cawley, J. (2004). The impact of obesity on wages. *The Journal of Human Resources*, 39(2), 468–496.

Chance, T., & Scannapieco, M. (2002). Ecological correlates of child maltreatment: Similarities and differences between child fatality and nonfatality cases. *Child & Adolescent Social Work Journal*, 19(2), 131–169.

Chen, H., & Guo, X. (2008). Obesity and functional disability in elderly Americans. *Journal of the American Geriatrics Society*, 56(4), 689–694.

Cheng, T. C. (2007). Impact of work requirements on the psychological well-being of TANF recipients. *Health & Social Work*, 32(1), 41–48.

Cherlin, A., Griffith, J., & McCarthy, J. (1983). A note on maritally-disrupted men's reports of child support in the June 1980 Current Population Survey. *Demography, 20*(3), 385–389.

Cherlin, A. J., Bogen, K., Quane, J. M., & Burton, L. (2002). Operating within the rules: Welfare recipients'experiences with sanctions and case closings. *The Social Service Review, 76*(3), 387–405.

Cherlin, A. J., Burton, L. M., Hurt, T. R., & Purvin, D. M. (2004). The influence of physical and sexual abuse on marriage and cohabitation. *American Sociological Review, 69,* 768–789.

Cherlin, A. J., & Fomby, P. (2004). Welfare, work, and changes in mothers'living arrangements in low income families. *Population Research and Policy Review, 23,* 543–565.

Choi, N. G., & Kim, J. S. (2007). Age group differences in depressive symptoms among older adults with functional impairments. *Health & Social Work, 32*(3), 177–188.

Christakis, D. A., & Zimmerman, F. J. (2007). Violent television viewing during preschool is associated with antisocial behavior during school age. *Pediatrics., 120*(5), 993–999.

Christakis, D. A., Zimmerman, F. J., DiGiuseppe, D. L., & McCarty, C. A. (2004). Early television exposure and subsequent attentional problems in children. *Pediatrics, 113*(4), 917–918.

Clarke-Stewart, K. A., Lee, Y., Allhusen, V. D., Kim, M. S., & McDowell, D. J. (2006). Observed differences between early childhood programs in the U.S. and Korea: Reflections of "developmentally appropriate practices" in two cultural contexts. *Journal of Applied Developmental Psychology, 27,* 427–443.

Clarke-Stewart, K. A., Vandell, D. L., McCartney, K., Owen, M. T., & Booth, C. (2000). Effects of parental separation and divorce on very young children. *Journal of Family Psychology, 14*(2), 304–326.

Cobb-Clark, D. A., & Hildebrand, V. (2002). The wealth and asset holdings of U.S.-born and foreign-born households: Evidence from Sipp data. *Social and Economic Dimensions of an Aging Population Research Papers 89,* McMaster University.

Cohen, D. A., Farley, T. A., & Mason, K. (2003). Why is poverty unhealthy? Social and physical mediators. *Social Science Medicine, 57*(9), 1631–1641.

Coile, C., Diamond, P., Gruber, J., & Jousten, A. (2002). Delays in claiming Social Security benefits. *Journal of Public Economics, 84*(3), 357–385.

Coley, R. L., & Morris, J. E. (2002). Comparing father and mother reports of father involvement among low-income minority families. *Journal of Marriage and Family, 64*(4), 982–997.

Coley, R. L., Morris, J. E., & Herandez, D. (2004). Out-of-school care and problem behavior trajectories among low-income adolescents: Individual, family, and neighborhood characteristics as added risks. *Child Development*, 75(3), 948–965.

Condliffe, S., & Link, C. R. (2008). The relationship between economic status and child health: Evidence from the United States. *American Economic Review*, 4, 1605–1618.

Connell, C. M., Bergeron, N., Katz, K. H., Saunders, L., & Tebes, J. K. (2007). Re-referral to child protective services: The influence of child, family, and case characteristics on risk status. *Child Abuse & Neglect*, 31(5), 573–588.

Connolly, L. S., & Marston, C. E. (2005). Welfare reform, earnings, and incomes: New evidence from the Survey of Program Dynamics. *Contemporary Economic Policy*, 23(4), 493–512.

Copeland, C. (2006). Debt of the elderly and near elderly, 1992–2004. *Employee Benefit Research Institute Notes*, 27(9), 1–16.

Copeland, C. (2007). Labor-force participation: The population age 55 and older. *Employee Benefit Research Institute*, 28(6), 1–8.

Corcoran, M., & Adams, T. K. (1997). Race, sex, and the intergenerational transmission of poverty. In G. J. Duncan & J. Brooks-Gunn (Eds.), Consequences of growing up poor (pp. 461–517). New York: Russell Sage Foundation.

Crocker, K. J., & Moran, J. R. (2003). Contracting with limited commitment: Evidence from employment-based health insurance contracts. *Rand Journal of Economics*, 34(4), 694–718.

Cross, T. P., Finkelhor, D., & Ormrod, R. (2005). Police involvement in child protective services investigations: Literature review and secondary data analysis. *Child Maltreatment*, 10(3), 224–244.

Cuevas, C., Finkelhor, D., Turner, H. A., & Ormrod, R. K. (2007). Juvenile delinquency and victimization: A theoretical typology. *Journal of Interpersonal Violence*, 22(12), 1581–1602.

Cunningham, J. S., & Donovan, E. (1986). Patterns of union membership and relative wages. *Journal of Labor Research*, VII(2), 127–143.

Curtin, S. C., & Hofferth, S. (2003, November). *Differences in time use among overweight and normal weight children 6–12 years of age.* Poster session presented at the 131st annual meeting of the American Public Health Association, San Francisco, CA.

Curtis, M. A. (2007). Subsidized housing, housing prices, and the living arrangements of unmarried mothers. *Housing Policy Debate*, 18(1), 145–170.

Dallo, F. J., Al Snih, S., & Ajrouch, K. J. (2009). Prevalence of disability among U.S.- and foreign-born Arab Americans: Results from the 2000 US Census. *Gerontology*, 44(2), 153–161.

Datar, A. (2006). Does delaying kindergarten entrance give children a dead start? *Economics of Education Review*, 25(1), 43–62.

Datta, S. D., Sternberg, M., Johnson, R. E., Berman, S., Papp, J. R., McQuillan, G., et al. (2007). Gonorrhea and chlamydia in the United States among persons 14 to 39 years of age, 1999 to 2002. *Annals of Internal Medicine*, 147(2), 89–96.

Davila, A., & Mora, M. T. (2004). The scholastic progress of students with entrepreneurial parents. *Economics of Education Review*, 23(3), 287–300.

Davis-Kean, P. E. (2005). The influence of parent education and family income on child achievement: The indirect role of parental expectations and the home environment. *Journal of Family Psychology*, 19(2), 294–304.

De Robertis, M. T., & Litrownik, A. J. (2004). The experience of foster care: Relationship between foster parent disciplinary approaches and aggression in a sample of young foster children. *Child Maltreatment*, 9(1), 92–102.

Dearing, E., McCartney, K., & Taylor, B. A. (2001). Change in family income-to-needs matters more for children with less. *Child Development*, 72(6), 1779–1793.

Dearing, E., Taylor, B. A., & McCartney, K. (2004). Implications of family income dynamics for women's depressive symptoms during the first 3 years after childbirth. *American Journal of Public Health*, 94(8), 1372–1377.

DeCica, P. (2007). Does full-Day kindergarten matter? Evidence from the first two years of schooling. *Economics of Education Review*, 26(1), 67–82.

Deleire, T., & Kalil, A. (2002). Things come in threes: Single-parent multi-generational family structure and adolescent adjustment. *Demography*, 39(2), 393–414.

Dembe, A., E, Erickson, J. B., & Delbos, R. (2004). Predictors of work-related injuries and illnesses: National survey findings. *Journal of Occupational and Environmental Hygiene*, 1(8), 542–550.

Desha, L., Ziviani, J., Nicholson, J., & Martin, G. (2007). Physical activity and depressive symptoms in American Adolescents. *Journal of Sport & Exercise Psychology*, 29(4), 534–543.

Dominguez, S., & Watkins, C. (2003). Creating networks for survival and mobility: Social capital among African-American and Latin-American low-income mothers. *Social Problems*, 50(1), 111–135.

Donohue, S. M., & Heywood, J. S. (2004). Job satisfaction and gender: An expanded specification from the NLSY. *International Journal of Manpower*, 25(2), 211–234.

Downey, D. B., von Hippel, P. T., & Broh, B. A. (2004). Are schools the great equalizer? Cognitive inequality during the summer months and the school year. *American Sociological Review*, 69(5), 613–635.

Doyle, J. M., & Kao, G. (2007). Friendship choices of multiracial adolescents: Racial homophily, blending, or amalgamation? *Social Science Research*, 36(2), 633–653.

Drukker, M., Buka, S. L., Kaplan, C., McKenzie, K., & Os, J. V. (2005). Social capital and young adolescents'perceived health in different sociocultural settings. *Social Science & Medicine*, 61(1), 185–198.

Du, J., & Huang, G. G. (2002). Computer use at home and at school: Does it relate to academic performance? *Journal of Women and Minorities in Science and Engineering*, 8(2), 201–217.

Dubowitz, H., Pitts, S. C., Litrownik, A. J., Cox, C. E., et al. (2005). Defining child neglect based on child protective services data. *Child Abuse & Neglect*, 29(5), 493–511.

Duggan, M. G., & Kearney, M. S. (2007). The impact of child SSI enrollment on household outcomes. *Journal of Policy Analysis and Management*, 26(4), 861–886.

Duncan, G. J. (2002). The PSID and me. In E. Phelps, F. F. Furstenberg, & A. Colby (Eds.), Looking at lives: American longitudinal studies of the twentieth century (pp. 133–166). New York: Russell Sage Foundation.

Duncan, G. J., & Hoffman, S. (1979). On-the-job training and earnings differences by race and sex. *The Review of Economics and Statistics*, 61(4), 594–603.

Dunifon, R., & Kowaleski-Jones, L. (2003). The influences of participation in the National School Lunch Program and food insecurity on child well-being. *Social Science Review*, 77(1), 72–94.

Dunn, J. S., Kinney, D. A., & Hofferth, S. L. (2003). Parental ideologies and children's after-school activities. *American Behavioral Scientist*, 46(10), 1359–1386.

Eamon, M. K. (2002). Effects of poverty on mathematics and reading achievement of young adolescents. *The Journal of Early Adolescence*, 22(1), 49–74.

Earle, K. A., & Cross, A. (2001). *Child abuse and neglect among American Indian/ Alaska Native children: An analysis of existing data.* Seattle, WA: Casey Family Programs.

Early, D., Rimm-Kaufman, S., Cox, M., Saluja, G., Pianta, R., Bradley, R., et al. (2002). Maternal sensitivity and child wariness in the transition to kindergarten. *Parenting: Science and Practice*, 2, 355–377.

Eckstein, Z., & Wolpin, K. I. (1999). Estimating the effect of racial discrimination on first job wage offers. *The Review of Economics and Statistics*, 81(3), 384–392.

Edin, K., & Reed, J. (2005). Why don't they just get married? Barriers to marriage among the disadvantaged. *The Future of Children: Marriage and Child Wellbeing*, 15(2), 117–138.

Ehrle, J., & Geen, R. (2002). Kin and non-kin foster care—findings from a national survey. *Children and Youth Services Review*, 24(1–2), 15–35.

Eilat-Adar, S., Xu, J., Loria, C., Mattil, C., Goldbourt, U., Howard, B. V., et al. (2007). Dietary calcium is associated with body mass index and body fat in American Indians. *The Journal of Nutrition*, 137(8), 1955–1960.

Elder, T., & Powers, E. (2006). Public health insurance and SSI program participation among the aged (Research Paper No. WP 2006-117). Retrieved May, 2010, from Michigan Retirement Research Center website: http://www.mrrc.isr.umich.edu/publications/papers/pdf/wp117.pdf

Evans, M. F., & Smith, V. K. (2005). Do new health conditions support mortality-air pollution effects?. *Journal of Environmental Economics and Management*, 50(3), 496–518.

Everson, M. D., Smith, J. B., Hussey, J. M., English, D., Litrownik, A. J., Dubowitz, H., et al. (2008). Concordance between adolescent reports of childhood abuse and child protective service determinations in an at-risk sample of young adolescents. *Child Maltreatment*, 13(1), 14–26.

Fairbrother, G., Kenney, G., Hanson, K., & Dubay, L. (2005). How do stressful family environments relate to reported access and use of health care by low-income children? *Medical Care Research and Review*, 62(2), 205–230.

Fairchild, G. B. (2008). Residential segregation influences on the likelihood of black and white self-employment. *Journal of Business Venturing*, 23(1), 46–74.

Falba, T. A. (2005). Effects of health events on the smoking cessation of middle-aged Americans. *Journal of Behavioral Medicine*, 28(1), 21–33.

Fang, X., &Corso, P. (2007). Child maltreatment, youth violence, and intimate partner violence: Developmental relationships. *American Journal of Preventive Medicine*, 33(4), 281–290.

Finkelhor, D., Ormrod, R. K., & Turner, H. A. (2007a). Poly-victimization: A neglected component in child victimization. *Child Abuse & Neglect*, 31(1), 7–26.

Finkelhor, D., Ormrod, R. K., & Turner, H. A. (2007b). Polyvictimization and trauma in a national longitudinal cohort. *Development and Psychopathology*, 19(1), 149–166.

Finkelhor, D., Ormrod, R. K., & Turner, H. A. (2007c). Re-victimization patterns in a national longitudinal sample of children and youth. *Child Abuse & Neglect*, 31(5), 479–502.

Finkelhor, D., Ormrod, R. K., & Turner, H. A. (2009). The developmental epidemiology of childhood victimization. *Journal of Interpersonal Violence*, 24(5), 711–731.

Finkelhor, D., Ormrod, R. K., Turner, H. A., & Hamby, S. L. (2005a). Measuring poly-victimization using the Juvenile Victimization Questionnaire. *Child Abuse & Neglect*, 29(11), 1297–1312.

Finkelhor, D., Ormrod, R.K, Turner, H.A., & Hamby, S. L. (2005b). The victimization of children and youth: A comprehensive, national survey. *Child Maltreatment*, 10(1), 5–25.

Finkelhor, D., Turner, H., & Ormrod, R. (2006). Kid's stuff: The nature and impact of peer and sibling violence on younger and older children. *Child Abuse & Neglect*, 30(12), 1401–1412.

Fitzgerald, J., Gottschalk, P., & Moffitt, R. (1998). An analysis of sample attrition in panel data: The Michigan panel study of income dynamics. *Journal of Human Resources*, 33(2), 251–299.

Fitzgerald, K. G. (2006). The effect of military service on wealth accumulation. *Research on Aging*, 28(1), 56–83.

Flaherty, E. G., Thompson, R., Litrownik, A. J., Theodore, A., et al. (2006). Effect of early childhood adversity on child health. *Archives of Pediatrics & Adolescent Medicine*, 160(12), 1232–1238.

Flegal, K., Graubard, B., Williamson, D., & Gail, M. (2007). Cause-specific excess deaths associated with underweight, overweight, and obesity. *Journal of the American Medical Association*, 298(7), 2028–2037.

Flegal, K. M. (2007). The effects of changes in smoking prevalence on obesity prevalence in the United States. *American Journal of Public Health*, 97(8), 1510–1514.

Fletcher, J., & Wolfe, B. (2008). Child mental health and human capital accumulation: The case of ADHD revisited. *Journal of Health Economics*, 27, 794–800.

Fluke, J. D., Shusterman, G. R., Hollinshead, D. M., & Yuan, Y.Y. T. (2008). Longitudinal analysis of repeated child abuse reporting and victimization: Multistate analysis of associated factors. *Child Maltreatment*, 13(1), 76–88.

Fluke, J. D., Yuan, Y.Y. T., Hedderson, J., & Curtis, P. A. (2003). Disproportionate representation of race and ethnicity in child maltreatment: Investigation and victimization. *Children and Youth Services Review*, 25(5–6), 359–373.

Fomby, P., & Cherlin, A. J. (2004). Public assistance use among U.S.-born children of immigrants. *The International Migration Review*, 38(2), 584–610.

Forshee, R. A., & Storey, M. L. (2006). Demographics, not beverage consumption, is associated with diet quality. *International Journal of Food Science and Nutrition*, 57, 494–511.

Foster, H., & Hagan, J. (2007). Incarceration and intergenerational social exclusion. *Social Problems*, 54(4), 399–433.

Foster, W., & Miller, M. (2007). Development of the literacy achievement gap: A longitudinal study of kindergarten through third grade. *Language, Speech, and Hearing Services in Schools*, 38(3), 173–181.

Fox, K. E. (2004). Are they really neglected? A look at worker perceptions of neglect through the eyes of a national data system. *First Peoples Child and Family Review*, 1(1), 73–82.

Frias, S. M., & Angel, R. J. (2005). Partner violence among low-income women and the need for more refined race and ethnicity categories. *Journal of Marriage and Family*, 67, 552–564.

Frisco, M. L., Muller, C., & Dodson, K. (2004). Participation in voluntary youth-serving associations and early adult voting behavior. *Social Science Quarterly*, 85(3), 660–677.

Fu, X. N. (2008). Interracial marriage and family socio-economic well-being: Equal status exchange or caste status exchange? *Social Science Journal*, 45(1), 132–155.

Funkhouser, E., & Trejo, S. J. (1995). The labor market skills of recent male immigrants: evidence from the Current Population Survey. *Industrial and Labor Relations Review*, 48(4), 792–811.

Gabriel, P. E. (2004). Differences in earnings, skills and labour market experience among young black and white men. *Applied Economics Letters*, 11, 337–341.

Gangl, M. (2006). Scar effects of unemployment: An assessment of institutional complementarities. *American Sociological Review*, 71(6), 986–1013.

Garasky, S., & Stewart, S. D. (2007). Evidence of the effectiveness of child support and visitation: Examining food insecurity among children with nonresident fathers. *Journal of Family and Economic Issues*, 28(1), 105–121.

Garces, E., Thomas, D., & Currie, J. (2002). Longer term effects of Head Start. *The American Economic Review*, 92(4), 999–1012.

Garrett, B., & Zuckerman, S. (2005). National estimates of the effects of mandatory Medicaid managed care programs on health care access and use, 1997–1999. *Medical Care*, 43(7), 649–657.

Gershoff, E. T., Aber, J. L., Raver, C. C., & Lennon, M. C. (2007). Income is not enough: Incorporating material hardship into models of income associations with parenting and child development. *Child Development*, 78(1), 70–95.

Gibson, D. (2004). Long-term Food Stamp Program participation is differentially related to overweight in young girls and boys. Journal of Nutrition, 134, 372–379.

Gibson-Davis, C. M. (2008). Family structure effects on maternal and paternal parenting in low-income families. *Journal of Marriage and Family*, 70(2), 452–465.

Gibson-Davis, C. M., Edin, K., & McLanahan, S. (2005). High hopes but even higher expectations: The retreat from marriage among low-income couples. *Journal of Marriage and the Family*, 67(5), 1301–1312.

Ginther, D. K. (2000). Alternative estimates of the effect of school on earnings. *The Review of Economics and Statistics*, 82(1), 103–116.

Goins, R. T., Moss, M., Buchwald, D., & Guralnik, J. M. (2007). Disability among older American Indians and Alaska Natives: An analysis of the 2000 census public use microdata sample. *Gerontologist*, 47(5), 690–696.

Goodwin, D. K., Knol, L. L., Eddy, J. M., Fitzhugh, E. C., et al. (2006). The relationship between self-rated health status and the overall quality of dietary intake of U.S. adolescents. *Journal of the American Dietetic Association*, 106(9), 1450–1453.

Gottlieb, S. L., Pope, V., Sternberg, M. R., McQuillan, G. M., Beltrami, J. F., Berman, S. M., et al. (2008). Prevalence of syphilis seroreactivity in the

United States: Data from the National Health and Nutrition Examination Surveys (NHANES) 2001–2004. *Sexually Transmitted Diseases*, 35(5), 507–511.

Gould, E. D., Weinberg, B. A., & Mustard, D. B. (2002). Crime rates and local labor market opportunities in the United States: 1979–1997. *The Review of Economics and Statistics*, 84(1), 45–61.

Graefe, D. R., De Jong, G. F., & May, D. C. (2006). Work disability and migration in the early years of welfare reform. *Population Research and Policy Review*, 25(4), 353–368.

Grafova, I. (2008a). Overweight children: Assessing the contribution of the neighborhood environment. *Preventive Medicine*, 47(3), 304–308.

Grandjean, A. C., Fulgoni, V. L., III, Reimers, K. J., & Agarwal, S. (2008). Popcorn consumption and dietary and physiological parameters of U.S. children and adults: Analysis of the National Health and Nutrition Examination Survey (NHANES) 1999–2002 dietary survey data. *Journal of the American Dietetic Association*, 108(5), 853–856.

Grinstein-Weiss, M., Yeo, Y. H., Zhan, M., & Pajarita, C. (2008). Asset holding and net worth among households with children: Differences by household type. *Children and Youth Services Review*, 30, 62–78.

Grogan-Kaylor, A., Ruffolo, M. C., Ortega, R. M., & Clarke, J. (2008). Behaviors of youth involved in the child welfare system. *Child Abuse and Neglect*, 32(1), 32–49.

Guo, S., Barth, R. P., & Gibbons, C. B. (2006). Propensity score matching strategies for evaluating substance abuse services for child welfare clients. *Children and Youth Services Review*, 28(4), 357–383.

Haberstick, B. C., Timberlake, D., Hopfer, C. J., Lessem, J. M., Ehringer, M. A., & Hewitt, J. K. (2007). Genetic and environmental contributions to retrospectively reported DSM-IV childhood attention deficit hyperactivity disorder. *Psychological Medicine*, 25, 1–10.

Hadden, W. C., & Rockswold, P. D. (2008). Increasing differential mortality by educational attainment in adults in the United States. *International Journal of Health Services*, 38(1), 47–61.

Hahm, H. C., Lahiff, M., & Barreto, R. M. (2006). Asian American adolescents' first sexual intercourse: Gender and acculturation differences. *Perspectives on Sexual and Reproductive Health*, 38(1), 28–36.

Hamilton, E. R., Hummer, R. A., You, X. H., & Padilla, Y. C. (2006). Health Insurance and Health-Care Utilization of U.S.-Born Mexican-American Children. *Social Science Quarterly*, 87(5), 1280–1294.

Han, W.-J., & Waldfogel, J. (2003). Parental leave: The impact of recent legislation on parents' leave taking. *Demography*, 40(1), 191–200.

Hanratty, M. J. (2006). Has the Food Stamp Program become more accessible? Impacts of recent changes in reporting requirements and asset eligibility limits. *Journal of Policy Analysis and Management*, 25(3), 603–621.

Hansen, M. E. (2007). Using subsidies to promote the adoption of children from foster care. *Journal of Family and Economic Issues*, 28(3), 377–393.

Harper, C., & McLanahan, S. (2004). Father absence and youth incarceration. *Journal of Research on Adolescence*, 14(3), 369–397.

Hayward, M. D., & Gorman, B. K. (2004). The long arm of childhood: The influence of early-life social conditions on men's mortality. *Demography*, 41(1), 87–107.

Hayward, R. A., & DePanfilis, D. (2007). Foster children with an incarcerated parent: Predictors of reunification. *Children and Youth Services Review*, 29(10), 1320–1334.

Heikes, K. E., Eddy, D. M., Arondekar, B., & Schlessinger, L. (2008). Diabetes risk calculator: A simple tool for detecting undiagnosed diabetes and pre-diabetes. *Diabetes Care*, 31(5), 1040–1045.

Heiland, F., & Liu, S. (2006). Family structure and wellbeing of out-of-wedlock children: The significance of the biological parents' relationship. *Demographic Research*, 15(4), 61–104.

Heintze, T. C., Berger, L. M., Naidich, W. B., & Meyers, M. K. (2006). Housing assistance and employment: How far-reaching are the effects of rental subsidies?. *The Social Service Review*, 80(4), 635–674.

Herbert, C. E., & Tsen, W. (2007). The potential of downpayment assistance for increasing homeownership among minority and low-income households. *Cityscape: A Journal of Policy Development and Research*, 9(2), 153–183.

Hidalgo, D. A., & Bankston, C. L. (2008). Military brides and refugees: Vietnamese American wives and shifting links to the military, 1980–2000. *International Migration*, 46(2), 167–185.

Hill, T. D., & Angel, R. J. (2005). Neighborhood disorder, psychological distress, heavy drinking. *Social Science & Medicine*, 61(5), 965–975.

Hill, T. D., Mossakowski, K., & Angel, R. J. (2007). Relationship violence and psychological distress among low-income urban women. *Journal of Urban Health: Bulletin of the New York Academy of Medicine*, 84, 537–551.

Hirsch, B. T., & Macpherson, D. A. (2003). Union membership and coverage database from the Current Population Survey: Note. *Industrial and Labor Relations Review*, 56(2), 349–354.

Hisnanick, J. J. (2004). A resource to evaluate welfare reform: The Survey of Program Dynamics (SPD). *Journal of Economic Issues*, 38(3), 846–853.

Hofferth, S. L., & Curtin, S. C. (2005). Poverty, food programs, and childhood obesity. *Journal of Policy Analysis and Management*, 24(4), 703–726.

Hofferth, S. L., & Reid, L. (2002). Early childbearing and children's achievement and behavior over time. *Perspectives on Sexual and Reproductive Health*, 34(1), 41–49.

Hofferth, S. L., Smith, J., McLoyd, V. C., & Finkelstein Payes, J. (2000). Achievement and behavior among children of welfare recipients, welfare leavers, and low income wingle mothers. *Journal of Social Issues*, 56(4), 747–773.

Hollar, D., & Moore, D. (2004). Relationship of substance use by students with disabilities to long-term educational, employment, and social outcomes. *Substance Use & Misuse*, 39(6), 931–963.

Hollenbeck, K., & Kimmel, J. (2008). Differences in the returns to education for males by disability status and age of disability onset. *Southern Economic Journal*, 74(3), 707–724.

Holloway, S. R., & Mulherin, S. (2004). The effect of adolescent neighborhood poverty on adult employment. *Journal of Urban Affairs*, 26(4), 427–454.

Honora, D., & Rolle, A. (2002). A discussion of the incongruence between optimism and academic performance and its influence on school violence. *Journal of School Violence*, 1(1), 67–81.

Horwitz, A. V., Videon, T. M., Schmitz, M. F., & Davis, D. (2003). Rethinking twins and environments: Possible social sources for assumed genetic influences in twin research. *Journal of Health and Social Behavior*, 44(2), 111–129.

Hovmand, P., Jonson-Reid, M., & Drake, B. (2007). Mapping Service Networks. *Journal of Technology and Human Services*, 25(4), 1–21.

Huang, Z., Wong, F., Ronzio, C., & Yu, S. (2006). Depressive symptomatology and mental health help-seeking patterns of U.S.- and foreign-born mothers (2007). *Maternal and Child Health Journal*, 11(3), 257–267.

Huang, Z. J., Yu, S. M., & Ledsky, R. (2006). Health status and health service access and use among children in U.S. immigrant families. *American Journal of Public Health*, 96(4), 634–640.

Huffman, S., & Jensen, H. (2003, July). Do food assistance programs improve household food security?: Recent evidence from the United States. Paper presented at the annual meeting of American Agricultural Economics Association, Montreal, Canada. Retrieved May, 2010, from http://ageconsearch.umn.edu/bitstream/22219/1/sp03hu01.pdf

Huffman, S. K., & Jensen, H. H. (2005). Linkages among welfare, food assistance programmes and labour supply: Evidence from the survey of programme dynamics. *Applied Economics*, 37(10), 1099–1113.

Hunt, C., & Johnson, L. K. (2007). Calcium requirement: New estimations for men and women by cross-sectional statistical analyses of calcium balance data from metabolic studies. *American Journal of Clinical Nutrition*, 86, 1054–1063.

Hurlbert, J. S., & Acock, A. C. (1990). The effects of marital status on the form and composition of social networks. *Social Science Quarterly*, 71(1), 163–174.

Hynes, K., & Dunifon, R. (2007). Children in no-parent households: The continuity of arrangements and the composition of households. *Children and Youth Services Review*, 29(7), 912–932.

Iritani, B. J., Hallfors, D. D., & Bauer, D. J. (2007). Crystal methamphetamine use among young adults in the USA. *Addiction*, 102(7), 1102–1113.

Jacknowitz, A., Novillo, D., & Tiehen, L. (2007). Special Supplemental Nutrition Program for women, infants, and children and infant feeding practices. *Pediatrics*, 119(2), 281–289.

Jackson, M. I., & Mare, R. D. (2007). Cross-sectional and longitudinal measurements of neighborhood experience and their effects on children. *Social Science Research*, 36(2), 590–610.

Jaeger, D. A., & Stevens, A. H. (1999). Is job stability in the United States falling? Reconciling trends in the Current Population Survey and Panel Study of Income Dynamics. *Journal of Labor Economics*, 17(S4), S1–S28.

Jaffee, S. R., & Gallop, R. Social, emotional, and academic competence among children who have had contact with Child Protective Services: Prevalence and stability estimates. (2007). *Journal of the American Academy of Child & Adolescent Psychiatry*, 46(6), 757–765.

Jeannotte, S. M. (2003, November). Just showing up: Social and cultural capital in everyday life. Paper presented at the colloquium "Accounting for Culture: Examining the Building Blocks of Cultural Citizenship," Gatineau, Quebec, Canada. Retrieved May, 2010, from http://www.socialsciences.uottawa.ca/governance/eng/documents/just_showing_up.pdf

Jee, S. H., Barth, R., Szilagyi, M. A., Szilagyi, P. G., Aida, M., & Davis, M. M. (2006). Factors associated with chronic conditions among children in foster care. *Journal of health care for the poor and underserved*, 17(2), 328–341.

Jencks, C., Perman, L., & Rainwater, L. (1988). What is a good job? A new measure of labor market success. *American Journal of Sociology*, 93, 1322–1357.

Jennison, K. M. (2004). The short-term effects and unintended long-term consequences of binge drinking in college: A 10-year follow-up study. *The American Journal of Drug and Alcohol Abuse*, 30(3), 659–684.

Jeynes, W. H. (2001). The effects of recent parental divorce on their children's consumption of alcohol. *Journal of Youth and Adolescence*, 50(3), 305–319.

Jeynes, W. H. (2003). The effects of religious commitment on the academic achievement of urban and other children. *Education & Urban Society*, 36(1), 44–63.

Johnson, E., Dominici, F., Griswold, M., & Zeger, S. L. (2003). Disease cases and their medical costs attributable to smoking: An analysis of the national medical expenditure survey. *Journal of Econometrics*, 112(1), 135–151.

Jones, S. J., & Frongillo, E. A. (2007). Food insecurity and subsequent weight gain in women. *Public Health Nutrition*, 10(2), 145–151.

Jonson-Reid, M. (2002). Exploring the relationship between child welfare intervention and juvenile corrections involvement. *American Journal of Orthopsychiatry*, 74(4), 559–576.

Jonson-Reid, M., Chance, T., & Drake, B. (2007). Risk of death among children reported for nonfatal maltreatment. *Child Maltreatment*, 12(1), 86–95.

Judge, S. (2005). The impact of computer technology on academic achievement of young African American children. *Journal of Research in Childhood Education*, 20(2), 91–101.

Judge, S., & Jahns, L. (2007). Association of overweight with academic performance and social and behavioral problems: An update from the Early Childhood Longitudinal Study. *The Journal of School Health*, 77(10), 672–678.

Kahn, R. S., Brandt, D., & Whitaker, R. C. (2004). Combined effect of mothers' and fathers' mental health symptoms on children's behavioral and emotional well-being. *Archives of Pediatrics & Adolescent Medicine*, 158(8), 721–729.

Kapur, K. (2004). The impact of the health insurance market on small firm employment. *Journal of Risk and Insurance*, 71(1), 63–90.

Kenney, C. (2004). Cohabiting couple, filing jointly? Resource pooling and U.S. poverty policies. *Family Relations*, 53(2), 237–247.

Kenney, C. T. (2006). The power of the purse: Allocative systems and inequality in couple households. *Gender & Society*, 20(3), 354–381.

Ketsche, P. G. (2004). An analysis of the effect of tax policy on health insurance purchases by risk group. *Journal of Risk and Insurance*, 71(1), 91–113.

Kimbro, R., Lynch, S., & McLanahan, S. (2008). The influence of acculturation on breastfeeding initiation and duration for Mexican-Americans. *Population Research and Policy Review*, 27(2), 183–199.

Kimmel, J., & Powell, L. (2006). Nonstandard work and child care choices of married mothers. *Eastern Economic Journal*, 32(3), 397–419.

Kirk, D. (2008). The neighborhood context of racial and ethnic disparities in arrest. *Demography*, 45(1), 55–77.

Kirk, D. S. (2006). Examining the divergence across self-report and official data sources on inferences about the adolescent life-course of crime. *Journal of Quantitative Criminology*, 22(2), 107–129.

Kotch, J. B., Lewis, T., Hussey, J. M., English, D., Thompson, R., Litrownik, A. J., et al. (2008). Importance of early neglect for childhood aggression. *Pediatrics*, 121(4), 725–731.

Kowaleski-Jones, L., Dunifon, R., & Ream, G. (2006). Community contributions to scholastic success. *Journal of Community Psychology*, 34(3), 343–362.

Kranz, S., Hartman, T., Siega-Riz, A. M., & Herring, A. H. (2006). A Diet Quality Index for american preschoolers based on current dietary intake recommendations and an indicator of energy balance. *Journal of the American Dietetic Association*, 106(10), 1594–1604.

Kreager, D. (2007). Unnecessary roughness? School sports, peer networks, and male adolescent violence. *American Sociological Review*, 72, 705–724.

LaKind, J. S., Barraj, L., Tran, N., & Aylward, L. L. (2008). Environmental chemicals in people: Challenges in interpreting biomonitoring information. *Journal of Environmental Health*, 70(9), 61–64.

Lang, K., & Zagorsky, J. L. (2001). Does growing up with a parent absent really hurt? *The Journal of Human Resources*, 36(2), 253–273.

Lau, A. S., Litrownik, A. J., Newton, R. R., Black, M. M., & Everson, M. D. (2006). Factors affecting the link between physical discipline and child externalizing problems in black and white families. *Journal of Community Psychology*, 34(1), 89–103.

Lee, L.-C., Kotch, J. B., & Cox, C. E. (2004). Child maltreatment in families experiencing domestic violence. *Violence and Victims*, 19(5), 573–591.

Leigh, J. P. (1981). Compensating wages for occupational injuries and diseases. *Social Science Quarterly*, 62(4), 772–778.

Leigh, J. P. (1985). Analysis of Workers' Compensation using data on Individuals. *Industrial Relations*, 24(2), 247–256.

LePore, P. C., & Warren, J. R. (1997). A comparison of single-sex and coeducational Catholic secondary schooling: Evidence from the National Educational Longitudinal Study of 1988. *American Educational Research Journal*, 34(3), 485–511.

Lewis, C., Garfinkel, I., & Gao, Q. (2007). Incarceration and unwed fathers in fragile families. *Journal of Sociology and Social Welfare*, 34(3), 77–94.

Lewis, T., Leeb, R., Kotch, J., Smith, J., & et al. (2007). Maltreatment history and weapon carrying among early adolescents. *Child Maltreatment*, 12(3), 259–268.

Libby, A. M., Orton, H. D., Barth, R. P., & Burns, B. J. (2007). Alcohol, drug, and mental health service need for caregivers and children involved with Child Welfare. In R. Haskins, F. Wulczyn, & M. B. Webb (Eds.), Child Protection: Using Research to Improve Policy and Practice (pp. 107–119). Washington, D.C.: Brookings Institution Press.

Lindsey, M. A., Browne, D., Thompson, R., Hawley, K., Graham, J. C., Weisbart, C., et al. (2008). Caregiver mental health, neighborhood, and social network influences on child behavioral functioning among African Americans. *Social Work Research*, 32(2), 79–88.

Litrownik, A. J., Newton, R. R., & Landsverk, J. A. (2005). Assessment of depressive symptomatology in young maltreated children. *Journal of Human Behavior in the Social Environment*, 11(3–4), 135–156.

Liu, R. X. (2004). Parent-youth conflict and school delinquency/cigarette use: The moderating effects of gender and associations with achievement-oriented peers. *Sociological Inquiry*, 74(2), 271–298.

Livermore, M. M., & Powers, R. S. (2006). Employment of unwed mothers: The role of government and social support. *Journal of Family and Economic Issues*, 27(3), 479–494.

Lochner, K. A., Kawachi, I., Brennan, R. T., & Buka, S. L. (2003). Social capital and neighborhood mortality rates in Chicago. *Social Science & Medicine*, 56(8), 1797–1805.

Lofstrom, M., & Wang, C. (2007). Hispanic self-employment: A dynamic analysis of business ownership (Discussion Paper No. 2101). Retrieved May, 2010, from Institute for the Study of Labor website: ftp://ftp.iza.org/dps/dp2101.pdf

Long, S. K., Coughlin, T., & King, J. (2005). How well does Medicaid work in improving access to care?. *Health services research*, 40(1), 39–58.

Long, S. K., King, J., & Coughlin, T. A. (2006). The health care experiences of rural Medicaid beneficiaries. *Journal of Health Care for the Poor and Underserved*, 17(3), 575–591.

López Turley, R. N. (2002). Is relative deprivation beneficial? The effects of richer and poorer neighbors on children's outcomes. *Journal of Community Psychology*, 30(6), 671–686.

Lucas-Thompson, R., & Clarke-Stewart, K. A. (2007). Forecasting friendship: How marital quality, maternal mood, and attachment security are linked to children's peer relationships. *Journal of Applied Developmental Psychology*, 28, 499–514.

Lumeng, J. C., Appugliese, D., Cabral, H. J., Bradley, R. H., & Zuckerman, B. (2006). Neighborhood safety and overweight status in children. *Archives of Pediatrics & Adolescent Medicine*, 160(1), 25–31.

Mancini, J. (1978, October). *Social indicators of family life satisfaction: a comparison of husbands and wives.* Paper presented at the annual meeting of the National Council on Family Relations, Philadelphia, PA.

Manning, W. D., & Brown, S. (2006). Children's economic well-being in married and cohabiting parent families. *Journal of Marriage and Family*, 68(2), 345–362.

Markush, R. E., & Bartolucci, A. A. (1984). Firearms and suicide in the United States. *American Journal of Public Health*, 74(2), 123–127.

Martin, S. P. (2006). Trends in marital dissolution by women's education in the United States. *Demographic Research*, 15, 537–560.

Matthews, M. D., Weaver, C. N., Ciscernos, D. I., & Franz, R. S. (1992). Financial satisfaction among teachers. *Journal of Southwest Society of Economists*, 19, 105–109.

Maule, L. S., & Goidel, R. K. (2003). Adultery, drugs, and sex: An experimental investigation of individual reactions to unethical behavior by public officials. *Social Science Journal*, 40(1), 65–78.

McBride, B. A., Schoppe-Sullivan, S. J., & Ho, M.-H. (2005). The mediating role of fathers' school involvement on student achievement. *Journal of Applied Developmental Psychology*, 26(2), 201–216.

McCarroll, J. E., Ursano, R. J., Fan, Z., & Newby, J. H. (2004). Patterns of mutual and nonmutual spouse abuse in the U.S. Army (1998–2002). *Violence and Victims*, 19(4), 453–468.

McCrae, J., Chapman, M. V., & Christ, S. L. (2006). Profile of children investigated for sexual abuse: association with psychopathology symptoms and services. *The American Journal of Orthopsychiatry*, 76(4), 468–481.

McKinnish, T. (2008). Spousal mobility and earnings. *Demography*, 45(4), 829–849.

McNamara, P., Belsky, J., & Fearon, P. (2002). Infant sleep disorders and attachment: Sleep problems in infants with insecure-resistant versus insecure-avoidant attachments to mother. *Sleep and Hypnosis*, 5, 7–16.

Mellor, J. M., & Milyo, J. (2002). Income inequality and health status in the United States: Evidence from the Current Population Survey. *The Journal of Human Resources*, 37(3), 510–539.

Merrick, M. T., Litrownik, A. J., Everson, M. D., & Cox, C. E. (2008). Beyond sexual abuse: The impact of other maltreatment experiences on sexualized behaviors. *Child Maltreatment*, 13(2), 122–132.

Milesi, C., & Gamoran, A. (2006). Effect of class size and instruction on kindergarten and achievement. *Education Evaluation and Policy Analysis*, 28(4), 287–313.

Mills, T. L., Gomez-Smith, Z., & Leon, J. M. D. (2005). Skipped generation families: Sources of psychological distress among grandmothers of grandchildren who live in homes where neither parent is present. *Marriage & Family Review*, 37(1/2), 191–212.

Mitchell, R. E. (2006). How many deaf people are there in the United States?: Estimates from the Survey of Income and Program Participation. *Journal of Deaf Studies and Deaf Education*, 11(1), 112–119.

Mitra, A. (2000). Cognitive skills and black-white wages in the United States labor market. *Journal of Socio-Economics*, 29(3), 389–401.

Moeller, J.F., Cohen, S.B., Hock, E., et al. (2002, February). *Projecting National Medical Expenditure Survey data: A framework for MEPS projection* (Methodology Report No. 13). Rockville, MD: Agency for Healthcare Research and Quality.

Moffitt, R. (2003). The role of nonfinancial factors in exit and entry in the TANF program. *The Journal of Human Resources*, 38, 1221–1254.

Moffitt, R., & Winder, K. (2005). Does it pay to move from welfare to work? A comment on Danziger, Heflin, Corcoran, Oltmans, and Wang. *Journal of Policy Analysis and Management*, 24(2), 399–409.

Molnar, B. E., Browne, A., Cerda, M., & Buka, S. L. (2005). Violent behavior by girls reporting violent victimization: A prospective study. *Archives of Pediatrics & Adolescent Medicine,* 159(8), 731–739.

Molnar, B. E., Buka, S. L., Brennan, R. T., Holton, J. K., & Earls, F. (2003). A multilevel study of neighborhoods and parent-to-child physical aggression: Results from the project on human development in Chicago neighborhoods. *Child Maltreatment,* 8(2), 84–97.

Molnar, B. E., Gortmaker, S. L., Bull, F. C., & Buka, S. L. (2004). Unsafe to play? Neighborhood disorder and lack of safety predict reduced physical activity among urban children and adolescents. *American Journal of Health Promotion,* 18(5), 378–386.

Molnar, B. E., Miller, M. J., Azrael, D., & Buka, S. L. (2004). Neighborhood predictors of concealed firearm carrying among children and adolescents: Results from the Project on Human Development in Chicago Neighborhoods. *Archives of Pediatrics & Adolescent Medicine,* 158(7), 657–664.

Moore, K. A., Vandivere, S., & Redd, Z. (2006). A Sociodemographic Risk Index. *Social Indicators Research,* 75(1), 45–81.

Morenoff, J. D. (2003). Neighborhood mechanisms and the spatial dynamics of birth weight. *The American Journal of Sociology,* 108(5), 976–1017.

Morenoff, J. D., Sampson, R. J., & Raudenbush, S. W. (2001). Neighborhood inequality, collective efficacy, and the spatial dynamics of urban violence. *Criminology,* 39(3), 517–560.

Munafò, M. R., Hitsman, B., Rende, R., Metcalfe, C., & Niaura, R. (2008). Effects of progression to cigarette smoking on depressed mood in adolescents: Evidence from the National Longitudinal Study of Adolescent Health. *Addiction,* 103(1), 162–171.

Neblett, N. G. (2007). Patterns of single mothers' work and welfare use: What matters for children's well-being? *Journal of Family Issues,* 28(8), 1083–1112.

Nepomnyaschy, L., & Reichman, N. (2006). Low birth weight and asthma among young urban children. *American Journal of Public Health,* 96(9), 1604–1610.

Novak, S. P., Reardon, S. F., & Buka, S. L. (2002). How beliefs about substance use differ by socio-demographic characteristics, individual experiences, and neighborhood environments among urban adolescents. Journal of Drug Education, 32(4), 319–342.

O'Brien, M., & Peyton, V. (2002). Parenting attitudes and marital intimacy: A longitudinal analysis. *Journal of Family Psychology,* 16(2), 118–127.

O'Brien, M., Peyton, V., Mistry, R., Hruda, L., Jacobs, A., Caldera, Y., et al. (2000). Gender-role cognition in three-year-old boys and girls. *Sex Roles,* 42(11/12), 1007–1025.

Obeidallah, D., Brennan, R. T., Brooks-Gunn, J., & Earls, F. (2004). Links between pubertal timing and neighborhood contexts: Implications for girls' violent behavior. *Journal of the American Academy of Child and Adolescent Psychiatry*, 43(12), 1460–1468.

Ogden, C., Carroll, M., & Flegal, K. (2008). High Body Mass Index for age among U.S. children and adolescents, 2003–2006. *Journal of the American Medical Association*, 299(20), 2401–2405.

Oh, H. J. (2001). Exploration of the influence of household poverty spells on mortality risk. *Journal of Marriage and the Family*, 63(1), 224–234.

Olfson, M., Gameroff, M. J., Marcus, S. C., & Jensen, P. S. (2003). National trends in the treatment of attention deficit hyperactivity disorder. *American Journal of Psychiatry*, 160(6), 1071–1077.

Olfson, M., S.C., M., Wan, G. J., & Geissler, E. C. (2004). National trends in the outpatient treatment of anxiety disorders. *Journal of Clinical Psychiatry*, 65(9), 1166–1173.

Olfson, M. K., Marcus, S. C., Druss, B., & Pincus, H. A. (2002). National trends in the use of outpatient psychotherapy. *American Journal of Psychiatry*, 159(11), 1914–1920.

Palusci, V. J., Smith, E.G., & Paneth, N. (2005). Predicting and responding to physical abuse in young children using NCANDS. *Children and Youth Services Review*, 27, 667–682.

Pandey, S., & Kim, J.-H. (2008). Path to poverty alleviation: Marriage or postsecondary education? *Journal of Family and Economic Issues*, 29(1), 166–184.

Parish, S. L., & Cloud, J. M. (2006). Child care for low-income school-age children: Disability and family structure effects in a national sample. *Social Work*, 51(3), 223–232.

Park, H.-O. H. (2006). The economic well-being of households headed by a grandmother as caregiver. *The Social Service Review*, 80(2), 264–295.

Park, J., Hogan, D., & D'Ottavi, M. (2005). Grandparenting children with special needs. *Annual Review of Gerontology and Geriatrics*, 24, 120–149.

Percheski, C., & Wildeman, C. (2008). Becoming a dad: Employment trajectories of married, cohabiting, and nonresident fathers. *Social Science Quarterly*, 89(2), 482–501.

Pettit, B., & Western, B. (2004). Mass imprisonment and the life course: Race and class inequality in U.S. incarceration. *American Sociological Review*, 69(2), 151–169.

Petts, R. J. (2007). Religious participation, religious affiliation, and engagement with children among fathers experiencing the birth of a new child. *Journal of Family Issues*, 28(9), 1139–1161.

Peyton, V., Jacobs, A., O'Brien, M., & Roy, C. (2001). Reasons for choosing child care: Associations with family factors, quality, and satisfaction. *Early Childhood Research Quarterly*, 16, 191–208.

Phillips, S., Burns, B., Wagner, H. R., & Barth, R. (2004). Parental arrest and children involved with child welfare services agencies. *American Journal of Orthopsychiatry*, 74(2), 174–186.

Pittman, L. D. (2007). Grandmothers' involvement among young adolescents growing up in poverty. *Journal of Research on Adolescence*, 17(1), 89–116.

Popkin, B. M., & Udry, J. R. (1998). Adolescent obesity increases significantly in second and third generation U.S. immigrants: The National Longitudinal Study of Adolescent Health. *The Journal of Nutrition*, 128(4), 701–706.

Porterfield, S. L. (1998). On the precipice of reform: Welfare spell durations for rural, female-headed families. *American Journal of Agricultural Economics*, 80(5), 994–999.

Potocky-Tripodi, M. (2006). Risk and protective factors in the perceived health of children of immigrants. *Journal of Immigrant and Minority Health*, 8(1), 85–97.

Quillian, L., & Pager, D. (2001). Black neighbors, higher crime? The role of racial stereotypes in evaluations of neighborhood crime. *American Journal of Sociology*, 107(3), 717–767.

Quinlivan, E. P., & Gregory, J. F., III. (2007). Reassessing folic acid consumption patterns in the United States (1999–2004): Potential effect on neural tube defects and overexposure to folate. *The American Journal of Clinical Nutrition*, 86(6), 1773–1779.

Raudenbush, S. W., & Bryk, A. (2001). *Hierarchical Linear Models: Applications and Data Analysis Methods*. Thousand Oaks, CA: Sage Publications.

Raviv, T., Kessenich, M., & Morrison, F. J. (2004). A mediational model of the association between socioeconomic status and three-year-old language abilities: The role of parenting factors. *Early Childhood Research Quarterly*, 19, 528–547.

Reardon, S., Yun, J., & Kurlaender, M. (2006). Implications of income-based school assignment policies for racial school segregation. *Education Evaluation and Policy Analysis*, 28(1), 49–75.

Reardon, S. F., Brennan, R. T., & Buka, S. L. (2002). Estimating multi-level discrete-time hazard models using cross-sectional data: Neighborhood effects on the onset of adolescent cigarette use. *Multivariate Behavioral Research*, 37(3), 297–330.

Reardon, S. F., & Buka, S. L. (2002). Differences in onset and persistence of substance abuse and dependence among whites, blacks, and Hispanics. *Public Health Reports*, 117(Supplement 1), S51–S59.

Rees, D., & Sabia, J. (2007). The relationship between abortion and depression: New evidence from the Fragile Families and Child Wellbeing Study. *Medical Science Monitor*, 13(10), 430–436.

Reichman, N., Hamilton, E., Hummer, R., & Padilla, Y. (2008). Racial and ethnic disparities in low birthweight among urban unmarried mothers. *Maternal and Child Health Journal*, 12(2), 204–215.

Ren, P. (2009). Do sub-cultural norms survive immigration? — Cantonese and Mandarin fertility in the United States. *Journal of Comparative Family Studies*, 40(1), 25–50.

Ribar, D. C., & Hamrick, K. S. (2003). *Dynamics of poverty and food sufficiency* (Food assistance and nutrition research report Number 36). Washington, D.C.: U.S. Department of Agriculture.

Robbins, S. M., & Barcus, H. R. (2004). Welfare reform and economic and housing capacity for low-income households, 1997–1999. *Policy Studies Journal*, 32(3), 439–460.

Romney, S. C., Litrownik, A. J., Newton, R. R., & Lau, A. (2006). The relationship between child disability and living arrangement in child welfare. *Child Welfare*, 85(6), 965–984.

Rosenberg, S., & Robinson, C. C. (2004). Out-of-home placement for young children with developmental and medical conditions. *Children and Youth Services Review*, 26, 711–723.

Rostosky, S. S., Danner, F., &Riggle, E. D. B. (2007). Is religiosity a protective factor against substance use in young adulthood? Only if you're straight! *Journal of Adolescent Health*, 40, 440–447.

Rotolo, T., & Wilson, J. (2004). What happened to the "Long Civic Generation?": Explaining cohort differences in volunteerism. *Social Forces*, 82(3), 1091–1121.

Rumberger, R. W., & Larson, K. A. (1998). Student mobility and the increased risk of high school dropout. *American Journal of Education*, 107(1), 1–35.

Rupp, K., Strand, A., Davies, P., & Sears, J. (2007). Benefit adequacy among elderly Social Security retired-worker beneficiaries and the SSI federal benefit rate. *Social Security Bulletin*, 67(3), 29–51.

Russell, S. T., Crockett, L. J., Shen, Y.-L., & Lee, S.-A. (2008). Cross-ethnic invariance of self-esteem and depression measures for Chinese, Filipino, and European American adolescents. *Journal of Youth and Adolescence*, 37(1), 50–61.

Russell, S. T., Franz, B. T., & Driscoll, A. K. (2001). Same-sex romantic attraction and experience of violence in adolescence. *American Journal of Public Health*, 91(6), 903–906.

Ryan, S., Franzetta, K., Manlove, J., & Holcombe, E. (2007). Adolescents' discussions about contraception or STDs with partners before first sex. *Perspectives on Sexual and Reproductive Health*, 39(3), 149–157.

Sampson, R. J., Morenoff, J. D., & Raudenbush, S. (2005). Social anatomy of racial and ethnic disparities in violence. *American Journal of Public Health*, 95(2), 224–232.

Sander, W. (2001). *The effects of Catholic schools on religiosity, education, and competition. Occasional Paper* (Report No. NCSPE-OP-32). New York: Teachers College.

Sander, W., & Testa, W. A. (2009). Education and household location in Chicago. *Growth and Change,* 40(1), 116–139.

Schieman, S. (1999). Age and anger. *Journal of Health and Social Behavior,* 40, 273–289.

Schwebel, D. C., Brezausek, C. M., & Belsky, J. (2006). Does time spent in child care influence risk for unintentional injury? *Journal of Pediatric Psychology,* 31(2), 184–193.

Sebastian, R. S., Cleveland, L. E., Goldman, J. D., & Moshfegh, A. J. (2007). Older adults who use vitamin/mineral supplements differ from nonusers in nutrient intake adequacy and dietary attitudes. *Journal of the American Dietetic Association,* 107(8), 1322–1332.

Seeman, T., Merkin, S. S., Crimmins, E., Koretz, B., Charette, S., & Karlamangla, A. (2008). Education, income and ethnic differences in cumulative biological risk profiles in a national sample of US adults: NHANES III (1988–1994). *Social Science & Medicine,* 66(1), 72–87.

Selden, T. M., & Banthin, J. S. (2003). Health care expenditure burdens among elderly adults: 1987 and 1996. *Medical Care,* 41(7), 13–23.

Shanks, T. R. W. (2007). The impacts of household wealth on child development. *Journal of Poverty,* 11(2), 93–116.

She, P., & Livermore, G. (2007). Material hardship, poverty, and disability among working-age adults. *Social Science Quarterly,* 88(4), 970–989.

Shen, Y.-C., & Long, S. K. (2006). What's driving the downward trend in employer-sponsored health insurance? *Health Services Research,* 41(6), 2074–2096.

Shen, Y.-C., & McFeeters, J. (2006). Out-of-pocket health spending between low- and higher-income populations: Who is at risk of having high expenses and high burdens?. *Medical Care,* 44(3), 200–209.

Shen, Y.-C., & Zuckerman, S. (2005). The effect of Medicaid payment levels on access and use among beneficiaries. *Health Services Research,* 40(3), 723–744.

Shopland, D. R., Hartman, A. M., Gibson, J. T., Mueller, M. D., Kessler, L. G., & Lynn, W. R. (1996). Cigarette smoking among U.S. adults by state and region: Estimates from the Current Population Survey. *Journal of the National Cancer Institute,* 88(23), 1748–1758.

Shusterman, G., Fluke, J., & Yuan, Y. T. (2005). Male perpetrators of child maltreatment: Findings from NCANDS. Washington, D.C.: U.S. Department of Health and Human Services, Office of the Assistant Secretary for Planning and Evaluation. Retrieved May, 2010, from http://aspe.hhs.gov/hsp/05/child-maltreat/report.pdf

Sigle-Rushton, W., & McLanahan, S. (2002). The living arrangements of new unmarried mothers. *Demography*, 39(3), 415–433.

Silenzio, V. M. B., Pena, J. B., Duberstein, P. R., Cerel, J., & Knox, K. L. (2007). Sexual orientation and risk factors for suicidal ideation and suicide attempts among adolescents and young adults. *American Journal of Public Health*, 97(11), 2017–2019.

Simpson, L., Zodet, M. W., Chevarley, F. M., Owens, P. L., Dougherty, D., & McCormick, M. (2004). Health care for children and youth in the United States: 2002 report on trends in access, utilization, quality, and expenditures. *Ambulatory Pediatrics*, 4(2), 131–153.

Slade, E. P., & Wissow, L. S. (2004). Spanking in early childhood and later behavior problems: A prospective study of infants and young toddlers. *Pediatrics*, 113(5), 1321–1330.

Smith, B. D. (2003). How parental drug use and drug treatment compliance relate to family reunification. *Child Welfare*, 82(3), 335–365.

Smith, K. R., & Zick, C. D. (1986). The incidence of poverty among the recently widowed: Mediating factors in the life course. *Journal of Marriage and the Family*, 48, 619–630.

Smulian, J., Teitler, J., Nepomnyaschy, L., Ananth, C., & Reichman, N. (2005). Intrapartum fever and newborn complications. *American Journal of Obstetrics and Gynecology*, 193(6), S193.

Solon, G., Page, M. E., & Duncan, G. J. (2000). Correlations between neighboring children in their subsequent educational attainment. *The Review of Economics and Statistics*, 82(3), 383–392.

Steinberg, K. S., & Rooney, P. M. (2005). America gives: A survey of Americans'generosity after September 11. *Nonprofit and Voluntary Sector Quarterly*, 34(1), 110–135.

Strauss, R. S. (2000). Childhood obesity and self-esteem. *Pediatrics*, 105(1), e15.

Stuhlman, M., & Pianta, R. (2002). Teachers'narratives about their relationships with children: Associations with behavior in classrooms. *School Psychology Review*, 31, 148–163.

Sturm, R., Ringel, J. S., & Andreyeva, T. (2004). Increasing obesity rates and disability trends. *Health Affairs*, 23(2), 199–205.

Swahn, M. H., & Hammig, B. J. (2000). Prevalence of youth access to alcohol, guns, illegal drugs or cigarettes in the home and association with health-risk behaviors. *Annals of Epidemiology*, 10(7), 452.

Takei, I., Saenz, R., & Li, J. (2009). Cost of being a Mexican immigrant and being a Mexican non-citizen in California and Texas. *Hispanic Journal of Behavioral Sciences*, 31(1), 73–95.

Teitler, J. O., Reichman, N. E., & Nepomnyaschy, L. (2007). Determinants of TANF participation: A multilevel analysis. *The Social Service Review*, 81(4), 633–656.

Teitler, J. O., Reichman, N. E., Nepomnyaschy, L., & Martinson, M. (2007). A cross-national comparison of racial and ethnic disparities in low birth weight in the United States and England. *Pediatrics*, 120(5), E1182–E1189.

Thompson, R. (2005). The course and correlates of mental health care received by young children: Descriptive data from a longitudinal urban high-risk sample. *Children and Youth Services Review*, 27(1), 39–50.

Thompson, R. (2006). Exploring the link between maternal history of childhood victimization and child risk of maltreatment. *Journal of Trauma Practice*, 5(2), 57–72.

Thompson, R. (2007). Mothers' violence victimization and child behavior problems: Examining the link. *American Journal of Orthopsychiatry*, 77(2), 306–315.

Thompson, R. (2009). The impact of early mental health services on the trajectory of externalizing behavioral problems in a sample of high-risk pre-adolescent children. *Children and Youth Services Review*, 31(1), 16–22.

Thompson, R., Briggs, E., English, D. J., Dubowitz, H., et al. (2005). Suicidal ideation among 8-year-olds who are maltreated and at risk: Findings from the LONGSCAN studies. *Child Maltreatment*, 10(1), 108–123.

Thompson, R., Dubowitz, H., English, D. J., Nooner, K. B., Wike, T., Bangdiwala, S. I., et al. (2006). Parents' and teachers' concordance with children's self-ratings of wuicidality: Findings from a high-risk sample. *Suicide and Life-Threatening Behavior*, 36(2), 167–181.

Thompson, R., Lindsey, M. A., English, D. J., Hawley, K. M., Lambert, S., & Browne, D. C. (2007). The influence of family environment on mental health need and service use among vulnerable children. *Child Welfare*, 86(5), 57–74.

Thompson, R., & May, M. A. (2006). Caregivers' perceptions of child mental health needs and service utilization: An urban 8-year-old sample. *The Journal of Behavioral Health Services & Research* 33(4), 474–482.

Thompson, R., Proctor, L. J., Weisbart, C., Lewis, T. L., English, D. J., Hussey, J. M., et al. (2007). Children's self-reports about violence exposure: An examination of The Things I Have Seen and Heard scale. *American Journal of Orthopsychiatry*, 77(3), 454–466.

Thompson, R., & Wiley, T. R. (2009). Predictors of re-referral to child protective services: A longitudinal follow-up of an urban cohort maltreated as infants. *Child Maltreatment*, 14(1), 89–99.

Timberlake, D. S., Haberstick, B. C., Hopfer, C. J., Bricker, J., Sakai, J. T., Lessem, J. M., et al. (2007). Progression from marijuana use to daily smoking and nicotine dependence in a national sample of U.S. adolescents. *Drug and Alcohol Dependence*, 88(2–3), 272–281.

Trzcinski, E., & Brandell, J. (2002). Adolescent outcomes, poverty status, and welfare reform: An analysis based on the Survey of Program Dynamics

(Working Paper No. 269). Chicago, IL: Joint Center for Poverty Research. Retrieved May, 2010, from http://www.northwestern.edu/ipr/jcpr/workingpapers/wpfiles/trzcinski_brandell_sg00_01.pdf

Trzcinski, E., Brandell, J., Ferro, L., & Smith, D. (2005). Adolescent outcomes and welfare reform: An analysis based on the Survey of Program Dynamics. *Journal of Human Behavior in the Social Environment*, 12(2), 63–87.

Tubbs, C. Y., Roy, K. M., & Burton, L. M. (2005). Family ties: Constructing family time in low-income families. *Family Process*, 44(1), 397–410.

Turner, H. A., Finkelhor, D., & Ormrod, R. (2006). The effect of lifetime victimization on the mental health of children and adolescents. *Social Science & Medicine*, 62(1), 13–27.

Turner, H. A., Finkelhor, D., & Ormrod, R. (2007). Family structure variations in patterns and predictors of child victimization. *American Journal of Orthopsychiatry*, 77(2), 282–295.

Van Den Oord, E. J. C. G., & Rowe, D. C. (1998). An examination of genotype-environment interactions for academic achievement in a U.S. National Longitudinal Survey. *Intelligence*, 25(3), 205–228.

Van Hook, J., & Glick, J. E. (2007). Immigration and living arrangements: Moving beyond the "Instrumental Needs Versus Acculturation" dichotomy. *Demography*, 44(2), 225–249.

Vandell, D. L., McCartney, K., Owen, M. T., Booth, C., & Clarke-Stewart, A. (2003). Variations in child care by grandparents during the first three years. *Journal of Marriage and Family*, 65(2), 375–381.

Vandewater, E. A., Shim, M., & Caplovitz, A. G. (2004). Linking obesity and activity level with children's television and video game use. *Journal of Adolescence*, 27(1), 71–85.

Vartanian, T. P., & Buck, P. W. (2005). Childhood and adolescent neighborhood effects on adult income: Using siblings to examine differences in ordinary least squares and fixed effect models. *Social Service Review*, 79(1), 60–94.

Vartanian, T. P., Buck, P. W., & Gleason, P. (2007). Intergenerational neighborhood-type mobility: Examining differences between blacks and whites. *Housing Studies*, 22(5), 833–856.

Vartanian, T. P., & Gleason, P. M. (1999a). Do neighborhood conditions affect high school dropout and college graduation rates? *Journal of Socio-Economics*, 28(1), 21–41.

Vartanian, T. P., & Gleason, P. M. (1999b). Income and job market outcomes after welfare: 1990–1995. Chicago, IL: Joint Center for Poverty Research. Retrieved May, 2010, from http://www.northwestern.edu/ipr/jcpr/workingpapers/wpfiles/Vartanian.Paper.SIPP.PDF

Vartanian, T. P., Karen, D., Buck, P. W., & Cadge, W. (2007). Early factors leading to college graduation for Asians and non-Asians in the United States. *Sociological Quarterly*, 48(2), 165–197.

Vartanian, T. P., & McNamara, J. M. (2004). The welfare myth: Disentangling the long-term effects of poverty and welfare receipt for young single mothers. *Journal of Sociology and Social Welfare*, 31(4), 103–138.

Veazie, M. A., & Smith, G. S. (2000). Heavy drinking, alcohol dependence, and injuries at work among young workers in the United States labor force. *Alcoholism: Clinical and Experimental Research*, 24(12), 1811–1819.

Vericker, T., Macomber, J., & Geen, R. (2008). The story behind kinship care caseload dynamics: An analysis of AFCARS data, 2000–2003. *Children and Youth Services Review*, 30(4), 437–451.

Videon, T. M. (2002). Who plays and who benefits? Gender, interscholastic athletics, and academic outcomes. *Sociological Perspectives*, 45(4), 415–444.

Von Secker, C. (2002). Effects of inquiry-based teacher practices on science excellence and equity. *Journal of Educational*, 95(3), 151–160.

Votruba-Drzal, E., Coley, R. L., & Chase-Lansdale, P. L. (2004). Child care and low-income children's development: Direct and moderated effects. *Child Development*, 75(1), 296–312.

Wall, A. E., & Barth, R. P. (2005). Aggressive and delinquent behavior of maltreated adolescents: Risk factors and gender differences. *Stress, Trauma, and Crisis: An International Journal*, 8(1), 1–24.

Wang, G. J., & Brown, D.R. (2004). Impact of physical activity on medical expenditures among adults downhearted and blue. *American Journal of Health Behavior*, 28(3), 208–217.

Wang, H., Kao, G., & Joyner, K. (2006). Stability of interracial and intraracial romantic relationships among adolescents. *Social Science Research*, 35(2), 435–453.

Wang, Q. (2008). Race/ethnicity, gender and job earnings across metropolitan areas in the United States: A multilevel analysis. *Urban Studies*, 45(4), 825–843.

Wang, Y., Rees, N., & Andreosso-O'Callaghan, B. (2004). Economic change and political development in China: Findings from a public opinion survey. *Journal of Contemporary China*, 13(39), 203–222.

Warren, J. R., LePore, P. C., & Mare, R. D. (2000). Employment during high school: Consequences for students' grades in academic courses. *American Educational Research Journal*, 37(4), 943–969.

Weinshenker, M. N. (2006). *A matter of timing: Delayed fatherhood in the United States*. Illinois: University of Chicago.

Weisbart, C. E., Thompson, R., Pelaez-Merrick, M., Kim, J., Wike, T., Briggs, E., et al. (2008). Child and adult victimization: Sequelae for female caregivers of high-risk children. *Child Maltreatment*, 13, 235–244.

Wen, M., Browning, C. R., & Cagney, K. A. (2003). Poverty, affluence, and income inequality: Neighborhood economic structure and its implications for health. *Social Science & Medicine*, 57(5), 843–860.

Wen, M., Cagney, K. A., & Christakis, N. A. (2005). Effect of specific aspects of community social environment on the mortality of individuals diagnosed with serious illness. *Social Science & Medicine*, 61(6), 83–96.

Wen, M., Hawkley, L. C., & Cacioppo, J. T. (2006). Objective and perceived neighborhood environment, individual SES and psychosocial factors, and self-rated health: An analysis of older adults in Cook County, Illinois. *Social Science & Medicine*, 63(10), 2575–2590.

Wertheimer, R., & Atienza, A. (2006). A Vulnerable Youth: Recent Trends. Baltimore, MD: Child Trends. Retrieved May 10, 2010 from http://www.childtrends.org/Files//Child_Trends-2006_04_01_OP_VulnYouth.pdf.

Whitaker, R., Orzol, S., & Kahn, R. (2007). The co-occurrence of smoking and major depressive episode among mothers 15 months after delivery. *Preventive Medicine*, 45(6), 476–480.

Whitaker, R. C., Phillips, S. M., & Orzol, S. M. (2006). Food insecurity and the risks of depression and anxiety in mothers and behavior problems in their preschool-aged Children. *Pediatrics*, 118(3), e859–e868.

Whitaker, R. C., Phillips, S. M., Orzol, S. M., & Burdette, H. L. (2007). The association between maltreatment and obesity among preschool children. *Child Abuse & Neglect*, 31(11/12), 1187–1199.

Whiteside-Mansell, L., Bradley, R. H., & Rakow, E. (2001). Similarities and differences in parental investment for mothers and fathers. *Journal of Family Issues*, 22(1), 63–83.

Wickrama, K. A. S., Elder Jr., G. H., & Abraham, W. T. (2007). Rurality and ethnicity in adolescent physical illness: Are children of the growing rural Latino population at excess health risk?. *Journal of Rural Health*, 23(3), 228–237.

Willetts, M. C., & Maroules, N. G. (2005, August). *Parental reports of adolescent well-being: Does marital status matter?* Paper presented at the annual meeting of the American Sociological Association, Philadelphia, PA.

Winicki, J., & Jemison, K. (2003). Food insecurity and hunger in the kindergarten classroom: Its effect on learning and growth. *Contemporary Economic Policy*, 21(2), 145–157.

Wolfe, B., & Vandell, D. L. (2002). Welfare reform depends on good child care. *The American Prospect*, 13(13), A19–A22.

Wu, C.-F., & Eamon, M. K. (2007). Public and private sources of assistance for low-income households. *Journal of Sociology & Social Welfare*, 34(4), 121–149.

Yeung, A. S., Marsh, H. W., & Suliman, R. (2000). Can two tongues live in harmony: Analysis of the National Education Longitudinal Study of 1988 (NELS88) longitudinal data on the maintenance of home language. *American Educational Research Journal*, 37(3), 1001–1026.

Young, T. M., S., Martin, S.S.,Young, M. E., & Ting, L. (2001). Internal poverty and teen pregnancy. *Adolescence*, 36(142), 289–304.

Yu, S. M., Huang, Z. J., Schwalberg, R. H., & Kogan, M. D. (2005). Parental awareness of health and community resources among immigrant families. *Maternal and Child Health Journal*, 9(1), 27–34.

Zaff, J. F., Moore, K. A., Papillo, A. R., & Williams, S. (2003). Implications of extracurricular activity participation during adolescence on positive outcomes. *Journal of Adolescent Research*, 18(6), 599–630.

Zedlewski, S. R., & Alderson, D. (2001). Do families on welfare in the post-TANF era differ from their pre-TANF counterparts? Washington, D.C.: Urban Institute.

Zimmerman, S. L. (2003). Child and family well-being in states with different political cultures. *Families in Society*, 84(2), 275–284.

Index

Note: Page references followed by "*t*" denote tables.

appropriateness and feasibility of,
17–22
dependent variables, 18
population based data sets, 18
independent variables, 19
study replication, 19–20
identifiers, 20
generalization of results, 20
authorization of data sets, 20–21
programming, 21–22
duration for getting results, 22
cross-sectional, 12
defining, 9–12
disadvantages of, 15–17
addition information, collection
of, 16
researcher control issues, 16–17
policy changes, current, 16
sample sizes, 16
wording of concepts, 15–16
longitudinal, 12
population-based, 9–10
research trend, 4
sibling studies, 85, 175
Small Area Health Insurance
Estimates, 24
Small Areas Income and Poverty
Estimates, 24
Snapshots of America's Families, 91
Social Security Administration, 56
Social Security Administration Survey
of Income and Program
Participation, 24
Social Service Review (*SSR*), 4
Sociometrics, Inc., 141
software. *See* programming
SPSS, 14, 15, 21–22, 29, 32, 40, 55,
103, 135, 175
STATA, 14, 15, 21–22, 29, 40, 55, 103,
135, 175
State Education Data Center, 119

stratified sampling, 115, 175
Study of Asset and Health Dynamics
among the Oldest Old
(AHEAD), 56, 58
Study of Early Child Care and Youth
Development (SECCYD),
96–98
application, 97–98
availability/accessibility, 98
phases, 96–97
study replication, 19–20
Supplemental Children's Survey, 37
Survey Documentation and Analysis
(SDA), 47–49, 93, 141
Survey for Income and Program
Participation (SIPP), 11,
123–27
availability/accessibility, 127
core content data, 124
Data Ferret, 125
information, 123, 125–27
panel and panel members, 123–24
topical content data, 124–25
two-stage sampling design, 123
waves, 124
Survey Net, 37
Survey of Economic Opportunities
(SEO) sample, 10
Survey of Income and Program
Participation (SIPP), 6, 7, 9,
11, 12, 127
Survey of Program Dynamics (SPD),
7, 24, 127–30
1992–1993 wave, 128
1997 wave, 128
1998–2002 wave, 128
application, 129
availability/accessibility, 129–30
CAPI questionnaire, 128
Children's Residential History
Calendar, 128–29